RIGHTS AND RESPONSIBILITIES IN RURAL SOUTH AFRICA

RIGHTS AND RESPONSIBILITIES IN RURAL SOUTH AFRICA

Gender, Personhood, and the Crisis of Meaning

—⁄⁄⁄—

KATHLEEN RICE

INDIANA UNIVERSITY PRESS

This book is a publication of

Indiana University Press
Office of Scholarly Publishing
Herman B Wells Library 350
1320 East 10th Street
Bloomington, Indiana 47405 USA

iupress.org

Manufactured in the United States of America
First Printing 2023

Library of Congress Cataloging-in-Publication Data

Names: Rice, Kathleen, author.
Title: Rights and responsibilities in rural South Africa : gender, personhood, and the crisis of meaning / Kathleen Rice.
Description: Bloomington : Indiana University Press, 2023. | Includes bibliographical references and index.
Identifiers: LCCN 2023011245 (print) | LCCN 2023011246 (ebook) | ISBN 9780253066169 (cloth) | ISBN 9780253066176 (paperback) | ISBN 9780253066183 (pdf)
Subjects: LCSH: Social change—South Africa—Eastern Cape. | Women—South Africa—Eastern Cape—Social conditions. | Human rights—South Africa—Eastern Cape. | Sex role—South Africa—Eastern Cape. | Intergenerational relations—South Africa—Eastern Cape. | Interpersonal relations—South Africa—Eastern Cape. | BISAC: SOCIAL SCIENCE / Ethnic Studies / African Studies | SOCIAL SCIENCE / Anthropology / Cultural & Social
Classification: LCC HN801.A8 R532 2023 (print) | LCC HN801.A8 (ebook) | DDC 303.40968—dc23/eng/20230309
LC record available at https://lccn.loc.gov/2023011245
LC ebook record available at https://lccn.loc.gov/2023011246

CONTENTS

ACKNOWLEDGMENTS

THE CONTROVERSIAL NATURE OF SOME topics covered in this book require me to protect the confidentiality of the people whose lives and community I discuss in the pages that follow. This means that the people who most deserve my most humble acknowledgment and thanks, including most Xhosa people who contributed one way or another to making this book what it is, must remain unnamed. To the staff of the Lodge, the NGO, and everyone who called Mhlambini home during the time that I have spent there, thanks always for your time, your patience, and your friendship. I acknowledge you most of all.

To my doctoral supervisors, Janice Boddy and Holly Wardlow, and to Mark Hunter (doctoral committee member), a huge thanks for all your thoughtful guidance and insight. Thanks also to Michael Lambek and my fellow members of the Dissertation Writing Group in the Department of Anthropology at the University of Toronto—this book is stronger for your feedback and encouragement. Thanks to Jennifer Cole and three anonymous manuscript reviewers for your wonderful feedback. I hope I've done justice to your vision of how much better this book could be. Brady G'Sell, your scholarly insights have been wonderful, but your encouragement and enthusiasm for my work are even more so. I look forward to collaborating with you in the years to come. Richard Lee, thanks for the opportunity that ultimately set me on this path. I'd never have guessed almost twenty years ago that a summer internship would tie me to South Africa the way it has. Fiona Webster, thank you so much for your years friendship and mentorship, and for trusting me to get my work done on my own time. Your encouragement and your trusting approach to postdoctoral supervision allowed me to keep this alive while we were working on other things.

The initial fieldwork that led to this book was funded by a doctoral fellowship from the Social Sciences and Humanities Research Council of Canada and a dissertation fieldwork grant from the Wenner-Gren Foundation. Subsequent fieldwork was funded through a Wenner-Gren Foundation Engaged Anthropology Grant, and the book writing itself was funded by a Hunt Postdoctoral Fellowship from Wenner-Gren Foundation. I am deeply grateful for the support of these funders. I am also deeply grateful for the patience and hard work of Nosabelo Futhu, Bohle Conference and Translation Services, and Anthony Sparg (especially) for their help with translation work.

To Annette Champion, thanks always for being a mom of sorts. Dave and Belinda Malherbe and all your staff, thanks for giving me a place to go. Meg Orton, KT Adams, Janene Marais, Kate Intlanzi, Nomonde Majongozi, and Michelle Whittal, thanks for the friendship and all the good times. Richard Coetzee and Marinda Louw, thanks always for your friendship and hospitality, both then and since. Thanks finally to my family—Mary Muckle (my mom), Jake Rice (my dad), my sister Joanna, and most of all to my much-loved husband, Kevin O'Neill, for your encouragement and for sticking with me through all of this.

RIGHTS AND RESPONSIBILITIES IN RURAL SOUTH AFRICA

INTRODUCTION

"THE PROBLEM THAT WE ARE having with rights," said Mbeko, "is that people are exercising their rights but ignoring their responsibilities." Mbeko, a man in his late twenties, was one of my most insightful interlocutors in the rural Xhosa village called Mhlambini, where I have carried out ethnographic field-work since 2010.[1] Contentions about human rights are ubiquitous in Mhlambini, and from prior conversations, I was aware of Mbeko's ambivalent feelings about them. This talk of responsibilities, however, was new to me.

"What do you mean, ignoring their responsibilities?" I asked.

Mbeko explained by way of example: children have a right to education, teachers have a responsibility to teach schoolchildren, and parents have a responsibility to support their children and to ensure that their children attend school. This, according to Mbeko, is as it should be. However, because of her rights, the child cannot be disciplined with a beating if she skips school. This is reprehensible, according to Mbeko, because the parents are fulfilling their responsibilities to the child by raising her, and the teacher is fulfilling her responsibility to the child by teaching her, but *because* of her rights, the child can ignore her responsibility to become educated.

As the conversation progressed, Mbeko offered further examples of what he termed "abuses" of human rights, and of the neglected responsibilities and disrespect that follow from these alleged transgressions. Several examples targeted unruly children, but his criticism was aimed especially at the young women who allegedly two-time their boyfriends, who go against Xhosa custom by "talking back" to men, and who taunt men by reminding them that they can no longer legally discipline women with violence. "So, you see," concluded

Mbeko, "I'm against the women. Because the women are the ones who have a lot of changing things."

I was initially skeptical of Mbeko's claims because I have seen little evidence of young women behaving in the ways that he contends they do. And although young women *do* reference human rights and civic freedom to explain social change and to support their aspirations and agendas, no young woman has ever claimed in my presence that rights can be deployed in the devious ways that Mbeko attributes to them. (Indeed, many explicitly deny the veracity of such accusations, which are widespread.) Nevertheless, Mbeko's concerns about wayward women and disobedient children reflect a real concern for many in the rural Eastern Cape, South Africa, today: How should old and young, male and female, live together in a time and place where a long-standing way of life is under heavy strain?

This book is grounded in long-term fieldwork in a rural Xhosa village and seeks to explain gendered and generational conflicts about social change in the rural Eastern Cape, South Africa, roughly twenty years after the end of Apartheid. As exemplified by Mbeko's critiques, debates about human rights lucidly expose gendered and generational tensions that are widespread today, because human rights are felt by many to privilege the individual in ways that decenter obligations and responsibilities toward others. Such uncertainties about how people should live together—in particular, disagreements about the relevance of age and gender for social life—are in constant negotiation in rural South Africa today, a place characterized by profound uncertainty about what it means to be a good person who knows their place in the world.[2]

RIGHTS AND RESPONSIBILITIES: SOCIAL
REPRODUCTION IN UNCERTAIN TIMES

Since the transition to democracy in the early 1990s, South Africa has become known as a place of sharp contradictions. On the one hand, it has one of the world's most liberal rights-based constitutions, one that guarantees equality and nondiscrimination across broad domains of life (Comaroff and Comaroff 2005; Davenport and Saunders 2000). Yet on the other hand, it continues to grapple with the effects of Apartheid,[3] and it has among the highest rates of economic inequality, interpersonal violence, gendered violence, and HIV/AIDS in the world. Numerous ethnographers have written about the effects of these circumstances on South African communities (e.g., Smith 2019; Mnisi Weeks 2017; von Schnitzler 2016; Ferguson 2015; Hickel 2015; Makhulu 2015; Decoteau 2013; Hunter 2010; Ashforth 2005), often framing them in terms of crises of youth (because unemployment precludes the formation of normative families for broad swathes of South African society) and, relatedly, of masculinity (because many men can no longer achieve long-standing ideals of provider manhood). A great strength of this work has been in exposing how contemporary practices of intimacy and sociality are inseparable from political economy, and this work has been influential in part because aspects of these trends are visible across the continent.[4]

I too am interested in the implications of these transformations for South African individuals and communities. However, this book departs from most recent research on this topic by focusing particularly on how *rural* people, especially women, experience and navigate these transformations and uncertainties in daily life.[5] Building on this earlier work on crises of social reproduction, masculinity, HIV/AIDS, and rights and personhood in South Africa and related contexts, this book shows that although rights-based public discourse and state practices promote liberal, autonomous, and egalitarian notions of the person, widespread unemployment and poverty in the Eastern Cape means that people are deeply reliant on one another, albeit often in configurations that are disruptive of the gendered and generational hierarchies that are framed as traditional and culturally authentic. Relationships are thus being reconfigured in ways that challenge entrenched hierarchies while leaving both personal aspirations and interpersonal obligations of care and respect—which Mbeko termed "responsibilities"—often unfulfilled. Moreover, where hierarchy and tradition are fundamental to the content of the cultural categories that organize experience and interpersonal sociality—categories such as "masculinity," "femininity," "youth," and "elderhood," for example—the idiom of rights and equality renders the content of these categories unclear. In this fraught environment, I suggest that the dissonance between these forces becomes apparent through gendered and generational conflicts that exemplify, sustain, and produce deep moral ambiguities about identity, gender, age, status, sexuality, and worthy personhood, played out through the messy intimacy of social reproduction and rural domestic life.

A word of caution: although egalitarian ideologies and practices have gained momentum since the transition to democracy, this book does not capture a point of transition between one (older) modality of personhood and another, more modern one. Rather, regardless of where they stand in relation to generational and gender hierarchies, and whatever their respective stakes may be in debates about the merit of a so-called traditional way of life, forthcoming chapters demonstrate that regardless of age and gender people in Mhlambini sometimes act—and justify doing so—in ways that resonate closely with liberal idioms of autonomy, and in other instances, they behave in ways that presume and reinforce their position within an interdependent hierarchy. This is often driven by the pragmatics of survival, but this unpredictability is itself a key contributing element to the moral ambiguities and uncertainties that characterize contemporary rural South African life. It will also become evident that what is at stake in gendered and generational contests is less a question of the degree to which a person is positioned in a relationship of interdependence with others and more *how* they are positioned as such, with whom, and on what premises (e.g., filial obligation, economic dependence, or romantic attachment). This ethnography does, however, reflect a moment in time where economic, political, and ideological apparatuses have aligned such that so-called traditional social structures are under heavy strain, and the conceptual tools most prominently available to challenge them are premised on the privileging of autonomy and equality as moral imperatives.

SOCIAL REPRODUCTION IN THE POST-APARTHEID COUNTRYSIDE

> Someone must come and educate the old ones about the rights of young people, and must make a case for us. We are living a life of oppression here. What we need is someone who can help the youth of this community, who can convince the old people to give us freedom. Me, I don't like to stay in the village because my father is oppressing me. I want to start a project [run a business], but my father says no. I even asked, at a community meeting, for land for my project, and my father stood up and said no. So, he is blocking that project. My father, he wants me to work on the mines, but I didn't find a job on the mines, or he wants me to stay home and farm our land. I don't like farming; you can't get rich quick from farming. Farming is my father's gift from God, not mine. Me, I want to support my children, but not in the old way. I want to build my own home, away from my father, but again, he says no. I am the oldest son; he says I must stay here at his home. So you see, I am living a life of oppression. Someone must educate the old ones about the rights of the youth.

This statement was made to me by Sibabalwe, a man in his midthirties, as part of a long, impassioned explanation of the problems that younger men like him are having with village elders. Like many village men of his generation, Sibabalwe is unemployed and unmarried, and although he aspires to both, he wants to achieve them on his own terms rather than those dictated by father. From Sibabalwe's perspective, the problems that he faces are grounded in the heavy-handed authority of his father (an influential, elderly patriarch) and are tied to his father's inflexible and outdated ideas about the kind of life that Sibabalwe should live. His financial dependency on his pension-earning father and employed younger sister, and the broader support that his father enjoys from other powerful elders, constrain his opportunities to live the kind of life that he considers appealing and worthy. The longer narrative from which this excerpt is taken makes it clear that he has left the village on several occasions with the hope of building a new life free from the hierarchies of village life, but opportunities outside the village were few given his limited education and lack of influential connections.

In contrast, the following statement was made by Sibabalwe's elderly father. In it, he positions himself as a morally upstanding man whose achievements are anchored in patriarchal lineage: "I have never been to school, but I am educated because I know a lot about cattle, and I built my father's homestead. My father helped me, by disciplining me to look after the cows properly. This is not my own house; this is my father's house. Our children are educated, but their education is not taking them anywhere."

Like most elders and many young men, Sibabalwe's father is deeply invested in this hierarchal social order, which is itself intimately connected to a particular kind of multigenerational patriarchal household. Many interpersonal conflicts in Mhlambini today stem from gendered and generational disagreements about the scope and value of this form of patriarchy and gerontocracy (Aguilar 1998)—that is, the clear authority of men and elders over women and younger men, as well as over the legitimacy of the rural patriarchal household as the appropriate site for social reproduction.[6]

By social reproduction, I mean the production of persons (sexually and socially), the reproduction of the home (socially and materially), and the reproduction of society. Where I discuss changes in social reproduction, I refer to transformations in household composition, as well as ideological transformations in idealized forms of family and household. Where I discuss *conflicts* about social reproduction, I refer to negotiations over how this can be achieved, and particularly over the legitimacy of other arrangements besides those considered traditional. In this way, this book is about the gendered and generational politics surrounding the reproduction of lineage, kinship, ideology, and lifeways at what Hylton White (2001, 458) termed "the crisis-ridden intersection of kinship and political economy" that is contemporary rural South Africa.

The observation that social, economic, and political transformations lead to a crisis of social reproduction is not new in Africanist scholarship.[7] Yet although these sorts of anxieties are neither new nor specific to South Africa, people in Mhlambini *experience* these changes as recent, pivotal, and rooted very close to home. Indeed, virtually everyone can tell me precisely from where and when these changes originate: with the government and with South Africa's democratic transition in the early 1990s. All these problems and all these conflicts between men and women, young and old, have, I am told, come about "since freedom," "since voting," "since democracy," and "since Mandela." Although I believe that the causes of current crises exceed the transition from an authoritarian to a democratic social order, in this book I take seriously people's claims that there is something unique and different about the contemporary moment, and that questioning the forms of subjectivity that "freedom" and "democracy" set in motion is a fruitful starting point for understanding gendered and generational conflicts in South Africa today.

The challenges that people in Mhlambini face as they struggle to get by and make sense of their world are moral ones. I draw on anthropological concepts of "moral worlds" and "moral economies," and by this I mean that they are emotive and contested and involve struggles, predicaments, and dilemmas at the intersection of political economy, ontology, subjective experience, and collective life (Willen 2015; Kleinman 2007). I refer to the positions, ontologies, and subjectivities that are adopted, deployed, and negotiated in these contests as "moral frames," a term borrowed from Sarah Willen's work on the politics of immigration in Israel. Although Willen's regional and topical focus are different from my own, the concept is fitting in the South African case because there too "we cannot fully understand the sides, stakes, or consequences of localized debates about highly controversial issues unless we consider the lively traffic between public assertions of value and personal, even intimate questions of 'what really matters' for individuals and communities with which they identify" (Willen 2015, 74).

In demonstrating what is at stake for people as they debate the merits of long-standing and emergent values and cultural forms, it will become clear that the rural Eastern Cape today is a place where singular moral frames are especially unworkable. In this precarious and uncertain environment, people encounter and deploy multiple, sometimes incommensurate moral frames as a pragmatic survival strategy, placing relationships under heavy strain while rendering moral action ambiguous and situational.

Take the ubiquitously mobilized Xhosa term *isithehe* (usually translated as "tradition," but it also means "culture"), for example: In recent decades, economic and political transformations have reduced the availability of jobs that have historically employed unskilled South African men, meaning most young men are unable to fulfill long-standing ideals of provider masculinity that are a cornerstone of this patriarchal tradition. Much has been written about the emasculation and suffering experienced by these men and the social ills that follow from their frustration.[8] In this context, claims to tradition have advantages for men: patriarchal tradition proffers authority and power over others by simple virtue of being male, and through the practice of *ukuthwala* (bride abduction), it offers a means to obtain a wife without the expenses of courtship and formal marriage. Motivated by such promises, young men like Mbeko are often the most vociferous critics of human rights and gender equality, yet as we see with Sibabalwe, young men also regularly draw on egalitarian ideologies to distance themselves from the demands of elder kin and, at times, to make claims on the South African state. Meanwhile, forthcoming chapters will show that younger women often distance themselves from tradition (in particular, from the hierarchical gender relations that characterize rural Xhosa marriages), yet young, wage-earning women deploy human rights to justify building homes for themselves that are modeled closely on the rural patriarchal homestead. Some even mobilize bridewealth (a form of interfamily exchange, primarily from the groom's family to the bride's, that is requisite for formal marriage) for their brothers and sons as a means of compelling poorer, less educated women to relieve them of the domestic chores that are solely women's responsibility. This, in turn, raises a new set of questions about the meaning of bridewealth: Is it a means of securing access to married women's labor, as these wage-earning, house-building women imply? Is it then also a means of buying gendered privilege, as many men and elders claim? If so, can it also be evidence of love, as many unmarried girls contend it to be? But many young village women espouse a widely held belief that love necessarily leads to egalitarian conjugal relations. It is a safer move, then, for a wage-earning woman to compel her son to marry a young woman with whom he is *not* romantically involved? But then can she really hold out for love marriage herself while denying others the opportunity to do the same?

It is difficult for people living amid these dilemmas to choose a course of action, and it is hard for them to predict what the future might look like, regardless of which option they choose. Yet daily life in the rural Eastern Cape is characterized by precisely these kinds of uncertainties, and people sustain, produce, amplify, and transform the conceptual categories upon which these multiple moral frames depend in their daily struggles to survive in a region characterized by long-standing marginalization and poverty.[9]

TRADITION, MODERNITY, AND HISTORY

Mhlambini is a village in Bomvanaland, situated roughly two hundred kilometers northeast of East London, on the coast of the Eastern Cape Province
of South Africa. It is home to roughly one thousand people living in approximately one hundred *imizi* (homesteads; singular, *umzi*), most of whom speak a
rural dialect of isiXhosa (the Xhosa language). These *imizi* consist of clusters of
cement and mud-brick huts, often with *kraals* (pens) for livestock and gardens
for growing subsistence crops, and they are spread out over the rolling green
hills that are characteristic of the subtropical region (see fig. 0.1). *Imizi* are connected to one another by trails, and to the outside world by a meandering dirt
road that was extended into the village in 2010. Villages blend into one another
in the rural Eastern Cape, and Mhlambini is situated in very close proximity to
other villages that range in size from between roughly five hundred and several
thousand people.

All land in Mhlambini is held communally. No one may buy or sell land, and
permission to build must be acquired from the subheadman. Informal ownership rights are inherited from elders and ancestors (who are typically buried
on that land) and are reinforced through continued land use. People who can
afford to maintain an independent household usually build near kin and typically remain heavily involved in the activities of their natal or marital home.
Many people also keep livestock, which graze freely in and around the village.

The following quote was made by twenty-nine-year-old Unathi, a Xhosa
nongovernment organization (NGO) employee who lives in Mhlambini but
grew up much closer to the nearest city, in a large village that is an infrastructure hub for surrounding rural areas. He juxtaposes his home village with
Mhlambini in the following way:

> In my village, we are very close to town. So, in my village, most people, they
> are educated. There are nurses, there are police, teachers, soldiers, you know,
> we've got the classes there. The middle-classes. You know, those class things.
> But here, I found out that this place is more backward-like. The cultures that
> we are no longer using, they are still operating here. So, this place is more
> traditional, and more peaceful. You see, in places like near town, you know,
> there's always violence and stuff like that. But here, it's quiet and peaceful.
> *Ja*, people are doing their own traditions. They've got the strong beliefs. You
> know, just like grabbing a girl.[10] If you want to marry a girl, you don't have to
> talk to her at all. If you want her, you just talk to the parents, and then you just
> grab the girl. Even if she doesn't want you. So that's some of the differences.
> We are more educated in my area. So here, education is not so important.

Figure 0.1. Typical *imizi* in Mhlambini, showing huts of different styles.

> That's another difference. And then, you know, we are kind of abandoning
> our culture, bit by bit. We are going far away with the culture. But here, they
> are still walking exactly on the culture.

As evident from this quote, Unathi views life in Mhlambini as deeply traditional and thus different from less remote Xhosa communities, like the one
where he grew up. This view is widely held in Mhlambini and echoes claims
made by earlier anthropologists, who have described the Bomvana as "fiercely
traditional" relative to other South African groups (Moodie 1992, 587; Cook
1931). I approach these claims carefully.

Debunking the long-standing fictional dichotomy between tradition and
modernity has been a major theme in Africanist anthropology for several decades. Building on the perspective that modernity is plural and that modernity
and tradition necessarily exist as conceptual categories in contradistinction to
one another, this work demonstrates that Africa is everywhere modern (the coexistence of thatched roofs, solar panels, ancestral spirits, and cellphones—all
present in Mhlambini—is an unremarkable feature of African modernity) and
that many practices colloquially associated with "otherness" and "primitive"

lifeways (e.g., witchcraft) flourish in the present precisely because they address contemporary concerns.[11] Moreover, many of the practices most staunchly defended as traditional arose through adaptation to colonial policies (Ngwane 2001; Piot 1999; Bozzoli 1983). Bearing this in mind, I approach tradition by asking what it means for local people, and by exploring how it is deployed.[12]

Defended most staunchly by elders and questioned most frequently by young women, the traditional way of life in this region is patriarchal, gerontocratic, and nostalgic, based on a widely held belief that the authority of elder men has been a cornerstone of Xhosa culture since time immemorial. We cannot confidently know the degree to which patriarchy and gerontocracy characterized this society in the precolonial era, and there are good reasons to be skeptical of claims about the timeless authenticity of contemporary forms of patriarchy and gerontocracy.[13] Yet scholarly insights notwithstanding, the authenticity of tradition is not up for debate in Mhlambini. Virtually everyone agrees that gendered and generational hierarchy is a fundamental principle of Xhosa *isiko* (culture and custom, also translated as ritual). Debates about tradition at the community level center instead on uncertainties about the continued merit of a traditional way of life.

Tradition in Mhlambini is therefore both active and emic. It is active in that it reflects "in practice the most evident expression of . . . dominant and hegemonic pressures and limits . . . an intentionally selective version of a shaping past and a pre-shaped present, which is then powerfully operative in the process of social and cultural definition and identification" (Williams 1977, 115). It is emic in that the concept of tradition is a rich and meaningful moral frame through which local people understand their world, which they then mobilize to influence contemporary practices and social relations. It is a framework through which people express a range of aspirations and anxieties about emergent forms of cultural practice. Put differently, people in Mhlambini evoke the past to describe the present. But that is not all that tradition is.

Tradition as Spatial-Moral Geography

Unathi's comments about differences in marriage practices between urbanized communities and the rural countryside in some ways reflect the skills that he regularly used as community liaison for a local grassroots NGO. His job itself entailed a kind of cross-cultural translation as he communicated back and forth between influential villagers and senior NGO personnel, relaying NGO business, gaining community input, and reporting back on its reception by the community. He is adept at reading his audiences and explaining things in terms that listeners understand, and he brings this skill to the insights he offers about marriage, family, power, and culture. In so doing, he shows that local ideas about tradition have both temporal and spatial dimensions, such that material differences between industrialized urban areas and rural regions are taken as evidence that older ways of life have been preserved in rural regions. Although this sort of temporal geography exists in many postcolonial societies,[14] the history of this region makes these assumptions particularly lucid for South Africans.

The land that is now South Africa was economically and politically complex long before the first Dutch colonists arrived in the mid-seventeenth century. This historical context, and the many phases of slow settler colonial expansion and conquest that followed, are well beyond the scope of this book.[15] For our purposes, suffice to say that by the late nineteenth century, British imperial, industrial, and colonial interests were firmly established, characterized by a strong impetus to mobilize African labor and land in the service of mining, industry, and the comfort of white colonial society. To that end, colonial administrators devised a system of indirect rule that ensured a supply of male African labor for industry while keeping most women, children, and elders on the land in rural reserves (Barchiesi 2008; Wolpe 1972). Buttressed by force and legislation that prevented nonworkers from residing outside these designated reserves, this model served the dual purposes of racial segregation and of ensuring that rural African households would assume the burden of producing and sustaining the labor force. Under Apartheid, these reserves officially became homelands or "Bantustans," self-governed territories that were cornerstones of Apartheid-era segregation policy. Mhlambini is in the heart of what was formerly a Bantustan called the Republic of Transkei (Transkei for short). Because the Transkei was alleged to be an independent, self-governing Bantustan, the South African government made little investment in infrastructure and services for the millions of people who were legislated to live there. Although it was reabsorbed into South Africa in the early 1990s, the impacts of past policy have left a visible mark on the landscape: much of the former Transkei is densely populated, overgrazed, and heavily eroded, and infrastructure is poor relative to areas outside its former boundaries. For example, in sharp contrast to formerly whites-only communities, Mhlambini lacks electricity (although this is apparently coming in 2023) and basic sanitation. It did not receive communal water taps until 2013, and they are usually dry. The nearest hospital is several hours' drive away, and the poorly maintained dirt road that used to end in the neighboring village, five kilometers away, was finally extended to Mhlambini only in late 2010. To this day, several nearby villages are reachable only by dirt trails.

Segregation in South Africa was thus a project that ossified hierarchies in the service of industry and white supremacy. Mahmoud Mamdani (1996, 27) has outlined in detail how "as a form of rule, apartheid—like the indirect rule colonial state—fractured the ranks of the ruled along a double divide: ethnic on the one hand, rural-urban on the other." This system was premised on a constellation of assumptions about cultural boundedness (the fiction of a coherent traditional Black culture, for example), the fundamentality of racial difference, and the synonymy of race and culture. These assumptions permeated most dimensions of public and private life during the colonial and segregation eras. A cumulative outcome of this is that stark differences in infrastructure between urban areas (especially heavily developed, infrastructure-rich areas that were formerly designated for whites only) and rural former Bantustans reinforce the popular perception that rural areas have been less touched by time, even as these places are believed by many Black South Africans to be strongholds of authentic cultural presence. As Hylton White (2010, 505) eloquently observes, the South African countryside thus continues to be thought of as "a realm of power and personhood fundamentally different from the domain of urban experience," one characterized by timeless lifeways, spiritual grounding, and ethnocultural authenticity. This ethnocultural authenticity was generally believed to be embodied in a combination of a gerontocratic patriarchy and dependent, domestic femininity in opposition to "whiteness" and to autonomous, liberal forms of personhood (White 2010; Comaroff and Comaroff 1987).

It also means that concerns and anxieties about social change are regularly articulated through a "rhetoric of contrasts" (Comaroff and Comaroff 1987), notably as distinctions between urban and rural, work and home, educated and uneducated, and Christian and those whose spirituality is focused on their relationship with ancestors and other spirits. A vast lexicon of practices and things give symbolic form to this dichotomous way of thinking about tradition, place, and culture, and many aspects of this tension feature in the chapters that follow. Examples include architectural forms, literacy and competence in English, forms of religious and ritual practice, habits of alcohol consumption, and companionate marriage based on love and mutual choice versus marriages negotiated primarily between senior members of extended kinship groups in accordance with elders' economic, affective, and sociopolitical agendas. It also includes adherence to or departure from gendered and generational *hlonipha* (respect) customs, which sustain and reproduce social hierarchies.[16]

The analytic purchase of this kind of dichotomous, categorical thinking has been a subject of bitter and long-standing discussion in regional anthropology, and my objective is not to adjudicate these debates.[17] Certainly in Mhlambini, differences between urban and rural, traditional and modern are oversimplified and overstated; people and things associated with town are present in the village (if they were not, many of the conflicts and tensions discussed in forthcoming chapters would not manifest), and village concerns are also town concerns because people regularly migrate back and forth between them. Accordingly, my approach aligns with recent scholars who have shown that regardless of their descriptive limitations, this kind of categorical thinking does offer conceptual tools—what I term moral frames—though which local people position themselves according to pragmatic personal and political projects (Bank 2011, 2002; Ferguson 1999, 82–122). These moral frames offer a kind of toolkit that people use to pursue their personal goals, position themselves vis-à-vis others, and make sense of their world. The manner and degree to which they can do so, however, is shaped by hierarchies of gender, age, and access to resources such as wealth and formal education.

Tradition as Constitutive of Gender

Theories that frame gender as performative (Butler 1990; West and Zimmerman 1987), fluid, multiple, ranked, and historically and culturally situated (Connell 2012; Connell and Messerschmidt 2005), have found strong analytic purchase in South Africa, as scholars and activists have sought to explain South Africa's notoriously antagonistic gender politics. I take gender to be all of these, while drawing particular attention to the performative nature of gender—that is, the notion that it is something one does and becomes—for understanding gendered sociality in Mhlambini today. As Cook writes in one of the earliest ethnographies of the Bomvana: "The work of the two sexes is, as it were, an integral portion of the very nature of their sex—almost a secondary sex characteristic. Thus, a woman by performing a woman's work well is more of a woman; the better a man succeeds in the tasks of men, the more manly he becomes" (1934: 14). The language of "the two sexes" here reflects a conflation of biology and gender that was normative in Cook's time, but this quote nevertheless captures what I have witnessed over and over in Bomvanaland and what was succinctly summarized for me by a village elder: "It is your *deeds* that make you a man [or woman]." As forthcoming chapters will show, in Mhlambini today these deeds are performed at times unreflexively, at times strategically, and often in negotiation with tradition.

Furthermore, while acknowledging the utility of mainstream gender theory, Africanist gender scholars have highlighted the culturally situated nature of gender theories and have questioned the ability of theories from the global North to fully explain what gender is and how it works in Africa.[18] For example,

Mfecane (2020) takes issue with gender theories that posit body and spirit as unimportant for gender, arguing that for Xhosa men, body modification through traditional circumcision and maintaining proper relations with ancestors through ritual are key constitutive elements of manhood. Moreover, Kopano Ratele identifies important parallels between gender and tradition, noting that they are both contingent, questioned, multiple, and negotiated, and amenable to emergent new forms under conditions of social change. He further points out that sexuality is always embedded within tradition, implying that reproduction and all the hierarchically oriented forms that go with it are inseparable from tradition as well. Ratele notes that "the regulation of sexual desire and the practices and relations which desire elicits—what people are encouraged or discouraged from feeling, doing, and with whom—which operates always in conjunction with the regulation of gender, thus is a critical set of pivots around which traditions revolve" (2013:141). Taken together, these insights lead him to conclude that tradition is co-constitutive of gender (Ratele 2018)—a point with which I concur.

In line with this theory, the following quote by a young man from Mhlambini demonstrates that tradition itself—both as an idea of how one should live and as a constellation of practices that sustain and produce relationships—is indeed constitutive of gender for people in Mhlambini:

> The thing is, if you are able to work and get married, that makes you proud. That makes you a man, you know? You see, everyone now is recognizing you as "Ya, that man has got a wife!" Even if you are just walking with your wife, you are proud because she is your wife. And when you see the people of that same age with you, they are just running, kicking the ball there, not having wives, you see you've achieved something. So, you see, it's an achievement to have a wife. Which you have paid *lobola* [bridewealth] for! (Unathi, unmarried man, age twenty-nine)

This goes some way to explain the persistence of traditional practices (e.g., bride abduction, bridewealth, rituals for ancestors) and social arrangements (e.g., gerontocracy, patriarchy) despite powerful pragmatic and ideological challenges (e.g., the unaffordability of bridewealth, human rights regimes): tradition is not just a tool to deploy—it is also part of who people *are*.

Tradition as Flexible Resource

When people in Mhlambini describe traditional practices and values, they usually speak as though these are fixed, unambiguous, inflexible, and timeless. This way of speaking about tradition offers an accurate description of normative ideals—for instance, people often tell you that *lobola* (bridewealth) is ten cows, maybe a bit more if the woman is well-educated, and maybe a bit less if she is already a mother—but poorly reflects how these practices and values are actually taken up and used in daily life. Far from being fixed and unchanging, Xhosa tradition can be flexible and accommodating—it is "usable" (Livermon 2015) and useful, and this too is a reason for its continued appeal.

For example, while many young adults are now unmarried in Mhlambini, marriage rates are nevertheless higher than in many low-income communities in South Africa. This intrigued me for a while—I knew that marriage is often a process in Southern Africa and that full upfront bridewealth payment is rare, and I also knew that the high cost of marriage is considered a key reason why so many young South Africans remain unmarried (Posel, Rudwick, and Casale 2011; Hunter 2010; Hosegood, McGrath, and Moultrie 2009). Once people started disclosing the details of specific recent marriages, however, I learned that in practice, some families agree to *lobola* payments as low as a single cow (or cash value equivalent)—and in some cases this low balance remained unpaid even after the couple had been living together as spouses for years. Reasons given for settling on such low *lobola* included sympathy for a young couple who were in love, already had a child together, and wanted to live together as a family;[19] sympathy for a poor but well-liked and newly employed young man who lived alone following the death of his parents and siblings; a widower with young children who was a migrant mineworker and who desperately needed someone present in the village to care for his children; and a mature widow keen for the companionship, labor, and prestige that a daughter-in-law would bring. Despite claims otherwise, in practice tradition surrounding bridewealth and marriage is flexible and accommodating, offering practical means of addressing pressing problems and profound desires. Forthcoming chapters will show various ways in which tradition is used by people of all ages, genders, and social positions to ensure security and achieve dignity for themselves and their families.

GENDER, POWER, AND AGE

Gender difference is a fundamental organizing principle of social life in Mhlambini. Boys and girls are held to different standards and expectations from an early age, and this is continually reinforced and reproduced through gendered spheres of activity and practice. Girls and women, for example, usually do all the cooking, cleaning, and most of the child-rearing, as well as the laundry, brickmaking, dung-collecting and floor-dunging, beer-brewing, and collecting of shellfish, firewood, and water. This constitutes the bulk of the manual labor that goes directly into the daily maintenance of an *umzi*. Men's activities include building (of houses, fences, and so forth), plowing, fishing, herding, and caring for livestock. Apart from occasionally being sent on errands, boys are not expected to do much work.

Despite the legislation of gender equality, in practice men have more power than women. However, as in many rural South African communities, a person's status and social power is always a factor of both gender and age. Elder men are the most powerful people in the village. They organize and dominate discussions at the community meetings that are the primary site for village politics, and as a cohort, they exercise ultimate authority to adjudicate domestic and community-level disputes. Having come of age in a time when jobs were more widely available, in many cases their patriarchal authority is buttressed by their economic status as retired mineworkers; many of them have modest wealth in the form of livestock, and most receive government old-age pensions as well.

Elder women are also generally accorded great respect, and in old age they are free of many of the restrictions that constrain young women, especially young wives. For example, many attend and participate in community meetings,[20] and they attend ritual events as they please. Although older men and women both explicitly claim that elder women are under the authority of their husband and his kin, this is exactly the kind of situation where we see huge variation in practice despite sweeping claims otherwise. As the mother of a friend of mine once explained, her husband is the boss of the household, but because she is old, her husband cannot really prevent her from visiting her natal village if she wishes, and indeed he always allows her to go. Women tend to outlive men, and widows are particularly unrestricted.[21]

This gender order aligns with what Deniz Kandiyoti (1988, 278) terms *classic patriarchy*. As Kandiyoti explains, women negotiate from a weaker position in all patriarchies, but under conditions of classic patriarchy, women participate in a patriarchal bargain whereby "the deprivation and hardship [a woman] experiences as a young bride is eventually superseded by the control and authority she will have over her own subservient daughters-in-law" (279). She cautions, however, that such patriarchal bargains are profoundly destabilized under both capitalism and in conditions of poverty. This describes Mhlambini, especially because recent economic transformations are destabilizing local patriarchies in ways that lead to heightened antagonism between genders and also between elder and younger women, resulting in increasing fragility of elder women's authority over their juniors. Forthcoming chapters delve deeply into how elder women go about reinforcing their authority over junior women in their households, as well as how some younger women maneuver around this.

Although elder womanhood is an esteemed status, most women do not experience a gradual, steady increase in social power from girlhood to old age. This is due to how marriage alters women's social position. On the one hand, marriage is a valued achievement for Xhosa women, and it is a steppingstone on the long temporal journey toward becoming *abafazi abadala* (old women): respected elderly matriarchs. On the other hand, although being a young wife is generally more *respectable* than being an unmarried mother, women's independence and autonomy is greatly diminished upon marriage, and their authority in the household is far less than that of unmarried women (see also Liebenberg 1997; Hunter [1936] 1961). In most households, they are expected to stay close to the *umzi* except on errands such as collecting water and firewood, and they are always expected to be busy with chores. Young wives are very often the hardest working people at the homes that they have married into, and the domestic labor these young wives provide is an asset to virtually any household fortunate enough to include one.

Furthermore, unless she is returning to her own people following mistreatment at her husband's home, a young wife would face serious consequences—quite possibly a beating—for leaving the village without permission from her husband and mother-in-law. In contrast, unmarried adult daughters are generally quite free to move about; many of them go to town or other villages as they please. Also, by their early twenties, most single women have a child or two and will regularly leave their children at home with their mothers and sisters-in-law.[22] Young wives can rarely do this. And although unmarried daughters generally contribute amply to the work of their homes, they also have more leeway than young wives do to avoid work by delegating chores to others. Visitors to a local *umzi* will quickly be able to identify who is a wife and who is a daughter not only by their clothing (which is an immediate giveaway given married women wear long skirts and head-coverings, whereas young unmarried women rarely wear these) but also by their comportment. Daughters will readily greet visitors and may drop what they are doing to eat, drink, and chat with guests. Young wives, however, remain busy in the background, breaking from their work only if invited to do so by their in-laws. When in Mhlambini, I regularly call on my unmarried friends at home unannounced, often staying a while to relax and catch up. In sharp contrast, I am usually able to speak with my young married friends only while helping them garden or fetch firewood, or in the context of formal interviews, and then only after we have both requested permission from their mothers-in-law. The significant curtailing of freedom and autonomy upon marriage is a key factor in young women's widespread ambivalence about marriage, and this ambivalence is a source of considerable conflict and antagonism in Mhlambini today.

Work, Marriage, and Migration

For much of the twentieth century, social reproduction in rural Xhosaland was shaped by the constraints of the migrant labor system (see Moodie and Ndatshe 1994; Manona 1980; Mayer 1980). Employment prospects in the Bantustans were such that labor migration was virtually the only way Black men could earn the wages needed to pay tax (see Redding 2006), invest in their future security, and support wives and families who remained, by law, in the rural Bantustan. Rural women, meanwhile, had few options besides wifehood, and in this way the countryside became a place of domesticity and feminized dependency.[23] During this time, the typical household consisted of a man (who was usually absent), his wife (or wives) and their children, and possibly married adult sons (also likely absent) and their wives and children as well (Bank 2015; Hunter [1936] 1961). Sustained and consolidated through the constraints of the migrant labor system, it is this household structure that is widely associated with tradition today,[24] and a rich body of ethnographic and historical work on gender, domesticity, and migrant labor attests to the "common motif [of] commitment to the independence and satisfaction of patriarchal proprietorship over a rural homestead" (Moodie with Ndatshe 1994, 21) as a linchpin of masculine identity, authority, and power (e.g., Steinberg 2013; Hunter 2010; Mayer 1980, 39–44; Qayiso 1964). Although many men pine for and romanticize this patriarchal rural home, the viability of this household form has been under strain for several decades (Bank and Qambata 1999; Mager 1999; Campbell 1994), and few young men are able to build homes of their own.

The dismantling of Apartheid in the early 1990s meant that the migrant labor system was no longer scaffolded by coercive restrictions on employment and residency. Economic transformations, however, have nevertheless contributed significantly to the decline of the traditional patriarchal home. Industrial restructuring combined with market liberalization in the 1980s and 1990s have diminished employment prospects in ways that impact young people in particular, to the point that most young South Africans have never engaged in formal employment, and quite possibly never will (see Ferguson 2015, 3–5). Unemployment has in turn undermined men's prospects for paying bridewealth and supporting a wife and children, contributing to South Africa's exceptionally low marriages rates and excluding most young people from an idealized form of social adulthood that is closely tied to marriage (Pauli and van Dijk 2016; Hunter 2010). Recent decades have also seen a modest increase in employment opportunities for South African women, offering a fortunate minority the possibility of freedom from economic dependence on men. Many of these women choose to remain unmarried.[25] Households composed of young married couples and their children are thus the exception rather than the norm in South Africa today, except among the affluent (Mupotsa 2015; Hunter 2010).

In many ways, these broad trends are present in Mhlambini. Most young men are unemployed and spend a lot of time hanging around the village. Although some young men invest great mental energy into dreaming up possible opportunities for entrepreneurship, at the time of writing, none of these plans had materialized. Moreover, it is mostly young women who can effectively compete for local jobs, which are primarily in the tourism and rural development sectors.[26] As mentioned, however, young people do marry in Mhlambini in greater numbers than in many low-income South African communities; a demographic survey that I conducted indicates that one-quarter of villagers between the ages of fifteen and forty are married or widowed. Women are disproportionately represented among this younger married cohort because there are several wives and widows who married older men.

In contrast to the recent past, most households in Mhlambini are composed of older married or widowed parents, unmarried sons and daughters, unmarried daughters' children, ancestral spirits, and in some cases, the wives and children of married sons who continue to live with their parents. Many households also include at least one member who resides in a more urban area, either as a labor migrant or as an unemployed jobseeker. If these would-be migrants are women, they usually leave their children in the village with their parents. New households are formed as established married couples eventually move out of the husband's parents' homestead, or when young family members with the means to do so build their own houses in proximity to their parents' *umzi*. These living arrangements are characteristic of most low-income rural parts of South Africa today (Klasen and Woolard 2009).

In this context, the gerontocratic authority of elders is buttressed by their economic power as gatekeepers to resources such as land and jobs through government job-creation schemes and as recipients of state old-age pensions.[27] And, as already mentioned, most elder men are retired mineworkers with wealth in the form of livestock. Yet this gerontocratic power is undermined not only by egalitarian ideologies but also by elders' weak demographic representation: more than half the village population is under fifteen years of age, and most are under thirty.[28]

Marriage

As evident from the quote by Unathi, in which he reflects on the connection between having a wife and being a man, marriage remains a key ambition for most young men and some women. Especially for men, this emotive attachment to the dignity of married manhood is buttressed by the fact that under Customary Law, men have no legitimate claim to their children unless they have at least compensated a woman's parents financially for impregnating her and, ideally, have married her.[29] Young women, for their part, have more complicated feelings about marriage, balancing a desire to find loving commitment against an aversion to the "controls" that characterize rural Xhosa marriages. This feeling is expressed in this statement by Mandisa, a single employed mother in her thirties:

> I don't think I will marry, because I don't want the man that wants to control me. I don't want anyone to control me. It's good to control myself. I need the man who is just equally [a man who will treat me as an equal]. We do things together. You see, in my village, most of the men, they will control you. Yeah, most of them, they need someone under him, you know? So, I don't know [that I will ever marry]. I don't know. I am looking [for my type of man]. But not in the village. Maybe one day I can [will] find him.

Typical of younger village women, Mandisa articulates a juxtaposition between the traditional village man and the modern city dweller: the man who could love her as his respected peer cannot, in her view, be found in the village. Her apprehensions about "control," meanwhile, are supported by statements made by young wives, many of whom have recounted to me how difficult they have found adjusting to married life. Perhaps the most poignant of these was made by a fifteen-year-old wife, who once quietly reflected, "I'm happy [in my marriage] in a hopeless kind of way. In the way that I don't have any say. I just don't choose anything anymore."

Although most young people do not marry today, these statements speak to how marriage remains, for many, at once an important aspirational goal and a site through which gendered and generational negotiations are waged on both pragmatic and ideological levels. These negotiations are particularly high stakes for young people because elders are deeply resistant to abandoning marriage as a prerequisite for legitimate reproduction and household formation.

The importance of marriage as an aspirational goal, a precondition for forms of social adulthood that are associated with tradition, constitutive of gendered identity for both men and women, *and* a pragmatic site of social reproduction means that marriage is a key domain where gendered and generational struggles are waged. Marriage presents challenges for many people in Mhlambini not only because it is a difficult goal to achieve but also because gerontocratic and patriarchal power is widely perceived as being legitimized through marriage at the same time that marriage occupies a prominent space in post-Apartheid images of freedom, personal choice, and social mobility. As such, it is an institution that has multiple, shifting meanings that variously align with both hierarchical and relational moral frames, and with both individualistic and egalitarian forms of personhood.

Most local marriages come about through a process of drawn-out negotiation between families. In theory elder kin can broker a marriage without consulting the prospective bride and groom, but in practice it is more common for men to feel great pressure to marry (especially if they have the means to do so) and to be allowed considerable leeway in choosing a wife.[30] In these cases, men typically choose a woman with whom they have an established relationship, and they usually propose to her in private prior to formally approaching her family.[31] However, the young married men whom I know emphasize that their choice of spouse was heavily constrained by obligations to kin.

This was especially so if they had already fathered children outside of marriage. These men also tend to consider their prospective spouses according to how they believe a given woman might adapt to married life, evaluating prospective spouses according to a complex bodily habitus that encompasses her speech, decorum, dress, sociality, schooling (or often lack thereof; less educated women are believed to be better adapted to the modesty and subservience that rural wifehood entails), and potential fertility. For example, as the eldest son, Fundile had been under great pressure to marry following the death of his father, because his mother "couldn't be left alone at home." Although Fundile had been living in Mthatha (the nearest city, some three hours' drive from Mhlambini) at that time and had a girlfriend in town whom he was especially fond of, in the end he decided to marry a former girlfriend from a village near his natal home, with whom he already a child. He explained that although he loved his city girlfriend, he was concerned that she would not adapt to married village life. I asked what had prompted this decision, and Fundile pulled out his phone to show me pictures of the two women. When I commented that they both looked like nice people, he patiently drew my attention to differences in their dress and bodily carriage: the city girlfriend, leaning against the gas pump in her work uniform and sporting a shiny purple weave, apparently had the wrong "style" for village life and would consequently be "lazy" and insufficiently deferential to Fundile's mother. Although Fundile's concerns may accurately reflect the respective dispositions of his two girlfriends, they also exemplify notions of difference between urban and rural forms of personhood.[32]

Besides marriages like those described earlier, many marriages come about through a long-standing form of bride abduction called *ukuthwala* (see Karimakwenda 2020, 2013; Thornberry 2019; Rice 2018, 2014; Smit and Notermans 2015). Meaning literally "to carry off," this term encompasses a range of scenarios that run the gamut from staged elopement through the abduction of a young women with her parents' consent to violent kidnapping of an unwilling and unsuspecting woman against her wishes and those of her family. Common to all *ukuthwala* is the forcible seizing of a young woman by a man and his allies, who take her to the aspiring groom's homestead with the aim of making her his wife. Regardless of the true impetus and degree of violent coercion that a given *ukuthwala* entails, in all cases once the girl has been taken to the groom's homestead, her family are given the choice to either enter bridewealth negotiations with the suitor or demand their daughter's return. As I elaborate in the final chapter, the parents' decision is always honored by the abductors, although the girl's wishes are frequently muffled. Both *ukuthwala* marriage and arranged marriage exemplify a notion of marriage as reproductive and socially embedded: the interests of the bride (especially) and groom are not necessarily considered; it is the interests of their elder kin that are paramount.

Conflicts about marriage in Mhlambini are particularly tense because patriarchal and gerontocratic influence in marriage sits awkwardly in relation to South African law, which protects the "right to culture" but stipulates that the decision to marry must be autonomous, freely chosen, and cannot involve legal minors. Contemporary rural marriage practices, including polygyny (which is permitted but uncommon; Wilson 1981), conflict with popular public discourse that privileges companionate monogamy and romantic love in marriage as moral goods and modern ideals. Anthony Giddens (1992, 14–15) describes this form of romantic love as quintessentially modern in that it is bound up with the cultivation of an individualized self—one who has a particular style, particular tastes, and a particular constellation of relationships independent of kinship, and who is most fully realized through a romantic relationship in which each partner recognizes the uniqueness of the other. Long promoted by church and school (Cole and Thomas 2009; Hunter [1936] 1961), this model of modern relationships resonates with images of love and marriage that are promoted through South Africa's robust consumer culture, as well as with post-Apartheid discourses of autonomy and freedom. Thus, like their peers in many societies, young people in Mhlambini—especially women—frame spousal choice and love marriage as a means through which to assert a modern identity, viewing their desire for companionate marriage as a point of distinction between themselves and their elders.[33] Although this perception oversimplifies past forms of intimacy, some aspects of contemporary intimacy are indeed novel in Mhlambini.[34] School, for example, offers younger people a place to meet and socialize with potential partners well away from the supervision of their elders, and cellphones afford young people a new and private form of intimacy given that few elders are literate.

How young people navigate the very different meanings that are attached to marriage will be elaborated on theoretically and ethnographically in chapter 5.

Education

As hinted at elsewhere in this introduction, the value of formal education is contentious in Mhlambini for the ways in which it is thought to orient young people's disposition away from submission to patriarchal and gerontocratic social forms. One elder notes, "Our parents taught us well even if they didn't send us to school. There are children who are educated, but their education is not taking them anywhere. They hurt their parents even though [school] gives them more brains. Sending a child to school should mean you are taking them away from bad things, but it doesn't work like that with our children."

For people in Mhlambini, these changes in subjectivity and behavior are closely connected to the transition from Apartheid to democracy: the first village school was established in 1996, two years after the democratic government was formalized (until 2019, it only went up to sixth grade). Prior to the mid-1990s, some wealthier families sent their children to schools elsewhere, and several of the older wives had been educated in their home villages before marrying into Mhlambini. Barring these exceptions, few people over the age of thirty have any formal education, making schooling a key point of generational distinction. Education (or its lack) is leveraged, for instance in young people's complaints that lack of education motivates elders to "block development," and in elders' wry observations that although schooling has made their children "clever," it has done little to make them respectable. Despite their complaints about the ways in which education leads to disrespect, many local parents and grandparents do try hard to ensure that their offspring receive educational opportunities that they never had.

Education is central to local identity politics because of how it resonates with notions of appropriate gendered and generational sociality. Recall, for instance, Unathi's claim that differences in practice and value between his home village and Mhlambini stem from differences in levels of education. This kind of thinking is also evident from a statement made by a young man named

Bongani during a conversation about the moral difference between men having multiple girlfriends (which many men frame as an extension of polygyny) and women having multiple boyfriends. Admitting that the issue is complex, he explained his ambivalent feelings in a way that frames patriarchal power as long-standing but outdated, while connecting education, romantic love, and transformations in gendered sociality:

> My main one, she knows I've got other girlfriends. But if you, the girl, are doing that? Wow! Then you are out! Yeah, mostly if the girlfriend cheats, then you just leave her. This mindset, this is the way we grew up, you know? This is something that has always been happening. But actually, I don't see why. Now that I'm educated, I've read, I've read, and then I've experienced. I see that I don't like to share my girlfriend with anyone. But if it happened, it wouldn't make any difference. If I love her, it doesn't make any difference, because she'll still be the one. So myself, I no longer mind.

Although many men and elders would scoff at Bongani's reasoning, elements of a moral frame linking education to particular forms of personhood are widely shared in the village. For instance, a man from a nearby village was chastised by Mhlambini elders for attempting to abduct and marry a teacher from the local NGO-run preschool. The young woman in question was from the former Ciskei (the other Xhosa Bantustan), and in keeping with her status as a schoolteacher, she was educated (and, not incidentally, a Christian) and for this reason was deemed to be "not his type." The man was disciplined, apparently, not for trying to obtain a wife through *ukuthwala*, but rather for selecting an inappropriate woman for that purpose.[35]

Although not mobilized in the same way in the context of gendered conflicts, education is also a point of gendered distinction to the extent that girls stay in school longer than boys and are consequently disproportionately represented among those who can compete for local employment.[36] As chapter 5 will demonstrate, this can alter the gendered and generational power dynamics in families, because brothers and parents are often dependent on the income that these young women generate.

OVERVIEW OF THE BOOK

Chapter 1 describes my entry into the community as a volunteer schoolteacher recruited through a grassroots NGO. It explains the ethical and methodological challenges of carrying out research in a community in which gaining the support, trust, and respect of diverse actors (e.g., NGO personnel, young local women, and local men and elders) necessitates the uptake of often incommensurate roles and identities. Through discussion of the role of the NGO and its affiliated backpacker lodge in rendering divergent moral frames both lucidly visible and ubiquitous in Mhlambini, in this chapter we begin to see the moral dilemmas, pragmatic challenges, and opportunities that arise for local people as they navigate daily life in a situation that requires them to variously embrace, refuse, and accommodate—often all of these, at different times—practices, bureaucracies, and institutions whose meanings are polysemic.

Chapter 2 explores how people deploy the idioms of human rights and equality, demonstrating how human rights regimes are central to the moral ambiguities that characterize rural life in the Eastern Cape. I explore a tension between rights and responsibilities as manifest in the concepts of *irhayti* (a Xhosaization of the English [human] right) and *amalungelo* (a more relational form of moral rightness). In analyzing local articulations and critiques of human rights, this chapter speaks to scholarly conversations about relational and more autonomous modes of personhood and raises the possibility of achieving social justice by mobilizing interpersonal obligations between persons whose relative social power may be interdependent but hierarchical. More broadly, this chapter introduces ethnographically both the ways that tradition sustains and reproduces gender hierarchy and difference, and the ways in which human rights discourse threatens identity and personhood by delegitimizing interpersonal violence—especially gendered violence—as a means through which a hierarchical and interdependent social order is maintained. The role of interpersonal violence in the moral shaping of the person, the maintenance of the social order, and the fluctuating tension between refusing and accommodating rights and responsibilities are key themes that are elaborated through the remaining chapters of the book.

Through a range of topics, including social security grants, young women's impetus for and experiences of wage labor, marriage, and bride abduction, the remaining chapters elaborate on the themes already outlined. Through these examples, I also show how envisioned futures are created from existing cultural categories as they are taken up in new ways, according to contemporary circumstances, thereby both sustaining and transforming long-standing cultural forms.

I conclude the book by fully articulating the implications of my ethnography for scholars working on issues of gendered and generational subjectivity, human rights, violence, political economy, personhood, and social reproduction both within and beyond the South African context. The book closes by exploring how we might reimagine contemporary forms of moral personhood and human rights in more relational terms that are both attentive to the difficulties and, in many contexts, undesirability, of taking up an intendent, autonomous subjectivity in conditions of material and social insecurity, and that allow people the practical and conceptual tools to both exercise their rights and fulfill their interpersonal responsibilities.

ONE

~m~

THE LODGE AND THE NGO

TWO INSTITUTIONS DISTINGUISH MHLAMBINI FROM many neighboring villages: an ethnotourism-oriented backpacker lodge (from here forward, referred to simply as "the Lodge"), and an affiliated grassroots nongovernmental organization (henceforth, "the NGO"). It is not my intention to evaluate the impact of these institutions on community life or to make ethnographically informed arguments about the value of ethnotourism and development work in the rural Eastern Cape. This was never my area of research focus, and I did not collect the kind of data that this would require. However, examining these institutions in relation to issues of gender, generation, and social change in Mhlambini is important because of how the Lodge and NGO channel people and things into and out of the community while making certain moral frames and modes of personhood locally palpable. Moreover, although transforming local politics and sociality are not explicit motivations of these institutions, they do foster initiatives and opportunities that sustain, reproduce, and challenge gendered and gerontocratic hierarchies. The opportunities that the Lodge and NGO have created in Mhlambini have also transformed horizons of opportunity (both real and imagined) for many villagers. For these reasons, the activities carried out by the Lodge and the NGO influence how local people experience, interpret, and respond to social change. Finally, the NGO was my own point of entry into the community, meaning my positionality in Mhlambini is bound up with what the Lodge and the NGO have come to represent.

This chapter brings these threads together to provide important context for the rest of the book, and several broader themes are introduced here that carry forward in what follows. I begin by briefly describing both institutions and explaining what they do on a pragmatic level. I then explain my involvement with the Lodge and NGO and outline my research methods. The chapter concludes with a reflection on what these institutions do in the community in a more conceptual sense.

Although the Lodge and the NGO distinguish Mhlambini from many surrounding villages and differ in some ways from many other touristic and development-oriented initiatives found along the former Transkei coast, backpacker tourism, NGOs, faith-based organizations, and small-scale government-funded initiatives of various kinds can be found throughout the region. As such, aspects of what I discuss here resonate in many communities.

THE LODGE

The Lodge was established in the early 2000s through a partnership between a white South African man from Cape Town named Stephen (a pseudonym) and Mhlambini villagers as a collective. From the outset the Lodge was founded on community-based principles, with the primary objectives being to alleviate rural poverty and uplift the villagers rather than to generate profit for Stephen. The initial agreement was that all funds invested in the Lodge would be Stephen's, that Stephen and the community as a collective would share ownership of the Lodge sixty/forty, and that the community would be actively involved in all Lodge-related decision-making. The goal was to have the Lodge be entirely staffed and run by people from the local community within two years of its opening; however, cultivating the necessary management skills took far longer than anticipated. When the Lodge opened, no one in the community had enough schooling to manage the logistics of running a tourism establishment, and years went by before a few young local people gained sufficient skills to take on this work independently. Because the objective was primarily to fight rural poverty through backpacker tourism, the intention was to hand over full ownership to the community once the business became sustainable; at that point, Stephen would no longer gain any income from the Lodge. This goal was achieved in late 2012, some months after I completed my most significant period of fieldwork.

The Lodge itself consists of a formerly derelict cottage that has been repaired and renovated and a collection of purpose-built huts and safari tents.[1] The business is advertised as offering a remote, scenic, eco-friendly backpacker tourism experience in a "deeply traditional" Xhosa community. Despite being small in scale and difficult to get to (dirt-road access was extended to Mhlambini only in late 2010), over the years the Lodge has accumulated national and international accolades for ethical ethnotourism and community development, including glowing endorsements from major guidebooks and travel agencies. It attracts a wider demographic of tourists than most backpacker lodges, both because of these rave reviews and because the kind of ethnotourism experience that is offered in Mhlambini is somewhat unusual. Consequently, in addition to more stereotypical backpacker tourists, the Lodge attracts a significant number of families and older, more affluent tourists. Due to the quiet, remote beauty of the setting, the Lodge also attracts many travelers—especially couples—who are keen to avoid the hedonism that characterizes most of the backpacker lodges along the Eastern Cape coast (which is famous for its excellent surfing and attracts a lot of young tourists who either surf or are drawn to the party scene that often accompanies surf-oriented tourism in South Africa). Finally, during South African school holidays, many urban middle-class South African families come to Mhlambini on vacation. The community encourages this by reserving a percentage of Lodge beds only for South Africans during the high season—an unusual policy for South African backpacker lodges. Although Lodge guests are free to move about the village as they please, many do not venture far from the Lodge and adjacent beach except on guided touristic activities. Consequently, unless they are Lodge employees or enjoy spending time at the Lodge (which some local people do), many villagers do not regularly interact with tourists.

Since its inception, all "unskilled" Lodge jobs have been filled by village residents who were chosen by the community at community meetings. When a new position becomes available (a rare occurrence, because these are coveted jobs and people rarely leave them), a community meeting is held, nominations are solicited, and a new employee is chosen through drawn-out deliberation and debate. The cooking, laundry, and cleaning are done by local women. It has been the community's policy to reserve these jobs for women who do not have the support of a spouse. Most of these women are widows, only one has some formal schooling, and none speak more than basic English. During my fieldwork, a position opened for a dessert cook, and I followed the process through which the position was filled. After lengthy debate among older people in the community, the job went to my neighbor, a young widow who was responsible for two small children she had had with her late husband, four older children from her late husband's first marriage (the mother of these children had died years before), and a baby who was born after her husband's death. Maintenance workers and security guards are all men with families to support, and they were also appointed to their jobs by the wider community through a deliberative process. In addition to the managers, cooks, and cleaning staff, the Lodge is also a base for tourism activities. These activities are all managed as microenterprises and are owned by the individuals who run them. Most of these individuals speak limited English, so the experience is different from what is typical of tourism establishments in South Africa, where proficiency in English accompanies greater professionalism.

At the time of writing, the Lodge was managed by four young people who grew up in the village. All four had fathers who were employed outside the village, and all four came from families that prioritized their education enough to devote precious resources to sending them outside the village to complete secondary school. This combination of very modest family wealth and commitment to education allowed them to acquire the literacy, numeracy, and English fluency necessary to manage the Lodge. Two female managers live in the village at their parents' homesteads. They are both unmarried mothers in their twenties who wish to remain unwed; as will be explored in chapter 5, wives rarely work for wages, and the young women managers value the freedom and opportunities that employment proffers. Two male managers live in the village with their wives and children.

THE NGO

Because the Lodge was founded on community development principles, it has served as a base for rural development projects since its inception.[2] Although it was initially feasible to run these projects through the Lodge, over time the Lodge's sustainable rural development arm grew too extensive to manage concurrently with the business of running a backpacker tourism establishment. The NGO consequently separated from the Lodge to become an autonomous but affiliated NGO.

The NGO has four main areas of focus: education, health and nutrition, basic services, and sustainable livelihoods. The education program entails running preschools in Mhlambini and three neighboring villages, offering after-school enrichment programming at Mhlambini's primary school and, recently, the establishment of a local secondary school.[3] The health and nutrition program offers a range of initiatives, including monthly health days in each of the four villages, coordination of visits by HIV- and TB-testing outreach workers from the nearest hospital, well-baby programs, home visits for disabled or ill villagers, assistance and support with accessing social grants and other government services, and more recently the establishment of a local health point.[4] Basic services entail expanding access to needed resources, primarily clean water.[5] Sustainable livelihoods involve supporting local entrepreneurs in developing their own microenterprises, such as a hair salon and a chicken-farming business.

When a new job becomes available at the NGO, it is filled by a local person, as long as a suitably skilled individual can be found. As with the Lodge, the community appoints their chosen candidate. However, some NGO jobs—especially managerial jobs—require skills and experience beyond the abilities of any local person, and these jobs are filled by South Africans from outside the community. By the time I left Mhlambini in June 2012, the NGO employed twenty-two full-time salaried staff (fifteen of them villagers) and a further one hundred people (all from Mhlambini and surrounding villages) under the government-funded Community Work Program (CWP).[6]

RESEARCH APPROACH

Early in my career, I worked as an anthropologist in the Social Aspects of HIV unit of a large South African research institute, and through that experience I developed an interest in the popular politics of HIV prevention along South Africa's eastern seaboard. I was initially intrigued by initiatives such as virginity testing, which entailed mobilizing generational power as a means of curtailing HIV transmission among girls and young women (e.g., Vincent 2006; Scorgie 2002). I felt it was important to query why communities were so committed to these kinds of strategies despite strong evidence that they are not effective at preventing HIV transmission and despite convincing critiques that they place responsibility for prevention squarely on the shoulders of an exceptionally vulnerable group: preteen and adolescent girls. As my interests evolved through professional experience and graduate training, with time I became focused less explicitly on HIV prevention and more on the gendered and generational politics of social change in rural communities. In the end, I sought out not a community that practices virginity testing (I am unaware of whether this is practiced in Mhlambini; I suspect it is not, given it has never come up in my research) but rather one where gendered and generational conflicts feature significantly in daily life.

Mhlambini became the site for this research because the NGO was looking for a volunteer to run an after-school English and math program for students in grades four to six at the local primary school. Job criteria included willingness to stay for at least six months without pay, teaching experience, and experience living in a rural area with poor infrastructure, ideally in southern Africa.

I applied for the position while being transparent about my research project and motivation for wanting to be in the community, and I was accepted as a volunteer after meeting with both senior NGO administration and the village elders during a community gathering.

I arrived in Mhlambini in February 2011 and stayed for sixteen consecutive months. This book is based primarily on long-term ethnographic fieldwork collected during that time, supplemented with periodic return visits of roughly a month apiece between 2013 and 2020. During the sixteen-month stretch of ethnographic fieldwork, I lived at a local *umzi* (homestead) and engaged in participant observation of many aspects of daily village life. I also collected dozens of interviews with villagers. The interviewees ranged from roughly fifteen years of age (the youngest interviewees were all young women who had experienced *ukuthwala*, abduction marriage, and those interviews focused primarily on their experiences of bride abduction) to over eighty. Most of the interviewees were women, although I interviewed men as well. Interviews with English-speaking people were always carried out by me alone; all these individuals were under thirty-five years old. All other interviews were carried out with support of one of three local young people whom I hired as research assistants. One assistant was an unmarried woman in her early twenties, one was an unmarried man in his midtwenties, and one was a wife in her midtwenties whose husband was a migrant mine worker. Although hiring an older assistant might have afforded easier access to certain community members—for instance, old men— no older people had the skills (literacy, command of English) that I required. I spoke only the most basic isiXhosa (the Xhosa language) when I arrived in the village in early 2011. Through dedicated daily study and immersion in an isiXhosa-speaking village, by the time I left, I had achieved a conversational level of fluency.

The ethnographic data that this research generated were supplemented by archival research and by unpublished transcripts of interviews carried out with elderly people in the general vicinity of Mhlambini in the late 1980s. These transcripts were acquired through personal correspondence with a professor of English at Rhodes University who had collected them for her own research project in the 1980s.[7] I also engaged in a range of activities as an NGO volunteer, and these activities likewise informed my research.

During my first eight months in Mhlambini, I ran the after-school program in collaboration with Unathi, who became a friend and key informant. As mentioned in the introduction, Unathi is a young Xhosa man from a large village near Mthatha who was employed by the NGO as their community liaison. Starting in September 2011, Unathi and I trained a local woman to take over my volunteer schoolteacher position. My teaching role finished at the end of the school year in December 2011, and when new schoolyear began in early 2012, she ran the program on her own as a paid job. Although my research does not focus on children, teaching local children gave me legitimacy in the eyes of community and meant that someone knew me in virtually every household. It also afforded me firsthand exposure to the educational challenges that local young people face.

In my capacity as an NGO volunteer, I also collaborated with Unathi on an oral history project called the Storytelling Project. Prior to my arrival in Mhlambini, village elders decided that it would be a good idea to collect oral life-history interviews with community elders. The reasoning was that elders have lived through a period of great social change, and that their life experiences would be a valuable resource for future generations. Although the project was originally solely Unathi's responsibility, he felt uncomfortable asking elders to speak openly about their lives. Once the community discovered that asking questions and listening to stories was something I was skilled at and keen to do, I was recruited to help Unathi collect the oral histories. Over the course of several months, we interviewed a total of fourteen elders, collecting both video and audio recordings. Material from the Storytelling Project has been helpful for my own research and features periodically in forthcoming chapters.

Profiling Research

Five months into my fieldwork, the NGO director (a South African woman from outside Mhlambini) approached me about what came to be known as the profiling research. As the director explained to me, the NGO relied on census data and feedback from community meetings to inform their goals and activities, but they had limited knowledge of the material and social circumstances of many local families. For some time, the NGO had hoped to profile all village households to get a better sense of local needs, and she wondered whether I would be willing to take on such as project. As an ethnographer by training, I had never imagined taking on a survey-style project. But the director was quite open to the possibility of me adapting the project to accommodate data that would be useful to my own research, and I could appreciate why better data might benefit the community through improved NGO programming. I agreed to lead the profiling research.

In collaboration with the senior NGO personnel, I developed a questionnaire that included both qualitative and quantitative components. This open-ended questionnaire was to be filled out at the household level. Questionnaire topics included the following:

- Basic demographic information on all members of the household (age, level of education, marital status, etc.)
- Employment status and access to social grants
- Health (health status, challenges with access to care, etc.)
- Child mortality (number of child deaths, approximate dates, and perceived cause)
- Access to basic needs (clean water, food, cooking fuel, etc.)
- Animal husbandry and agriculture (number and kind of livestock, types and quantities of crops, challenges to caring for livestock, etc.)
- Difficulties faced as a household (broadly defined) and how household members imagine these difficulties could be overcome
- Views on both traditional and governmental leadership and on policing
- Opinions about local generational and gendered politics
- Hopes and concerns for the future

The questionnaire also included a section for recording general impressions of the *umzi* (condition of huts, presence or absence of tanks to collect rainwater, presence of and condition of gardens and livestock pens, evidence of stored food and what kinds of food, presence and condition of animals, apparent welfare of the people at the homestead, and anything else that seemed relevant). Filling out the full questionnaire took between one and three hours per homestead, depending on household size and the verbosity of the family. Although no households were obligated to participate in the profiling research, none declined to do so, and most were glad to have the opportunity to voice their needs and circumstances. We worked three mornings per week, and it took seven months to profile all 112 households in the village.

For the first three months, I worked with the NGO's community health worker, Guma, a young Xhosa woman with a bachelor's degree in social work who grew up in a large village some twelve kilometers from Mhlambini.[8] As Guma and I went from homestead to homestead, she would typically pose the questions, fill in the questionnaire form, and translate for me where necessary. While she asked the questions, I took observational field notes. After the interview was finished, we went through my notes together, and she elaborated or amended my notes as she saw fit. After three months, the NGO hired a young woman named Fundumi, a secondary school graduate from the next village over, to work with me two mornings per week. With Fundumi, I would pose the questions mostly in isiXhosa and fill in the questionnaire in English. She would watch what I wrote, translate for me where necessary, and contribute her insights.[9]

In late November 2011, I compiled all the quantitative data into tables, analyzed the qualitative data thematically, and wrote a report for the NGO. All personal details were anonymized in this report. This report was presented to one of the NGO's major Cape Town–based funders, and the funders were so impressed with the research that they offered more funding should the NGO wish to expand this project. The director was keen to profile the three other villages that they served, and their expanded budget allowed me to hire a research team (two per village) to profile the other three villages concurrently, as well as two data-entry staff through the CWP. By April 2012, all four villages had been profiled, encompassing approximately four hundred rural Bomvana households across four villages.[10]

A Note on Positionality

Over years of sharing my research with scholars, development workers, and laypeople, I have found that many people hold assumptions that shape how they imagine the Lodge and NGO. These preconceptions run the gamut from romanticized ideas about uplifting poor Africans to negative assumptions about the ways in which NGOs frame communities' needs and essentialize local values and power relations. I embarked on this research with apprehensions about my affiliation with the NGO in part because I shared some of these latter biases. At that point, my training as an anthropologist had equipped me with a solid foundation in ethnography that critiques development (e.g., Piot 2010; Li 2007; Ferguson 1990). These works are exemplary, important, and apt. I remain critical of the depoliticizing, individualizing politics of empowerment that have underscored many development projects. However, though I remain critical of the Lodge and NGO in some respects, over the course of my research, I struggled to see my biased expectations accurately mirrored in the local model of rural development embraced by both the Lodge and the NGO. Although it will become clear that I have not always agreed with all administrative decisions and priorities, and although I remain skeptical of some of the principles that guide these institutions, I certainly did not find myself amid a team of sincere foreign dupes, busy "helping" poor people while wedded to a myopic vision of the "problem" at hand.[11] And I did not find that these organizations, to quote Charles Piot (2010, 160), are engaged in "stopgap charity work [rather than] development that raises the living standard and advances the material life of communities." Indeed, I usually found the opposite.

Furthermore, people in Mhlambini themselves readily claim that they benefit greatly from the Lodge and the NGO, and I take their views seriously. No villager has ever said anything explicitly negative to me about either institution, whether in passing or in response to my pointed queries. When prompted to reflect on how the Lodge and NGO influence village life, local people draw my attention to the material benefits that these institutions have enabled, including the presence of water tanks and the better condition of people's homes. Some also speak of the improved health and welfare of local people; access to clean water has apparently greatly reduced the number of child and infant deaths in the community, and many of the widowed women who work at the Lodge were reportedly destitute before obtaining employment as cooks and cleaners. These kinds of changes matter to the people I write about here. Knowing this, I ask the reader to proceed with a critical yet open mind.

DEVELOPMENT, PERSONHOOD, AND SUBJECTIVITY: UNINTENDED IMPACTS OF THE LODGE AND NGO

The Lodge and NGO impact community life in Mhlambini in many ways that extend beyond the scope of this book. For my purposes here, I focus on two issues: how the Lodge and NGO relate to gendered and generational politics of social reproduction, and the ways in which they influence local subjectivities and modes of personhood. I stress that I do not conceptualize these institutions as agents that have caused transformations in subjectivity in a linear sense. Instead, I suggest that how the Lodge and NGO operate, their materialities, and the ways in which they are deployed by local people render more tangible certain local conflicts—specifically gendered and generational conflicts—and the modes of moral personhood that they entail.

Gender, Generation, Social Reproduction

The Lodge and NGO aim to transform the local economy through the generation and investment of capital, yet they strive to do so without challenging local norms and values. At times, this entails misalignment between the demands of the market and locally meaningful ideas of worth and worthiness, as well as tensions between egalitarian, rights-based ideologies and established social hierarchies. For example, the NGO does not engage with local gender politics and turns a blind eye to widespread gender violence in the village. Stephen has told me that the NGO has tried to broach the issue of gender inequality in the past but backed down in the face of powerful resistance. In Stephen's words, resistance to intrusions into local gender politics—gender violence especially—is so extreme in Mhlambini that "it undoes the trust that we [the Lodge and NGO] have built in the community and jeopardizes all the other work that we do."

Relatedly and somewhat paradoxically, the NGO and Lodge embrace a logic of rural upliftment grounded in neoliberal modes of empowerment (fostering "confidence," emphasis on the dignity of work, and so forth) yet aim to carry out their work through traditional structures of authority and governance. This approach is framed by both institutions as evidence that NGO and Lodge programming are community led, respectful of local values, and likely to succeed because they are grounded in deep knowledge of the local context. The fact that dominant sensibilities in the community are neither egalitarian nor concerned with the empowerment of all community members is generally ignored.

Recall, for instance, that where possible, both the Lodge and the NGO defer to the community's choice in the allocation of jobs. With respect to the Lodge in particular, community leadership in hiring is intended to counter a widespread tendency within the South African tourism industry for decisions to be made by white business owners, then implemented by a staff of non-white employees who earn low wages and have little decision-making power. As such, the community-led approach is designed to amend long-standing inequalities that are perpetuated in the tourism industry, and to contribute toward the creation of a more egalitarian society. However, although the term *community* implies inclusiveness, Mhlambini community-level decisions disproportionately reflect the interests, priorities, and values of those who have a powerful voice in village politics. These people are overwhelmingly male, and older. In this environment, a young single mother with the "initiative" and "confidence" to improve her life through employment may have little opportunity to do so if powerful village patriarchs decide that a married man with dependents is the more obvious and worthy candidate for a job.

Following on that point, the community thus defined seems deeply committed to the idea that all households should be headed by a provider—an ideal that resonates closely with long-standing cultural ideals of masculine status and achievement being tied to paid work (see Hunter 2010). Accordingly, unskilled jobs deemed suitable for men (e.g., security guards and manual laborers) are preferentially allocated to poor men with dependents. Unskilled jobs held by women (e.g., jobs as cooks and cleaners) are primarily allocated to women who have formerly been wives—and have therefore colluded in upholding long-standing ideals of rural masculinity—but who have been widowed or abandoned. In this way, hiring decisions serve to alleviate suffering for individuals and households who are in legitimate need of support—an objective that aligns closely with the principles that underscore the NGO and the Lodge—but also serve to reproduce a mode of personhood that is fundamentally inegalitarian. They also potentially neglect needy individuals and households who do not embody the model of the rural patriarchal home that powerful elders consider ideal, namely young single mothers and unmarried men.

Furthermore, local ideas about who deserves work and elders' assessments of why certain candidates are more suitable than others do not always align with the demands of the market. In other words, the impetus to run a successful community-owned business and the impetus to mobilize opportunities within that business to advance community interests (with further underlying impetus to sustain and reproduce the rural patriarchal home) are sometimes at cross-purposes. This tension was summed up succinctly by the owner of another tourism establishment elsewhere along the coast who once asked me, rhetorically, "Is the Lodge [in Mhlambini] for the community, or does it exist to make money for the community?" To illustrate this tension by way of example, at one point during my fieldwork community elders selected a man with an intellectual disability to work as a nighttime security guard. This man's family had recently arranged a marriage for him, a decision that was apparently based on a local belief that people who are "not right" mentally can benefit cognitively from the company of a spouse who is neurotypical. Although it quickly became apparent that the man was not able to effectively do the job, it proved difficult to replace him because of strong convictions from the community—and from the man's influential elderly father in particular—that this man was the most appropriate candidate for the job because the man's new wife was pregnant, and the household needed a provider.

Such situations notwithstanding, the most lucrative jobs at both the Lodge and NGO require skills that few local people possess, and where necessary, employees will be chosen from the small pool of qualified local candidates. This means individuals from wealthier families can get further ahead through employment in the NGO and the Lodge.[12] Furthermore, because young women tend to stay in school longer than men, they are often the best—indeed, only—local candidates for skilled jobs. This can destabilize the authority that elders and men have held over their juniors even as job allocation works through community forums that privilege men and elders. As such, the Lodge and NGO have a polysemic quality; they can be mobilized to multiple ends and enable and achieve outcomes that are often contradictory. They are simultaneously sites where gerontocratic and patriarchal values are reinforced (e.g., through hiring decisions) and challenged (e.g., through opportunities that they create for the employment of young women) and a means of making money for the community's benefit.

Subjectivity and Personhood

The presence of South African and foreign tourists at the Lodge means that local people regularly encounter outsiders whose lifestyle and means differ from their own. This has several effects on subjectivity and practice in Mhlambini, especially for young people. First, the Lodge presents an opportunity for local people to engage with patterns of sociality and consumption characteristic of wealthier communities, which resonate with local imaginaries of urban life. Although local people's means are far more limited than those of Lodge guests, activities such as purchasing commercially produced beer and snacks at the Lodge, charging cell phones, and maintaining social media accounts using the Lodge's satellite internet and solar-generated electricity, befriending Lodge guests and, occasionally, pursuing romantic and sexual relationships with tourists are some ways that local young people try out forms of being and socializing that differ from established ways of life in Mhlambini, and through which they position themselves as particular kinds of modern subjects. This, in turn, has implications for domestic village life because of how others interpret and respond to this positioning. As will be discussed in depth in chapter 4, for example, the young local women who are most viewed with reproach by men and elders tend to be those who spend quite a bit of time at the Lodge, whereas virtually all the young village woman who have married in the past few years avoid the Lodge and do not partake in activities such as drinking at the Lodge bar and socializing with tourists.

Furthermore, the Lodge offers opportunities to witness and interact with people from different race groups, and this also dovetails with perceptions of socioeconomic distance between guests and local people in ways which that shape local subjectivities. Although I have not systematically documented the demographic makeup of Lodge guests, based on years of ad hoc observation, my impression is that more than half of the Lodge's guests are young, university-educated, white Western and Northern European women (as opposed to North American, Australian, or South African) traveling alone or in the company of either a boyfriend or other young women of similar background. These female guests enjoy freedom of mobility and standards of consumption that are not attainable for village women. And although many of the Lodge guests are young budget travelers, they are all wealthier and more educated than local people. Observing and interacting with these tourists influences the life trajectories that local young people imagine for themselves. When asked about their hopes and dreams for the future, for instance, several of my local friends have listed activities such as wanting to go away and see other countries, go on tours to Cape Town, and own things like cars and computers, despite lacking the means to achieve any of these goals and, in most cases, lacking basic knowledge about these "other countries." And dishearteningly, some young people compare themselves to young foreigners and feel they come up short both materially and morally. These impressions show an acute sense of racial and classed difference between themselves and Lodge guests alongside a tendency to blame their own race and culture for perceived disparities between themselves and Lodge guests rather than viewing such disparities as outcomes of systemic, historically rooted processes of marginalization and inequality. For instance, a local friend once commented to me that white people are "better at romantic relationships" than Black people. I tried to counter this claim by suggesting that stable relationships are much harder to sustain peacefully in conditions of poverty and extended separation (as with migrant labor), but she was dismissive of my argument. Instead, she pointed out what to her was obvious: the Lodge attracts many white couples, and they never seem to quarrel, beat one another, or cheat on each other. Rather, these couples exemplify popular images of romantic love: they walk hand in hand on the beach, kiss as the sun sets, and snuggle around the fire pit.[13]

Like the Lodge, the NGO serves as an avenue for people and things from outside, because some NGO staff are not native to the village and have habits and values grounded in their own ethnic and socioeconomic backgrounds. Unlike Lodge guests, however, NGO personnel reside in rented housing at local homes in the village, usually for extended periods. Most of these people are South African (of various ethnicities, including some Xhosa from more affluent urban areas) or Zimbabwean, but they also include the occasional white, middle-class person from overseas—like me. Because NGO personnel reside for a longer term in Mhlambini, live among village households, and usually get to know local people in a way that Lodge guests cannot, villagers have much greater opportunity to observe and reflect on how these insider-outsiders live. Whereas NGO staff are perceived as different from local people (e.g., in how they present themselves, in how they interact with others, in terms of their explicitly stated beliefs and values), these differences are interpreted through established cultural categories and, at times, challenge local moral frames. The following ethnographic example demonstrates how this relates to contemporary moral ambiguities in Mhlambini.

"No One Is the Boss"

More than a year prior to my initial fieldwork in Mhlambini, an American woman named Janet came to Mhlambini for six months from the United States to volunteer for the NGO. She was an early childhood educator by profession and had taken a leave of absence from her job in the Pacific Northwest to help the NGO establish the first village preschool. Roughly six months into my stay in Mhlambini, I was informed that Janet would be coming to the village for a few weeks to run some workshops at the preschool, and she would be housed in the spare bedroom of my three-room hut.

By that point, I had heard a lot about Janet from NGO staff. I knew that she was in her late fifties and was well liked by everyone at the NGO. The preschool staff in particular spoke fondly of her kind patience and her valuable knowledge and skills. An additional fact that I had been told about her was that she was married to a woman—Janet's American wife had apparently visited her for a couple weeks during her stay as a volunteer.

One evening a week or so before Janet's arrival, I was chatting at the Lodge with two of the managers, Sipho and Amahle. I mentioned that Janet would be arriving soon and would be staying at my house. Sipho asked if she was bringing her wife with her, and I responded that I believed Janet's wife was staying home. Amahle commented that she knew she could not possibly "be gay" because she "loves men so much," and then she launched into a graphic description of what exactly she enjoys most about sex with men. Sipho roared with laughter, sat back thoughtfully, and remarked, "The thing I find so funny is, okay, you have two men: husband and husband. I don't like it, but okay, I get it. But wife and wife?"[14] Erroneously assuming Sipho was questioning how two women could have sex together, I began to offer a different perspective. Sipho quickly cut me off by instructing me, "Just think about it. Wife and wife. Wife, and *wife*." Again I attempted to disagree with him, and this time he laughed in my face. "Katie!" he exclaimed. "Think about it. This one calls this one wife, and this one calls this one wife [both partners refer to the other as wife]. Wife and wife. So it can't work, you see, because no one is the boss!"

Sipho's confusion about how same-sex marriages "work" is a common one in Mhlambini. When the topic came up (for instance, when same-sex couples stayed at the Lodge as guests, and when two teenaged girls from the next village over were caught having sex with one another), local people spoke of it with amusement and confusion. And yet this kind of confusion is familiar to everyone in Mhlambini because it centers on a way of being that is felt to be both foreign yet also familiar in how it resonates with broader uncertainties about identity and moral personhood that are characteristic of contemporary village life.

That is, despite popular discourse that positions same-sex sexuality as un(South) African, the rights of sexual minorities are heavily protected in South African law. South Africa was one of the first countries in the world to legalize same-sex marriage, on the basis that denying this right would violate rights to nondiscrimination on grounds of gender and sexuality as outlined in the constitution. These legislative endorsements are scaffolded by the presence of same-sex sexuality in South African popular culture; domestic soap operas, for instance, feature gay and lesbian characters and plotlines, and individuals who have spent time in town have often seen or heard about these shows when visiting friends and family. As such, even in deeply rural areas, most South Africans know that same-sex sexuality is present in South Africa and that the rights of sexual minorities are legally enshrined. People in Mhlambini are aware that same-sex marriage is an aspect of South African society, yet they are confused by it.

And yet the source of confusion is precisely not the mechanics of intercourse; Sipho himself assured me repeatedly that his concern is about power and authority in a relationship, not what same-sex couples do together with their bodies. The issue, rather, is that without the hierarchy inherent in the local gender order, the entire institution of marriage, all forms of sociality and domestic practice that it married life entails, and all sense of how to be as a married person fall away. As several people have asked me rhetorically, "In same-sex marriages, who *hloniphas* who [which partner engages in respect behaviors vis-à-vis the other]?" It is no coincidence that a number of people have offered same-sex partnerships as sine qua non examples of how life and morality are completely arbitrary in the post-Apartheid era, and as quintessential evidence that the government itself compels people to embrace an incomprehensible way of life through rights-based laws. Tellingly, when I asked Fundumi what she understood rights to mean, she responded, "Now, what I am understanding about rights, rights . . . some are just allowing us to do something that is not believable. You know? For example, that thing of a girl marrying another girl. It is happening, but is not believable, you know? But because of the right, it is happening now. So we just . . . we just . . . accept it."

On one level, Janet and her wife, as well as other same-sex couples who visit Mhlambini as tourists, are examples of how the Lodge and NGO help bring up close things that villagers are already aware of but previously viewed as distant and removed from village life. But Janet and her wife also exemplify a broader issue that carries forward in forthcoming chapters: that gendered personhood—especially with respect to marriage and domestic life—is almost impossible for most rural Xhosa to conceive of without hierarchy, at the same time that they live in a time and place where they are confronted with this notion both top-down through policy and law and in more immediate form through people and things that they see right in front of them. This, in turn, speaks to what I am referring to as moral ambiguity in the rural Eastern Cape today. "Not believable" things are happening all the time. They are a ubiquitous fact of life, and forthcoming chapters will show that navigating and even, at times, mobilizing such often incommensurate modes of personhood can be instrumental for getting by day to day.

In closing, beyond describing the Lodge and the NGO, the purpose of this chapter is emphatically not to suggest that by facilitating the local presence of different subjectivities, modes of consumption, and forms of sociality, such moral ambiguities originate with the Lodge and the NGO. However, by facilitating the movement of diverse people and things into Mhlambini, the Lodge and NGO have the effect of giving concepts like same-sex gay marriage, but also simply more egalitarian gendered dynamics in any intimate relationship, more tangible form.

TWO

—◊—

RIGHTS AND RESPONSIBILITIES

IN THIS CHAPTER, I DEVELOP and further explain the conflict between rights and responsibilities with which I introduced the book, thereby expanding upon Mbeko's assertion that human rights enable the neglect of responsibilities. Central to this discussion is a tension between *amalungelo* (a socially embedded and relational form of rights) and *irhayti* (a widely used Xhosaization of the English "[human] right"). This chapter takes the incongruency between these two kinds of rights as a starting point to investigate the interpersonal tensions that arise through the production and contestation of the subject positions that human rights set in motion. I focus on how people define and mobilize rights in the context of gendered generational conflicts, and I ground this chapter in men's and elders' explanations of how human rights enable morally reprehensible actions and how they are implicated in what they perceive to be a pervasive climate of interpersonal neglect. In so doing, it becomes apparent that human rights are central to the moral ambiguities of rural South African life in that they challenge the content of subject positions that are fundamental to identity, social relations, and personhood. It also becomes clear that tradition (as idiom, as a collection of practices, as a way of organizing relationships) sustains and produces gender hierarchy and difference, and that human rights discourse threatens identity and personhood by refusing gendered violence as a mechanism through which this social order is maintained. An oscillating tension and accommodation between rights and responsibilities—and the moral frames and modes of personhood that underpin them—are elaborated through the remaining chapters of this book.

HUMAN RIGHTS AND POPULAR JUSTICE IN
CONTEMPORARY SOUTH AFRICA

Though contested, human rights command special attention in contemporary South African life. Resistance to Apartheid, both within South Africa and abroad, was largely framed in reference to notions of universal rights to human dignity and equality, with powerful critiques of the former regime aimed at exposing the ways in which it had denied such rights to the majority. Accordingly, during the transition out of Apartheid in the early 1990s, global human rights discourse provided a framework for the transformation of South African society, as reflected in a constitution and bill of rights that are widely recognized as among the most liberal-democratic in the world (Davenport and Saunders 2000). The constitution explicitly states not only that all people are equal before the law but also that it is unlawful to discriminate against anyone on grounds of "race, gender, sex, pregnancy, marital status, ethnic or social origin, colour, sexual orientation, age, disability, religion, conscience, belief, culture, language, and birth" (Constitution of the Republic of South Africa 1996, 6). Consequently, a key outcome of the transformation into human rights–based democracy has been the increased centrality of rights-based politics and legal practice in South African life. Many of these rights—and their centrality to governance and politics—have been welcomed by South Africans, but in the years since the democratic transition, it has become vividly clear that there is widespread disagreement within society about what these rights actually mean and how they should be implemented, as well as sharp awareness of the limitations of these constitutional rights as a governing framework for South African society (Posel 2004).

First, there is the ongoing struggle between liberal notions of democracy founded on individual rights and understandings of democracy that reflect Black nationalist emphases on sovereignty and self-determination of the previously repressed majority (Johnson and Jacobs 2004). Moreover, liberal claims to universal human dignity and equality are confounded by the blatant socio-economic inequalities that characterize post-Apartheid life.[1] This speaks to a much larger paradox about rights, capital, and autonomy in the neoliberal world. As Julia Paley writes,

> The nature of democracy and the influence citizens could have on policy in the late twentieth century were shaped not only by national politics, but also by international economic processes. In public discourse, . . . policymakers

and . . . politicians have linked free market economic policy to democracy, seeing them as twin pillars of freedom around the world. Yet as citizens in places as diverse as Africa, Latin America, and countries of the former Soviet Union acquired the right to vote in the 1980s and 1990s, they often had little ability to influence public policies. By the 1980s and 1990s, these countries' economic frameworks were largely determined not by citizens but by employees of multinational corporations, experts within financial institutions, or staff of transnational lending bodies such as the International Monetary Fund. . . . At the very moment when countries regained democratic political institutions, key decisions about public life and the economy had moved outside the ambit of elections, beyond the reach of the electorate— indeed, beyond the reach of the nation-state. (2001, 4; see also Makhulu, Buggenhagen, Jackson 2010)

Proponents of human rights rarely acknowledge this stalemate, which is implicit in the marriage of the rights-bearing autonomous individual to an economic system that renders self-determination extremely difficult for so many to obtain. Thus, "debates in South Africa test the capacity of the dominant, international liberal paradigm to be meaningfully implemented or effective in local contexts where vast socio-economic and racial inequalities persist" (Johnson and Jacobs 2004, 86).

Furthermore, the notion of universal human equality and the primacy of state and law enforcement as the arbitrators of justice do not align with the moral sensibilities of many South Africans, especially in communities where gerontocratic and gendered hierarchies are deeply important. Heated conflicts over rights to gender equality are a particularly volatile example of this disagreement, both in South Africa and abroad.[2] This is complicated from the perspective of South African human rights law because, as we have seen, gendered and generational hierarchies are understood by many to be fundamental to tradition and culture, and the "right to culture" is itself guaranteed in the constitution and bill of rights. Indeed, respect for cultural diversity has been part of the governing African National Congress (ANC)'s[3] guiding philosophy for decades and has been explicitly affirmed in party documents since long before the democratic era (Venter 1995). Finally, beyond merely outlawing discrimination on grounds of culture, the South African constitution explicitly guarantees the right to participate in the cultural life of one's choosing while also recognizing the legitimacy of traditional legal systems (Comaroff and Comaroff 2005; Davenport and Saunders 2000; Himonga and Bosch 2000).

In this legal, political, and socioeconomic climate, it is unsurprising that ambiguities have arisen because it was not explicitly stated how constitutional rights, traditional legal systems, and rights to culture would be achieved in practice. Writing shortly after the transition to democracy, legal theorist Venter (1995, 4) summarizes this conundrum: "It is unclear just what role will be played by customary law within the new legal system. Their [the legislators'] reticence is perhaps understandable, since an emphasis on cultural rights might lead tribal groups... to pursue secession. Nonetheless, allowing cultural groups to practice customary law without any limitation makes a mockery of the protection that the Constitution affords women."

These conundrums are far from resolved, especially with regard to gender equality. Their rights to equality notwithstanding, ample evidence suggests that in rural communities like Mhlambini, women are often barred from representing themselves in traditional courts and often do not have access to civil courts.[4] Beyond the conundrum of reconciling women's status under customary law with their constitutionally sanctioned right to freedom from discrimination on grounds of gender and sex, further complications stem from the fact that the territories overseen by elected officials in rural municipalities overlap with those of traditional authorities whose claim to their position is hereditary rather than democratic (Rangan and Gilmartin 2002; Ntsebeza 2002).

These contradictions are resolved in Section 30 of the constitution, which privileges rights to equality over customary hierarchies in proclaiming that "everyone has the right to use the language and to participate in the cultural life of their choice, but no one exercising these rights may do so in a manner inconsistent with any provision of the Bill of Rights" (see also Comaroff and Comaroff 2005, 302; Davenport and Saunders 2000, 579).[5] The use of the term *choice* here causes further logistical and legal challenges, however, because it implies that culture is a closed, fixed, and unified package of logics and practices that can be freely chosen or put aside through will rather than an open-ended constellation of constantly shifting meanings and practices that are fundamental to subjectivity and (gendered and generational) personhood.[6]

Finally, although this emphasis on constitutional rights and equality is productive of new forms of justice, it also eclipses other avenues and paradigms through which justice could be pursued (von Schnitzler 2016; Hornberger 2011; Manicom 2005). For instance, through the example of a civil court case over water rights, Antina von Schnitzler (2016, 2014) shows how appeals to human rights and dignity not only serve to define the state's obligation to its citizens in particular ways but also produce specific forms of citizenship, justice, and politics through universalist claims to human dignity. Similarly, through her analysis of human rights policing in Johannesburg, Julia Hornberger (2011) contends that for human rights to be liberating, a particular subject position is required. Through detailed ethnography, she exposes how producing this subject position in conditions of its absence is a hegemonic project that delegitimizes other forms of moral good.

Like Hornberger and von Schnitzler, my discussion here contributes to anthropological understandings of the productive nature of human rights by examining the ways in which rights are implicated in the (re)production of popular justice. In shifting my focus to the level of interpersonal social relationships and intimate daily life, I show that obligations and rights are also useful lenses though which to theorize the implications of human rights for personhood more broadly.

RIGHTS AND PERSONHOOD

People in Mhlambini consider a hierarchical patriarchal and gerontocratic social order to be the traditional and long-standing Xhosa way. The social norms that this order entails are also exemplary of a relational notion of personhood that has long been recognized as constitutive of personhood in some non-Western contexts and that is taken up in Africanist philosophy as the concept of *ubuntu* (humanism, often summarized through the Xhosa idiom *umntu ngumntu ngabantu* [a person is a person through other persons]).[7] In such societies, full personhood is "attained in direct proportion as one participates in communal life through the discharge of the various obligations defined by one's stations" (Menkiti 1984, 176), and whereby the person is best "understood in large part as constituted by those relations to which his position in the system is connected" (Riesman 1986, 100). This means that an individual's humanity is a work in progress, that personhood and status are not qualities equally shared among people by virtue of their common humanity but are rather produced through social relationships and are worked toward and continually constituted over the life-course. Anthropologists have shown that the relations within which the person is embedded have long been characterized by hierarchical dependencies that are premised on both a very different understanding of value and a lesser valuing of autonomy relative to Western individualism. Speaking of African personhood in the precolonial past, Harri Englund (2004, 17) writes, "Security in its widest existential sense was achieved through the accumulation of people. . . . 'Wealth in people' sustained a logic of value that was clearly different from the logic of accumulation in a capitalist sense. . . . Its particular historicity involved a specific form of personhood for which 'freedom' lay not in a withdrawal into meaningless and dangerous autonomy but in attachment to a kin group, to a patron, to power' (Kopytoff and Miers 1977: 17) . . . 'Freedom' was 'belonging' rather than 'autonomy.'"

This has more recently been echoed by James Ferguson, who writes of the Ngoni state in Southern Africa that "hierarchical dependence here . . . throughout the region, was not a problem or a debility—on the contrary, it was the principal mechanism for achieving social personhood. Without networks of dependence, you were nobody—except maybe a witch" (2013, 226–27).

Such relational notions of personhood become significant when we consider the ways in which rights are discussed, contested, and deployed in the rural Eastern Cape today. In this region, as in much of Nguni-speaking South Africa, human rights are widely translated as *amalungelo*. However, *amalungelo* and human rights are not neatly equivalent concepts.[8] The term *amalungelo* is derived from the verb *ukulungisa*, meaning to make things nice, pleasant, correct, or good in a moral sense. By examining how the concepts of *amalunglo* and *ukulungisa* are used in context, we begin see the challenges that human rights pose for established, locally meaningful notions of moral personhood. Anette Wickström, for example, focuses on acts of *lungisa* to understand Zulu concepts of health and wellness. Drawing on ethnographic fieldwork in KwaZulu-Natal, Wickström defines *ukulungisa* as "to correct" or "to put in order" and says that *ukulungisa* "refers to efforts to improve a person's situation when there has been disorder" (2014, 213). Acts that foster *lungisa* result in the reestablishment and fortification of relationships with kin and ancestors (these especially), as well as friends and neighbors.

Patrick McAllister (2002) also refers to *amalungelo* in an analysis of sociopolitical implications of Xhosa beer-drinking rituals. According to McAllister, the term *amalungelo* refers to the significant portion of beer that must be allocated to privileged persons who are close neighbors of the host and who can be called on for assistance. Historian Jeffery Peires defines *lunga* as a combination of "order" and "justice." Drawing on a range of historical texts, he explains that misfortunes such as cattle sickness, poor harvests, and personal injury were historically interpreted as "evidence of divine displeasure . . . due to one's own shortcomings and *derelictions of duty*" (Peires 1987, 48; emphasis added). Such misfortunes could be corrected through acts of *ukulungisa* (to make it right). Finally, in the village where I carried out fieldwork, Nokulunga is the most popular women's name. Although this name could literally be translated as "mother of rights," local people told me that it means "mother who makes it nice [in the home]." In a community like Mhlambini, a mother who makes it "nice in the home" is not one who ensures equality between all members of the household, but rather one who maintains peace and well-being in a household composed of members whose relative authority is unequal.

What emerges from this inquiry into the concept of *amalungelo* is a socially embedded idea of moral rightness, especially regarding close kin. Among rural Xhosa, these are ties of obligation between persons whose relationships are characterized not by parity in status but rather by gendered and generational hierarchy. This constitutes a different way of framing rights compared with the constitutional forms of rights-based justice that dominate South African public discourse. In part because of the difficulty in reconciling *amalunglo* with human rights, many local people use the term *irhayti* in some contexts, and *amalungelo* in others.

RIGHTS, OBLIGATIONS, AND GENERATION

Elders in the village are the most vociferous critics of human rights. Their critiques often center on the ways in which rights seem to justify young people's failure to meet their obligations to elders—a complaint that is ubiquitous. Over and over, I am told of the problems caused by young people's disrespect and neglect in the name of freedom. Acts that are perceived as disrespectful included evading housework, publicly displaying romantic affection, drinking alcohol, and, especially for young wives, depriving elder women of their companionship and labor.[9]

For example, the elderly subheadman once brought up rights in the context of changing gender relations and disorderly social reproduction:

[Nowadays] there's rights, so if there is someone you want to be intimate with, you will just phone the person and say, "At such and such a time I want you here!" It's not the man, it's she, the woman, who will be made ready for sex here, not so? [It's the woman who wants sex, and who phones the man.] Those are the things of you young people. It's not the game that people in my day used to play. And we no longer ask any questions, because we can see that the country is messed up. Is it not so that these days it is permitted for a Black person and a white person to marry, and nothing is seen to be wrong with that? It wasn't like that in my day. In my day, if you met a white person and you fell in love with her, you would have made a big mistake. Do you know that if that happens these days, you haven't made a mistake? What kind of law is that? It's the current law!

I believe that the subheadman's statement should be viewed with a mind to broader concerns about the way that rights provide legitimacy for sexual and reproductive norms that undermine generational obligation and authority. Lydia Boyd's (2013) work on rights and same-sex sexuality in Uganda offers a useful comparison. Boyd notes that for many Ugandans, there is a fundamental distinction between same-sex sex acts and the social sanctioning of the "right" to homosexuality. Despite vociferous popular claims that homosexuality is un-African, Boyd notes with surprise that many people readily acknowledge that same-sex sex acts have long been practiced in Uganda and that these acts in themselves pose no great threat to society. Yet as a pastor explained to Boyd, the *social sanctioning* of homosexuality through rights discourse is a completely different affair: by granting a right to same-sex sexuality, Ugandans would be condoning a new freedom from cultural norms, including obligations to family. In other words, it is not the sex itself that is disruptive of the social order but rather an implicit rejection of socially embedded sexuality and thus the rejection of the centrality of kinship and family for moral personhood.

Rights are threatening to elders in the village for similar reasons. Indeed, the subheadman's statement should not be taken at face value given that he knows interracial intimacy is not novel in South Africa. As mentioned in the previous chapter, the largest clan in the village, called *Abelungu* (white people), proudly claim descent from shipwrecked Europeans. The subheadman is certainly aware of this. But he is also keenly aware that human rights have brought about a fundamental change in the social *legitimacy* of interracial sex.

Elders also link rights and freedom to other examples of a decline in generational respect. For example, many elders are critical of overt displays of affection between unmarried young people, which they experience as a deplorable affront. Examples of such displays include young couples walking down the road together, or young men chatting with their girlfriends by the riverside while the girlfriends wash laundry. Yet elders never complain about the actual intimacy itself; they assume that all normal young people have boyfriends and girlfriends. What they take issue with is the public nature of it. One elderly woman expressed this to me as follows: "In the old days, we would meet in the forest, or meet after our parents were sleeping! If we saw anyone older, day or night, we would run and hide! If I was caught, my father or brother could beat me!" That young people carry out their affairs more publicly suggests to elders that they embrace a public sanctioning of sexuality outside the constraints of reproduction and family life.

However, elders' paramount critique of human rights stems from the way that they are seen to justify young people's failure to meet their obligations to their elders. I am repeatedly told of the problems caused by young people's disrespect in the name of freedom. Here are but a few examples:[10]

Young women are disrespectful. They "move up and down" [the road] with men. They like having boyfriends, and they don't respect people. And then they get babies at a young age. They don't take care of their elderly people anymore. (Elderly woman)

Young men have no dignity. They are just outside all day, doing what they please. They do nothing to help at home. Then they come home after dark and expect to be fed. (Middle-aged woman)

The youth are not the same as the old generation. The girls and young men are lazy, and they are busy with their own things. They do not take care of their families anymore. (Middle-aged man)

Complaint is an important symbolic practice through which elders can reinforce social norms and remind others of their obligations to one another.[11] Andreas Sanger, for instance, found that township-dwelling Xhosa elders offered similar complaints to those of my elderly collaborators. He writes: "For older people, to embrace a girl or boy in front of older persons was certain evidence of the young people's rejection *of all moral obligations* towards the elderly. . . . Disrespect, defined as divergence of younger people's behaviour from 'traditional' cultural behavioural norms, thus involved a threatening . . . and paralysing . . . experience. Disrespect . . . bore witness to the ineffectiveness of social relationships and thus of *selves*. In view of the aged, it negated both their dignity and personhood" (Sanger 2002, 50; emphasis added).

For people who have grown up in a gerontocratic and interdependent society where status and full personhood are owed to the elderly by virtue of their life experience and connection with ancestors, disrespect and neglect from youth robs elders of their very personhood. Human rights are understood to be a key enabling force in this because they justify autonomous action and equality as parity between the old and the young. Importantly, however, elders express concern not only for their loss of personal dignity but also that this lack of interpersonal care threatens the well-being of everyone in the village. For example, one of the subheadmen once told me that he is afraid people will starve in the future because they are not farming maize anymore. He framed this problem as a lack of interpersonal care. In his words, "[This change] is something that is killing us, that is going to kill us. All these things that are happening are afflictions [*ingcinezelo*].[12] They're afflictions. But we do it to ourselves, because we don't help each other. One can't do things on one's own."

Although rural women arguably stand to benefit most from the legislation of rights and equality, elder men and women are in fact largely united in their critiques of *irhayti*. A few older women reflect that rights are good "in some respects," but most lament that they feel frankly bewildered by rights, and they express skepticism that *irhayti* applies to them at all. Indeed, what emerges from my conversations with elder women is a sense that *irhayti* implies a fundamentally foreign form of womanhood. These differing forms of womanhood are even referenced occasionally as evidence of generational rupture. For example, while I was attempting to discuss rights with an elderly woman named Nokhumbulele, she asserted that *abantwana* [children] like my research assistant and me (we were both well into our twenties at the time) have rights, but women like her do not. When my research assistant tried to counter this assertion by arguing that she too was a woman rather than a child (interestingly, as a married mother, she took issue with being positioned as a child rather than with the assertion that older women lack rights), Nokhumbulele interrupted her by saying, "No, I mean you and Katie are not living like we are living. Even you can see that." Although generational conflicts among women are rarely as overtly antagonistic as conflicts among elder men and their juniors, women like Nokumbulele invest great energy in compelling younger women to assume roles that are domestic and supportive and are thus in keeping with a hierarchical and dependent notion of feminine morality.

RIGHTS, OBLIGATIONS, AND GENDER

I now return once again to Mbeko, the young man whose views I used to introduce this book, to provide an illustration of how rights destabilize gendered identities. I will do so by examining a widespread local perception that young women are intentionally abusing their rights at men's expense. This is best shown by way of example. One day, I was grilling fish on my firepit with Mbeko and Jono. Both young men attested, as many men do, that women often abuse their rights in ways that are damaging to men. I asked them to explain how women are abusing their rights, and how men are harmed through this abuse. Without pause, Jono offered the hypothetical example of a woman who has sex with a man, only to discover that he does not have as much money in his wallet as she had previously thought. According to Jono, because she has rights, this woman can now go to the police and claim that she was raped. Mbeko concurred that this was a strong example of how women abuse their rights.

Somewhat skeptical, I asked Jono and Mbeko whether they had personally had an experience like this, and they conceded they had not. However, Jono offered the following personal anecdote instead: Several years back, he had a girlfriend who grew tired of him and pushed him aside. Then she discovered that Jono had been cheating on her. According to Jono, the girlfriend confronted him about his affair, saying terrible things to him in a vicious and unjustified verbal attack. Jono claimed that she explicitly taunted him, stating, "You're going to just listen to me now! Because whatever you do [to me], I will phone the police, and they will arrest you!"

Jono knew that his girlfriend's claims were factually correct: he could not legally retaliate against her with physical violence. Yet he could not stomach being taunted in this way, so he decided to "sacrifice his life" (risk getting sent to jail) by beating her up.

Both Jono and Mbeko agreed that this was another telling example of the ways that women abuse their rights. In Mbeko's words, this is evidence that "now even the girls, when they want to do anything they want to say, like *terrible* things, they say, 'You can't do anything to me because I can call the police. We have *irhayti*.' They can talk what they want to say [they say whatever they want] about *amadoda* [men], even though *amadoda* are respected people in our culture."

Contrary to the perception of Jono, Mbeko, and other men like them, in my experience, women do not draw on rights as a means of unduly punishing men. And although material provision and sexual intimacy are certainly connected in this community, I have never personally encountered a woman who deployed human rights in a way that struck me as blatantly instrumental, let alone weaponized. Rather, I have found that young women express their own ambivalence and contradictory feelings toward rights versus gendered social structures: although most claim to approve of rights for women, they are also very unlikely to exercise these rights if beaten by male friends, family members, or lovers. As a case-in-point example, Zanele (early twenties, unmarried) lamented to me at length that her boyfriend regularly beats her if he suspects her of infidelity—a suspicion that could apparently be provoked by leaving the house looking too well-groomed or speaking to other men in his presence. Although Zanele claimed that she could never report her boyfriend to the police for domestic violence, when I asked her about how rights have changed life in the village, she immediately referenced the right to police recourse in the event of domestic violence as an example of what has changed. This kind of reluctance to pursue rights-based justice even where legally justified to do so suggests that Jono and Mbeko's fears are exaggerated, at the very least.

Nevertheless, over the years, I have been frequently struck by the impression that many young men genuinely feel that their perceptions are accurate; however selective Jono's version of events may have been, he truly felt that he had been deeply wronged. In this way, young men's anxieties over rights to gender equality are like the sense of marginalization expressed by enthusiasts of the men's right's movement, where "the anguish, confusion, and pain . . . is real and well-grounded. [Yet] real, here, is not to be confused with true" (Coston and Kimmel 2013, 373). As such, analyzing men's felt experience of abuse and manipulation by women can productively inform understandings of rural South African gender politics more broadly and can speak to how human rights are often felt to conflict with local notions of gender difference. Like the American men's rights activists whom Michael Kimmel has analyzed, men like Jono and Mbeko "may not currently feel powerful, but they feel *entitled* to feel powerful" (Coston and Kimmel 2013, 377; emphasis in original). Romit Chowdhury's recent work on men's rights groups in India is also helpful here. Chowdhury is intrigued by the fixation of many men's rights activists on the poorly documented phenomenon of women who allegedly demonize innocent men by claiming in court to be victims of domestic violence. Citing figures that suggest most Indian men (and many Indian women) feel that wife beating is morally justified in some instances, Chowdhury argues that rights-based legislation about gender violence is threatening to many men because of a widespread patriarchal expectation from men that they must punish women for violating the codes of feminine propriety. Here, "false accusation" becomes the linchpin of men's rights articulation precisely because these men feel they are being criminalized for actions proper to their gender roles (Chowdhury 2014, 44).

This clarifies narratives such as Jono's. Similar to what Chowdhury describes, gender violence is widespread and widely condoned in Mhlambini, and most people concur that men are justified in disciplining women provided the woman misbehaves (that is, fails to fulfill her obligations toward a man within the parameters of normative gendered social roles or fails to acknowledge his authority). Recall from the previous chapter Stephen's report that the NGO does not address gender violence due to the vehement pushback that they have received when they tried to do so. Explicit questioning about motivations for gendered violence clearly showed that it is ubiquitous and unremarkable, as shown in the following exchange with an older woman:

Research assistant: What would cause a man to beat his wife?
MamQadi: Isn't it so that all the men here beat their wives?
Research assistant: Maybe . . . but why would you get beaten?
MamQadi: For various reasons. Sometimes there's something that I've done clumsily [*endiyimoshileyo*], you see? Or something that he was wearing, you understand? I can't remember where I put it. That causes us to have a disagreement, and I end up getting beaten.

When my research assistant and I pressed MamQadi to explain why beating in necessary in this situation (as opposed to a verbal reprimand or peaceful discussion, for instance), MamQadi defended conjugal violence at length on grounds that it is, in her view, at once a long-standing Xhosa practice, an unremarkable feature of all marriages, the only effective tool that husbands have to instruct their wives about their likes and dislikes, and essential for maintaining gender hierarchy. She concluded a long monologue by stating, "He doesn't want you to get too familiar with him. He wants you to know that he is the father [of the family]; [*Akafuni umqhele. Kufuneka umazi ukuba ungutata*]," adding for emphasis that these are the old-fashioned ways [*sisiphatho sakudala*].

The ubiquity of violence, the perception of its legitimacy in the context of marriage, and the ways in which rights are perceived to limit it all come together in the following conversation with Sipho, which I audio-recorded and have abridged below. What cannot be conveyed in text is his deeply agitated tone when speaking (in purely hypothetical terms) about his wife drinking alcohol in public, as well as his frank and unapologetic tone when describing "doing something to her" if she did so.

> The married women, once they got married and are under the control of the husband and the husband's family, they can't go to the *shebeen* [tavern]. My wife can't go to the *shebeen*. She knows that I have the right to . . . well, I can say that she knowns that I won't like that, and that I can do something [beat her], if she does that. Because why does she need to go there? She has to look after children, she has to do all kinds of things. But unmarried girls, they're free. Their boyfriends don't have the right [to beat them for going out drinking].

Taken together, these examples—and innumerable others like them—suggest that violent discipline is a significant dimension of how gendered subject positions are constituted and produced here. Violent discipline is so wrapped up in the local gender order that is appears to be a component of how masculinities and femininities are experienced and conceptualized for rural Xhosa. Indeed, one older woman once referred to her husband beating her "when she's guilty" as quintessential evidence that she is a real Xhosa woman. As such, it becomes easier to understand why human rights and the idiom of gender equality are experienced as threatening to the social order. In such a context, "it becomes possible to understand that for men [in these societies], the existence of a set of [rights-based] laws which criminalises domestic violence in an overall culture that authorizes violence against women as a script of male honour puts the very meaning of masculinity under pressure" (Chowdhury 2014, 44).

Put differently, by upsetting the conjugal gender hierarchy, human rights are experienced as rendering proper gendered social relations unclear. Tellingly, the above conversation with Jono and Mbeko flowed quickly into an impassioned critique of young women who have several boyfriends concurrently and who become pregnant but do not know which man is the father. This hypothetical scenario is frequently brought up by young men as the ultimate evidence of young women's abuse of rights in the democratic era.[13] To apply Mbeko's reasoning from the initial discussion of rights and responsibilities to this example of wayward pregnancy, women may have a right to freedom and autonomy, but that right entails a responsibility to deploy their sexuality judiciously, in ways that will not result in a pregnancy of uncertain paternity. But such women cannot be beaten even for these kinds of indiscretions—a situation that most people view as reprehensible. In a sense, by exercising *irhayti*, these women can disregard *amalungelo*. This potential for human rights abuse, according to men like Mbeko, is at the root of gendered and generational antagonisms about human rights.

Finally, the fact that violence seems related to how gender difference is produced here is particularly insightful—albeit troubling—when connected to the notion that tradition is constitutive of gendered identity. Although I do not suggest that beating women is a traditional Xhosa practice (and no one has claimed that to me in such bald terms), narratives like Mbeko and Jono's suggest that the gender hierarchy that *irhayti* upends is felt to be a cornerstone of tradition. Indeed, though many men deplore violence, most nevertheless vociferously claim that their authority over women is traditional and culturally authentic, and they clearly feel that violence is warranted as a means of reconsolidating that in situations where women fail to behave in ways that uphold this or act in ways that leave their obligations to men unfulfilled. Moreover, narratives like Nokumbulele's suggest that gendered violence is a ubiquitous, long-standing, and unremarkable element of gendered social structures. Taken together, this raises the question of whether human rights may lead to *more* violence given they empower women to behave in ways that, by a certain logic, *invites* this violence as a means of reinstating a gender order that is bound up with tradition and is fundamental to identity. Efforts to mobilize human rights to tame South Africa's exceptionally high rates of gendered violence might do well to consider how human rights set in motion transformations in gender-based hierarchies that then justify (in the minds of people for whom a hierarchical and relational social order is common-sense) gender violence as a mechanism of ensuring gendered difference. This predilection for violent enforcement of inequalities may be exacerbated in times and places where other anchors for gendered identity (work, married fatherhood, and so forth) are harder to achieve.

Among the most sophisticated anthropological critiques of human rights have been those that have exposed the ways that human rights and equality, being premised on liberal idioms of individuality and autonomy, are frequently experienced as destabilizing of social hierarchies which have long formed the foundation for personhood and moral action (e.g., Boyd 2013; Englund 2004; Taylor 2008; Nyamnjoh 2004). Using the examples of men's and elders' critiques of human rights in the rural Eastern Cape, this chapter demonstrates how and why rights pose a significant challenge for rural Xhosa people. For men and elders in particular, rights encourage a neglect of interpersonal obligation and responsibility in ways that undermine masculine and gerontocratic dignity and are thus seen to justify behaviors that negate the personhood of others. This critique of human rights, of course, neglects to acknowledge the manner in which young men are themselves often unable to fulfill their obligations to women and elders, for instance by not finding work, not supporting their children, and not paying bridewealth. This inability to live up to long-standing expectations of worthy manhood is felt to further undermine young men's dignity, as ample ethnographic data shows (e.g., Bank 2011; Hunter 2010; Ngwane 2001). Yet I argue this insecurity over failures to fulfill their traditional duties as men serve only to compound the suffering that young men claim to experience because of women's alleged emphasis on rights over social obligations, thus fueling rather than undermining their indignation. Moreover, where discipline is intrinsic to gendered subject positions, rights to equality render the meaning of these positions themselves unclear. As exemplified by the moral distinctions between *amalungelo* and *ukulungisa*, on the one hand, and *irhayti* on the other, contests about rights are fundamentally moral arguments about proper social relations between men and women and between young and old. Furthermore, the very content of gendered and generational subject positions is increasingly unclear, not only due to rights-based claims about equality but also because the modes of social reproduction upon which the normative gender and generational order has been premised are increasingly untenable. That *rights* and *amalungelo* are often used interchangeably in public life renders the meaning of rights and obligations all the more unclear. Human rights thus expose the deepest conundrums for contemporary rural Xhosa: they enable many welcome forms of justice, but they also contribute toward moral ambiguity over what it means to be a good person who knows their place in the world.

THREE

—ɯ—

SOCIAL GRANTS AND THE MORAL
BUREAUCRACY OF MERIT

BEYOND THE RACIAL, ETHNIC, GENERATIONAL, and gendered equities guaranteed in the constitution, South African policy and legislation also reflect the importance of socioeconomic equity as a post-Apartheid goal, to be achieved through access to social goods such as education, health care, fair labor practices, and social security (Seekings and Matisonn 2010; Brand and Heyns 2005). Yet despite this legislative framework, life in the rural Eastern Cape is in many ways far removed from the South Africa that the constitution calls into being. Previous chapters have demonstrated that gendered and generational equality is often confounded by long-standing gerontocratic and patriarchal hierarchies. Legislative guarantees to socioeconomic equality are also confounded in the former Transkei. Services such as schools, clinics, and hospitals are underresourced in rural Eastern Cape, and unemployment is ubiquitous.[1] Given such widespread poverty and unemployment, people experience the state—and its attendant institutional rationalities—primarily in the capacity of being recipients of state social security grants (specifically child support, foster care, and disability grants) and old-age pensions. Available to all low-income South Africans who meet the required criteria, these grants are the primary manifestation of South Africans' right to social security (Jelsma et al. 2008; Nattrass 2006), and evidence shows that they are effective in relieving extreme poverty (OECD 2020; DSD, SASSA, and UNICEF 2012).

It is within this context of both state dependency and socioeconomic exclusion that I examine the "social life" of social security grants in the rural Eastern Cape as an entry into considering how state practices intervene in and transform notions of age, status, and worthy personhood. This chapter traces the productive power of a social security system premised on an aspirational and fictitious model of South African society in which most adults are both economically productive and can easily be categorized as able, old, young, healthy, and so on. I explore how the assumptions, values, and rationalities that give the social security system meaning and purpose are distorted through local moral frames in a region with high unemployment, widespread social grant fraud, and weak state capacity to administer the social grant system. Through the examples of old-age pensions and disability grants, this chapter exposes tensions between age and ability as moral concepts bound up with living a "good life" by local metrics, as well as age and ability as bureaucratic constructs used by institutions to bestow economic rights. In so doing, I show that where economic and political transformations enable and foreclose particular kinds of social maturation, what it means to be a moral person of a particular age becomes unclear through ambiguities in temporalities of aging—what local women refer to as "age problems"—and as disability is reframed as a coveted opportunity to finally succeed in the domain of paid work. Beyond exposing uncertainties in the conceptual categories that shape identity and social roles in Mhlambini, it will also become clear that the seemingly arbitrary reasoning behind who is deemed to merit grants combined with widespread need for these resources raises moral questions about who is and is not deserving of state care and poses powerful questions as to why the struggles of some are deemed more worthy than those of others.

OLD-AGE PENSIONS AND "AGE PROBLEMS"

The South African pension system is premised on the assumption that aging is a biophysiological process that can be accurately measured based on citizens' progression through time. All human bodies develop and mature, but age and aging, though embodied, are nevertheless social constructs whose contents are variable and are indicative of societal values and expectations associated with progression through the life course (Settersten and Hagestad 2015; Aguilar 2007). Recent studies, notably of youth, unemployment, and transformations in life course, demonstrate the ways in which notions of age are shaped by political economic circumstance, and insights from medical anthropology show that even bodily transformations associated with aging are experienced and understood through categories that are culturally produced and are thus fluid. As such, my approach here is informed by the anthropological perspective that social maturation is shaped by political and economic forces, and that normative ideas of age and life stage are cultural products that are socially produced through practice and indicative of societal values. Grounded more in the social experience of aging than in the challenges of bodily transformation and de-cline, this discussion of "age problems" takes an anthropological approach to the aging process.

"Age Problems"

"Payday," as social grant day is colloquially called, is the most important day of the month in Mhlambini. Starting very early in the morning, nearly everyone begins walking up the steep road to "the pay place," leaving the village nearly deserted. In contrast, the pay place is a hive of activity. Traders arrive early from town to set up all manner of wares, and people line up to receive their grants long before the armed delivery truck arrives to disburse their cash payments. When the truck does arrive, recipients quickly line up in order of their status in the gerontocratic patriarchal hierarchy: male pensioners first, then female pensioners, then middle-aged mothers, and finally younger wives and young, unmarried mothers collecting their child support grants. By midmorning, most people have finished their shopping and have turned to socializing; old people sit in the sunshine to gossip and smoke, some people head off to one of the local shops to pay off their accumulated debts, and others head off to celebrate at one of the local *shebeens* (informal taverns).

According to elder women, the R1,500 (just over 100 US dollars at the time of writing) that pensioners receive resolves many household problems, but the system is not perfect.[2] If it were, there would be no age problems. Age problems arise due to the requirement that to qualify for an old-age pension, one must possess a valid identity document (ID) that indicates the bearer is at least sixty years of age.

Receiving a sizable payment in recognition of one's advanced age resonates with gerontocratic sensibilities; this money can be interpreted as an acknowl-edgment that one has reached a respectable age, and in privileging the elderly, it reinforces their status. Using sixty years as the defining criteria, however, is bewildering to many. First, many people over thirty are at best semiliterate, and many have difficulty interpreting the information on their ID. In some cases, the information is blatantly wrong due to bureaucratic error. For example, one local woman has been trying unsuccessfully to access child support grants for several years due to a bureaucratic error that has left her with an ID with her correct image but with the name and associated fingerprints of a woman who died years ago. Furthermore, many older people do not know their birth year, meaning the date on their document is the outcome of educated guesswork. Over the years, I have heard many stories of the challenges faced by govern-ment personnel following the democratic transition in the mid-1990s, as they tried to estimate the ages of people from the former Transkei who applied for identity documents ("Do you remember the years when the locusts ate everything?" "Do you remember Hitler's war?"). They were thus left to guess peoples ages through an improvised triangulation of the applicant's appearance and reported memory of historical events. Furthermore, some people admitted to me to having intentionally misreported their age to qualify for some privilege, usually a work permit or social benefit.[3] The following vignette provides a typical example of social grant fraud in Mhlambini:

Three local NGO employees and I are working at our desks in the large, one-room hut that serves as the NGO office. Suddenly, Guma (the wellness director) breaks the silence by asking, "Katie, when someone lies to the government so they can get money, is it called fraud?"

"Yeah, I think so," I respond uncertainly. "Why do you ask?"

"*Haibo* [wow]!" she says. "I think I am dealing with another fraud here."

Guma's responsibilities at the NGO are broad, covering not only community health and wellness activities but also work that would ordinarily be the jurisdiction of a social worker, if social workers would come this far from town. A large portion of Guma's workday is therefore devoted to helping people navigate the intimidating maze of paperwork involved in accessing necessities such as social grants and IDs, child support from absentee fathers, and compensation from mining companies. Today's case is typical in that Guma is trying to help someone whose inexpert attempts to work the system have landed them in difficulty. As she explains to us, she is trying to help a family get an ID and child support grant for a newborn. The complication is that the father is unemployed, and the family's only source of income is an old-age pension collected by the woman who has just given birth to the baby who needs an ID. We all wince at this woman's conundrum. Pensions and child support grants are processed through the same government ministry, and although IDs are processed through a different ministry, the mother will be asked to show her own ID when registering her child. Government personnel are sure to recognize that a sixtysomething pensioner could not possibly be a new mother. If this woman tries to register her child, she will get an ID and gain access to a child support grant, but she may lose her pension. A pension is four times more money than a child support grant, and the family would certainly forgo the child support in favor of the pension. Yet doing so would mean that the child would have no ID. This would probably have no immediate impact on his life but will present obstacles when he registers for school or requires medical care.

No one in the office seriously considers that the mother should come clean about her fraudulent pension, although all of us know that she is perhaps forty years old and may continue to collect fraudulent pensions for another twenty years. The family's survival is dependent on this money. Jabulile (the micro-enterprise project manager) and I come up with the same solution almost simultaneously: Is there a teenaged daughter who could claim to be the mother? Guma shakes her head. "They already tried that. But this baby was born in hospital, so he has a clinic card. They need that clinic card to the get the ID. And look what they did. This is how the problem started in the first place." Guma passes around the child's clinic card, a familiar yellow pamphlet documenting the child's vitals. The information on the card is filled out by hand, in black pen, by someone with delicate penmanship. It is painfully obvious that someone has scratched out the mother's name and has penned a new name in its place. The new name is written in blue pen, in the awkward scrawl of someone who can barely write. Guma sighs. "I don't know what to do with this one. Maybe their best option is to pretend they lost the clinic card and try to get a new one with the teenaged daughter's name."

I emphasize the pervasiveness of inaccurate and fraudulent pensions not to pass judgment on people who benefit from them. Many people who access fraudulent grants are living in desperate circumstances and are doing their creative best to survive. Instead, I offer these examples to underscore the degree to which access to grants can seem arbitrary, dissociated as they often are both from local ideas of age based on status and achievement and from the facts (of chronometric age, of maternity) that they are intended to represent.

Pension-collecting mothers, such as the woman whom Guma attempted to help, contribute to the age problems that plague some people in the village, especially women. These problems arise when the numerical age on an individual's ID does not align with their achieved social status in a community that marks life-stage transitions through ritual, and through conventions of dress, speech, and spatial mobility. There were a number of women—some almost certainly long shy of sixty—who complained to me that they are older than their IDs indicate. These were invariably women who had married an older man when they were quite young, and who had achieved all the markers of senior status for a mature woman: grown sons, daughters, and daughters-in-law to take over the work of running the home; grandchildren; widowhood or ongoing conjugal partnership with an elderly man; and completion of the rituals that mark their transition into the senior status of *abafazi abadala* (elder women). Given that most women who marry and bear children do so at a young age, some women achieve this status by their early forties. Watching some of their peers collect old-age pensions—or worse, watching chronometrically mature but never married or childless women collect pensions while they get nothing—is bewildering and frustrating for women who are, by local standards, "old." Moreover, in a community in which accessing a pension usually entails a dramatic improvement in quality of life, the indignity of being denied a pension is compounded by the distress and indignity of struggling in conditions of poverty.

Although age problems are in some ways particular to the local context, they also speak to broader issues surrounding the meaning of age in bureaucratic states. In a discussion of age and social structure in small-scale societies, Meyer Fortes (1984, 105) reminds us of incongruence between understanding age and generation as a "combination of conjugal and reproductive relations," and bureaucratic institutions such as old-age pensions. Of relevance in the case of people experiencing age problems, Fortes suggests that ambiguities arise because "pensions are awarded by the state not on the basis of kinship, family, or generational status but on the basis of the rights and duties of citizenship, that is, of membership in the political community" (108). As such, age problems illustrate an incompatibility between social status as achieved, and rights-based status based on fixed and impersonal criteria.

Moreover, age problems also demonstrate the ways in which bureaucratic artifacts are not neutral purveyors of discourse, despite their alleged impartiality.[4] Indeed, although the age listed on an ID may or may not be an accurate reflection of the chronometric age of the person that the document represents, the (oftentimes arbitrary, if not fraudulent) information inscribed on the document enables and forecloses opportunities that have important material and social effects. It also changes what it means to be old given the way that access to money can transform an individual's social power regardless of their position in a gerontocratic hierarchy.

Furthermore, although old-age pensions can consolidate gerontocratic power, they also present an irony in that, by design, they are intended to reflect industrial notions of age-based productivity (Livingston 2003). Within such systems, older people's status is presumed to be marginal rather than superior relative to the young due to their comparatively limited capacity to labor. Here, chronometric age serves as the impartial criterion by which to distinguish those who require specific forms of care and consideration because they can no longer access capital through paid work.[5] That most young people are "unproductive" in their allegedly productive years renders local understandings of the social grant system even more distant from its official rationale.

Furthermore, women in this region have not historically been expected to engage in wage labor, but rather in the reproduction of the domestic realm. If pensions are viewed as a means of supporting those who can no longer engage in wage labor, then allocating pensions to elderly women could be interpreted as subversive of local gender norms. Yet in many cases, women do begin to receive old-age pensions roughly concurrent with their transition into elderhood. Understanding pensions as a form of state recognition of elder status rather than compensation for economic unproductivity makes ironic sense in a historically gerontocratic society; people expect to wait a long time to assume a respected, powerful role in the community, and now access to state cash is a component of the privileges that old age entails. My interactions with elder women suggest that they understand their pensions primarily in this sense—as state recognition of their needs and seniority and not as a program that supports people who are no longer able to earn a living through wage labor. The problem, from their perspective, is that the state exercises poor judgment in determining who is worthy of such recognition, privileging some (socially) young women while neglecting some deserving elders.

The Moral Bureaucracy of Aging

By at once providing needed resources and challenging local notions of age and status, old-age pensions expose the ways in which bureaucratic policies, documents, and processes simultaneously shape the aging experience and provoke uncertainty about what elderhood means in Mhlambini today. Although rural households are increasingly reliant on state social grants, allocating these grants based on (alleged) chronometric age alone destabilizes what status and age are understood to be for older people—women especially—for whom age and status are bound up with marriage and reproduction. As these bureaucratic processes enable and foreclose particular kinds of social maturation, the content of generational subject positions is destabilized through contradictions in temporalities of aging. At the same time, the resulting age problems also expose dissonance between conceptualizing need and merit in accordance with industrial capitalist notions of ability and productivity versus with locally significant notions of achievement, status, and moral worth. This disconnect carries forward into the next section, which examines how people in Mhlambini experience and understand disability grants.

DISABILITY GRANTS IN THE RURAL EASTERN CAPE

As with other social grants, disability grants (DGs) are an outcome of the human rights–based rationalities that have shape the post-Apartheid South African state. The country's long history of discrimination on grounds of embodied difference gave disability rights activists a persuasive voice in both critiques of the Apartheid system (Graham, Moodley, and Selipsky 2013), and in successfully arguing for supports and protections for the differently abled as a right of citizenship (Kelly 2013; Graham, Moodley, and Selipsky 2013). As of 2015, an estimated 1.1 million South Africans received monthly DGs, which are equivalent to old-age pensions in monetary value (Ferreira 2017). They are also the only social grants typically available to working-aged men and constitute an important source of income for many households.[6] A 2008 study shows that in the rural Eastern Cape, households that include DG recipients have higher overall incomes and more material assets relative to households without (Jelsma et al. 2008), and the authors of a regional ethnographic study note that "in this setting, disability grants are a tool of survival for both the person with a disability and the household" (Hansen and Sait 2011, 110).

WORK AND WORTHINESS: DISABILITY GRANTS AND MORAL PERSONHOOD IN MHLAMBINI

I first met Sibabalwe in late 2011. He was in his early thirties at the time and had returned to Mhlambini after an extended absence with plans to open a gym and tavern in the village. He is the eldest brother of one my women friends, his father is a retired mineworker and influential village elder, and his mother is a *sangoma* (traditional spiritual doctor). When Sibabalwe is in the village, he lives at his parents' homestead, a large household consisting of Sibabalwe's mother and father, his two younger sisters, his sisters' children, and Sibabalwe's son by a former girlfriend. Another brother is employed as a migrant agricultural worker. Through the combined wealth and security generated by his father's old-age pension and investment in livestock, his mother's earnings as a *sangoma* and from the produce from her large garden, and the wages earned by his two younger sisters (both of whom run small businesses out of the backpacker lodge), the homestead is prosperous by village standards.

In many ways, Sibabalwe exemplifies the stereotype of the young man who is stuck in a state of thwarted adulthood, burdened by standards and expectations (including his own) that he struggles to meet. Besides being financially dependent on his pension-earning father and wage-earning sisters, he has fathered five children with different women, and these women periodically request financial support from Sibabalwe's family. Even worse, he has served jail time for his involvement in armed carjacking. He laments that he got involved in crime and insists that he wants to support his children but has never had the means. He has often assured me that he has changed his ways, although I remain skeptical. For as long as I have known Sibabalwe, he has sported stylish and expensive clothing, and it is unclear to me where he gets the money to pay for this.

As quoted in the introduction, Sibabalwe says that he enjoys the peacefulness of life in Mhlambini, but he finds village life difficult because of what he considers the backward mentality of local elders, and because his father constantly finds ways to let Sibablwe know that he is a disappointment. As Sibabalwe explained to me, his father had expected him to either find a job in mining or farm the family's land. However, like most of his peers, Sibabalwe has been unable to find mine work, and he is reluctant to farm. He has told me that farming is "not his gift from God" and that he resents his father's ongoing efforts to force him to live the "old way," off the land. Sibabalwe also suffers, he says, because his sisters are treated with more respect in his parents' home. He believes this is because they contribute toward the financial security of the household. Having only completed primary school education, Sibabalwe's work prospects are poor, hampering his efforts to, as he puts it, "get rich quick." Local opinions of him echo his father's assessment: he is widely considered lazy and irresponsible.

Perhaps unsurprisingly, as the months went by, Sibabalwe's gym-cum-tavern never materialized. Facing financial obstacles, strong resistance from elders (including from Sibabalwe's own father), and a lack of necessary skills, his vision seemed ill-fated from the start. Young people laughed when I asked them what they thought of Sibabalwe's plan: "That guy of all people, he could never start a business!" I was told. "He's always scheming to make money, but he is lazy. His plan will never work."

By my most recent visit to Mhlambini, Sibabalwe's business was no closer to being realized, and he seemed to be spending his time the way he always had: by wandering around the village and hanging out in the bar at the Lodge. While catching up with some young male friends, however, I soon learned that Sibabalwe's fortunes had changed: he was now receiving a DG. "Oh!" I remarked. "I didn't know that he is disabled."

Several young men simultaneously snorted. "He *isn't* disabled!" one said.

Willing to give Sibabalwe the benefit of the doubt, I countered cautiously, "Perhaps he was ill, and is now feeling better?"[7]

My speculation was greeted with laughter. "Of *course!*" someone responded. "He was ill. He probably couldn't get that grant otherwise! *Ja*, he was even using a wheelchair for a while. But he recovered a long time ago; you can see yourself that he is walking by himself all over the village! But he is still getting that grant!"

In the weeks that followed, it became apparent that Sibabalwe's grant was widely assumed to be fraudulent. But as with the previous example of a pension-collecting new mother, the receipt of an allegedly fraudulent grant was itself unremarkable. What surprised me was that people disapproved of a fraudulent grant in Sibabalwe's case because this grant was, apparently, "wasted" on Sibabalwe. In other words, it seemed that his peers deemed him undeserving of accessing a DG through (alleged) fraud. "Why is it wasted on him in particular?" I asked.

"Because of how he is. You know. Lazy," people explained.

I was initially perplexed. Perhaps Sibabalwe's grant was fraudulent, but what kind of opportunity was he squandering? His work prospects were poor regardless of his initiative; a fraudulent DG offers more security than most of the limited opportunities that are available to a young rural man without training or education.

My patient friend Sipho explained to me,

> Katie, you know Sibabalwe has this plan to start his business, but he was never having the money [he lacked the necessary funds]. Now, finally he has the money! Now, he's getting 1,500 [Rand], same as an old-age pension. It's a lot of money! Now, he can actually save his money, open his bar or gym, support his children finally! But he still just hangs around doing nothing. So, you see, he just wants the money, but he doesn't want to work. He never wanted to work, and now he's getting the grant, so he could be working! It's like I was telling you, he's just lazy, just wanting to get money fast. Some others, if they were getting that money, they could use it to start a business, maybe open a *spaza* [informal store] or *shebeen*. And they could even hire others to work in that *spaza*. So you see, others, they would be working with that grant.

Social welfare systems are regularly interpreted through local categories of deservingness and moral character;[8] at one level, local criticism of Sibabalwe's grant is likely an extension of the negative judgments that long precede his DG. But Sipho's explanation suggests that there is much more going on here. What Sipho makes clear is that in Mhlambini, a grant intended to support someone who is *unable* to work can be viewed not as an *alternative* to labor for someone whose impairment excludes them from the workforce, but rather as a valuable opportunity to create a job for oneself and potentially for others. In a community where jobs for young people are scarce, where social grant fraud—both intentional and accidental—is mundane, and where social grants are the primary source of income for many households, a man like Sibabalwe can be judged to be wasting a precious opportunity that would better have gone to a young man of generous, reputable, and industrious character. A man like that might be able to finally achieve the form of social adulthood that so many young people want, and that Sibabalwe himself had coveted for years. If the entrepreneurial venture was successful, this young man might also be able to fulfill further social obligations by employing other people as well.

Similar to those who believe that pensions should recognize socially achieved age, in Sibabalwe's case, people evaluate DG deservingness according to logics that are misaligned with those of the state. The pervasiveness of fraudulent grants combined with the seeming randomness of who can access DGs further contributes to the sense that grants—and the categories and values that scaffold them—are arbitrary, even as they have important material and social effects. With this in mind, I consider this ethnography in relation to broader research on disability grants and poverty in South Africa, ultimately illustrating how these grants contribute to moral ambiguity about social reproduction, work, status, and worthy life.

DISABILITY GRANTS, POVERTY, AND MORAL AMBIGUITY IN RURAL SOUTH AFRICA

At the policy level, DGs exist to support low-income citizens whose disabilities render them unable to engage in paid work. It is thus the socioeconomic dimension of disability that DGs are intended to address, leaving aside questions of how disability may be understood, experienced, and lived differently across the diverse strata of South African society. Moreover, although guidelines exist for how disability should be evaluated, disability itself is not defined in legislation or related literature (Kelly 2017, 2013). This opens the door for considerable polysemy because, similar to age, disability is both an embodied and socially constructed category, one that reflects standards of bodily, cognitive, and behavioral normativity that are cross-culturally variable.[9] With respect to DG policy, the responsibility for navigating this ambiguity falls upon physicians, whose approval is required for all individuals who hope to access a DG. Given DGs are only available to low-income South Africans, these physicians are gatekeepers who hold power to bestow or withhold economic security for the poor. The uncertainty about what constitutes disability combined with the requirement of physicians' clinical judgments as prerequisite for access renders the system highly vulnerable to bias and manipulation (Kelly 2017; MacGregor 2006). Although the precondition of a physician assessment ensures that a biomedical understanding of disability underscores the DG system, physicians' judgments are necessarily subjective, meaning there is considerable scope for variation in grant allocation according to how individual physicians interpret and apply guidelines. Applicant age—already itself ambiguous, as we have seen—is the primary factor that has been found to sway physicians in favor of or against approving claims by potential DG recipients (Kelly 2017, 2016a), but depth of poverty[10] (Kelly 2016a; de Paoli, Mills, and Grønningsæter 2012; MacGregor 2006; Simchowitz 2004), perceived merit as demonstrated through compliance to treatment regiments (Simchowitz 2004; Segar 1994; Baron 1992), and the nature of physicians' own commitments to social justice (Kelly 2016a; MacGregor 2006) have all been found to influence the outcome of a DG assessment. As a further complicating factor, effective communication about disability can be inhibited by language barriers (which are ubiquitous between physicians and patients in the rural Eastern Cape); whether a disability grant is recommended can be contingent on the accuracy of the translation offered by a third-party interpreter (Kelly 2017; Segar 1994).

DGs thus entail several levels of nested ambiguities and moral judgments, with the potential for multiple interpretations at every stratum.[11] At the policy level, a rights-based moral judgment has been made in favor of socioeconomic security for those who cannot work due to disability. The ambiguity at that level is around what constitutes impairment. That decision is left to physicians, who make their own moral judgments about deservingness that encompass biomedical notions of debility but exceed them as well. Moreover, there is ample opportunity for uncertainty at the level of the clinical encounter, from divergent illness etiologies between patients and physicians (e.g., Mkhonto and Hanssen 2018; Lourens 2013; Kahn and Kelly 2001) to inadequate translation between physician and patient (e.g., Deumert 2010; Grant 2006; Schlemmer and Mash 2006). And then, from Sibabalwe's case, we can see that civil society exercises further moral judgments about who and what DGs are actually for. At that point, the meaning of DGs is far removed from the institutional rationalities of governance upon which the social grant system is premised.

These nested ambiguities have opened the door to a widespread sense that DGs are a catch-all category to support for those who cannot find work and cannot access social security in other ways. Indeed, broader research suggests that across many communities, low-income South Africans view socioeconomic circumstances as the primary factor that should determine their eligibility for a DG.[12] Certainly in Mhlambini, there is a pervasive sense that certain people should be entitled to DGs on grounds of poverty alone, independent of bodily or cognitive limitations. This was believed especially by women experiencing age problems; a fair number of interlocutors referenced their advanced age (within the locally salient parameters of achieved elder status) to justify their entitlement to either old-age pensions or disability grants—they were indifferent to which grant. But many people who were too young to credibly claim entitlement to pensions either through local logics of achieved status or through state-recognized bureaucratic mechanisms simply referenced their poverty as grounds for deserving a social grant independent of any other consideration. When I asked them to clarify which grant they thought they might receive, many responded that they thought they should be able to access DGs. My efforts to elicit explanations of why a DG would be appropriate in their cases usually elicited circular emphases on poverty and renewed efforts to draw my attention to the meager materiality of their homes. Beyond pointing to an empty stomach, not once did anyone draw my attention to bodily or cognitive impairment as justification for why they should receive a DG. Unlike earlier research (e.g., Segar 1994), my interlocutors in Mhlambini make no claims to patient status. Most are able and well other than being hungry, and they are bewildered as to why the state supports some of their peers while neglecting others.

Finally, local perceptions of Sibabalwe speak to larger questions about employment, the limits of capitalism, and the politics of wage labor exclusion in South Africa. Using the example of widespread labor market exclusion alongside a robust system of social security grants in South Africa, James Ferguson (2015, 2013), for example, has argued that labor is being displaced as a source of value, and that greater analytic focus on the politics of distribution in such context may point to new political forms. Yet perceptions of Sibabalwe indicate that the dignity of work remains powerful in rural South Africa despite limited employment and widespread dependency on security grants. Indeed, it appears that accessing and generating paid employment remains more desirable and perhaps morally superior to supporting oneself through state welfare.[13] I think it is no accident that the nearly everyone who has argued they should be entitled to a DG was either a middle-aged or older woman without a pension—a demographic that faces less pressure to secure wage labor than their male counterparts given the tight, long-standing connection between wage work and valued forms of masculinity.

CONCLUSION

Local interpretations of social security grants demonstrate the absurdity of determining merit for social security according to capacity to engage in wage labor in circumstances in which paid work is virtually nonexistent. This absurdity is especially biting in and around Mhlambini given the widespread presence of government-funded public works programs (the CWP), which reflect the state's preference for addressing poverty by making work as opposed to making the current social security system more inclusive. As previously mentioned, these programs, which include maintenance of roads and public spaces, offer part-time work for very low wages. Although these programs could indeed have presented an alternative to social grants for the working-age young people who are currently excluded from the social grant system, in the interest of "respecting" local authority structures, the responsibility for allocating these jobs was bestowed upon community leaders. These mature and elderly men decided to reserve the jobs for those they deemed most deserving: widows with children, and elders experiencing the age problems discussed earlier.

In a discussion of the politics of social security provision in South Africa, Simchowitz (2004, 16) writes, "In order for South Africa to realise the constitutional right to social security, the country needs to move towards a system of social assistance not premised on the illusion of full employment." This imperative has led for calls from policy advisers (e.g., Taylor Commission 2002) and scholars (e.g., Ferguson 2015; Seekings and Matisonn 2010) to replace South Africa's current system with a universal basic income grant (BIG).[14] These grants would be small, but South African citizenship would be the sole criteria for eligibility.

Solving age problems and protecting unemployed youth from potentially undue moral judgments are surely not motivating factors for the policy advisers and scholars who have called for BIGs. Many of the problems I have discussed in this article, however, would be resolved through a more egalitarian allocation of social security. And yet the previous chapters have exposed some of the deep challenges posed by the promotion of egalitarian policies in a community where most espouse the notion that resources and influence should reflect an individual's social standing within a gerontocratic and patriarchal hierarchy. More equitable access to social security would likely address some local problems—for instance, households that lack wage-earners, DG recipients, and pensioners would have better food security, as would women with age problems and individuals who cannot access the grants to which they are legally entitled due to bureaucratic errors. But distributing economic power more equally would also fuel gendered and generational tensions, for instance by giving young people greater autonomy from pension-earning elders, and young women greater autonomy from both elders and men. Furthermore, though I doubt anyone in Mhlambini would refuse a grant if it was offered to them, the continued value placed on work—as evidenced, for instance, in the harsh judgments aimed at Sibabalwe—suggests that what people (men especially) want most are more jobs, not a new politics of distribution. In the meantime, widespread poverty and the reliance of rural communities on social security grants mean that addressing the limitations of the current social security system is both imperative and urgent.

Furthermore, the effective disbursal of social security grants in the former Transkei is impeded by the legacy of South Africa's Bantustan system. The logistics of rapidly extending the benefits and entitlements of citizenship to several million people (many of them illiterate) in the mid-1990s has left many rural dwellers with records and identity documents that misrepresent their bearers. This misrepresentation can manifest at both the level of pragmatic facts (e.g., incorrect birth date, name, photo, or fingerprints) and in misalignment between how their content is interpreted locally on the one hand and by bureaucrats on the other. Either way, people's access to state resources depends on the often inaccurate (and sometimes fraudulent) information that their records and IDs contain. These logistical challenges are further complicated by the deeply stratified nature of social life in these communities; allocating state benefits according to an egalitarian, rights-based idiom of social justice is out of keeping with lived experience and with the conceptual categories of gender, generation, and worthy life that organize daily life. In these ways, bureaucratic processes designed to support the most marginalized come into friction with local moral frames, taking on new meanings while destabilizing existing categories. An unintended outcome of this is that the allocation of grants seems at best arbitrary and at worst reprehensible in its implementation given the apparent tendency to exclude the deserving and reward the lazy. This perceived arbitrariness raises meaningful moral questions about who deserves state care and about why the suffering and poverty of some is deemed more worthy of compassion than the suffering of others.

FOUR

—ω—

WORKING WOMEN, WIVES, AND RURAL FEMININE PERSONHOOD

"THERE ARE A FEW PATHS here. So, if you can't go this side, you just have to go that side, you know?" Fezeka, a woman in her late twenties, spoke those words in response to my query about a what a good life looks like for a woman in the Eastern Cape today. I had asked this at the end of a long interview during which Fezeka, like many young, single women, criticized the patriarchal and gerontocratic gender order and described the life that she aspired to: she hoped to find employment, build her own house, help support her family, and never marry. Although many women—Fezeka included—emphasize the novelty of such ambitions, historical and contemporary sources nevertheless confirm that throughout Africa, some women have long rejected marriage in favor of opportunities that wifehood might preclude.[1] Alternatives to marriage have varied according to time and place, but this literature demonstrates these women are often motivated by an impetus to further their social position, to protect and augment their wealth, or both. Although there are ready examples of single working women in positions of relative wealth and authority in and around Mhlambini, I was surprised that for all her strong feelings about what she wanted for herself in life, Fezeka nevertheless felt that the form and content of a good life is unclear, contingent, and entails adaptability in conditions of constraint. With time, her words have helped me understand that for young women in the rural Eastern Cape today, it is difficult to know how to live and be a good person who knows her place in the world.

This chapter probes this uncertainty about moral personhood and the meaning of a worthy life course by focusing on how young women in the rural Eastern Cape are building lives for themselves in conditions of material scarcity, heightened gendered and generational antagonism, low marriage rates, and rapid political, legislative, and ideological change. In so doing, it bridges analyses of South Africa's political economy and fractious gender politics (e.g., Bank 2011; Hunter 2010) and a modest body of Africanist research on the topic of female life course (e.g., Cole 2010; Johnson-Hanks 2006; Bledsoe 2002). Grounded in the lives of young women whom I have come to know over the past decade, it explores what making a good life entails for young rural women. It will become clear that in their daily lives they are interpellated as autonomous, rights-bearing subjects with the capacity to achieve. However, they live in circumstances that simultaneously preclude most women from taking up such roles and reward some women for *disavowing* such subjectivities. Under these conditions, most women's lives entail a constant oscillation between divergent ideals of moral femininity as a means of survival. The opportunities available to these women are contingent on moral evaluations of identity and character that create opportunities at the same time that they foreclose others; there is constant friction between incommensurate moral frames and their attendant forms of gendered personhood. Political, economic, and ideological transformations have specific and undertheorized implications for women with which they must contend as they forge lives for themselves in conditions of constraint.

"THERE ARE A FEW PATHS HERE": FIVE STORIES ABOUT YOUNG WOMANHOOD

As Fezeka states, there are several paths available to women in the rural Eastern Cape. In keeping with the temporal moral geography outlined in the introduction, some young women feel that rural areas lag behind the times and that village life excludes them from the rights, entitlements, and opportunities that they imagine flourish in town. Although urban South Africa is characterized by exclusion arguably more so than opportunity, migration to town can hold the promise of relative freedom from domestic rural femininity and obligations to kin. Accordingly, some young women have left Mhlambini to seek better lives in the urban areas.

Urban life is widely regarded as dangerous, however, especially for those with little education and few connections. For every young woman who leaves the countryside, another opts to remain in her rural village. With few prospects for marriage or employment, most of these women make ends meet in a similar manner to that of many women in urban townships: through a piecemeal combination of child support grants, the assistance of kin with jobs or pensions, and support from their lovers.[2] And yet a few employment opportunities do exist in the tourism, social development, and public services sectors, and some young women have succeeded in securing these jobs. These young women can support both themselves and, invariably, their large networks of dependent kin. Although women who succeed in doing so are relatively few, the following example will show that opinions about working women seem to concentrate broader societal ambivalence and anxiety about social change.

Mandisa

Mandisa was one of my first friends in Mhlambini. Our acquaintance was facilitated by the fact that we were both single women in our late twenties and by certain attributes that rendered our friendship mutually appealing. Mandisa was one of few villagers who spoke English well, so especially in the early days, I could converse more freely with her than with most of our peers. The fact that we lived on opposite ends of the village gave me an opportunity to learn about village life as I journeyed back and forth from her home. From Mandisa's perspective, she found in me a rare friend who, like her, enjoyed and could afford the occasional beer at the backpacker Lodge bar. And she appreciated associating with a young woman who seemed to have achieved what she aspired to: financial autonomy and a house of her own.

In contrast with my circumstances, in the early months of my fieldwork, Mandisa's living situation afforded her little privacy. She lived with her parents at their large *umzi*, along with her elder brother, eight younger siblings, a sister-in-law, Mandisa's two young sons, and three nieces and nephews. Yet Mandisa is an intelligent and ambitious woman, and she had stayed in school longer than all her brothers and sisters. She was one of few villagers to have completed secondary school, and shortly before I met her, she managed to secure a rare government job as a fisheries monitor. To this day, she can often be found pacing the coast in her orange uniform, recording the catches of local fishermen and reprimanding them for catching undersized or out-of-season fish. Her salary is the largest source of income in her parents' household, although her elder brother is also employed as a mine worker and the family receives several social security grants.

Over the years, Mandisa has told me many times that employed single motherhood is preferable to the dependency and gendered subordination that village wifehood would, in her estimation, inevitably entail. Much better, she believes, is a life more reminiscent of idealized forms of rural manhood: from the time I met her, she aspired to build her own homestead in the village and support her children, parents, and siblings. Over the course of my fieldwork, she did just that, building a two-room square flat at the far end of her family's garden plot. There she lives with her two sons, "controlling herself," as she puts it. Although her father occasionally reminds her that he will likely accept a proposal should a man approach Mandisa's family about bridewealth, as time goes by, his words ring increasingly hollow as she becomes simultaneously more established as an independent wage earner and less appealing as a bride. When her parents compel her toward more established forms of adult feminin-ity, Mandisa continually repositions herself as their provider. In her words, "If someone comes to marry me, I have a [human] right now, and I will just say no. But anyway, no one is coming to marry me. And I am always saying [to my parents], If there is anything you suffer to buy [without my bridewealth], I will buy it for you instead."

Mandisa is a somewhat archetypical figure in the village, and opinions about her concentrate widely felt ambivalence over the changes that are claimed to accompany the civic freedom and *irhayti* that Mandisa herself regularly deploys to justify living as she does. Although many concede that she is a devoted mother and a reliable provider for her large family, she has a reputation for being too willful and insubordinate for marriage and for embracing a lifestyle and pattern of consumption that is too far removed from the traditional way of life. This is evidenced by her wayward patterns of reproduction (one child is expected, but two by different fathers implies, in the words of Unathi, that she "has no value"), by her patterns of dress (she usually wears form-fitting jeans or tracksuits and almost never wears skirts), and her habit of rewarding herself with a bottle or two of beer after work. The fact that she used her wages to fi-nance the building of her own house is viewed by some as proof of her wayward nature, enabling the promiscuity that men claim accompanies women's new rights to gender equality. Contentions about human rights and gender equality are intertwined with controversies about working women more broadly and, as shown in chapter 3, are regularly evoked in a manner that positions young women, law enforcement, and the government in opposition to men, elders, and Xhosa culture.

As a result, beyond offering an example of what a life can look like for ru-ral women who manage to secure lucrative employment, Mandisa demon-strates that young working women are often considered morally problematic in Mhlambini, regardless of how dependent their families may be on the income that they provide. This holds true even in families that readily embrace many other changes (for instance, Christianity, schooling, and contemporary archi-tectural styles) that they associate with town life and with a post-Apartheid so-cial order. With this in mind, I turn now to the example of another Mhlambini woman, which shows the lengths that some men and elders go to in their efforts to keep working women within the orbit of patriarchal control.

Busi

The youngest of five siblings, Busi lives in a large homestead with her father (a retired mine worker), her mother (a traditional healer), her elder sister and brother, her sister's three children, one of her unmarried brother's four children, and her own young son. Like many young women, Busi stopped schooling when she became pregnant in her midteens. By her account, her son's father's parents occasionally give her money to clothe the child, but this support is unreliable. By time I met Busi, her son was six years old, and her relationship with her son's father was long over.

For a short time following her son's birth, Busi supported herself with a single child support grant and depended heavily on her family for support. Up to that point, her circumstances were typical of most of young local women who experience unplanned pregnancies. However, when her son was very young, she managed to secure a position as apprentice to a massage therapist who was passing through the region on holiday. Deemed by her teacher to be an exceptionally gifted masseuse, by the time I met her in early 2011, Busi ran a lucrative one-woman business offering massages to tourists.

Unlike Mandisa, Busi is content to live at her parents' *umzi*—albeit in her own square hut. But like Mandisa, she makes limited effort to observe customs of gendered and generational respect. She travels to town periodically to visit a boyfriend, moves freely around the village, wears stylish trousers and weaves, and frequents local taverns on occasion. It was this latter activity that was a catalyst for elder men in the community to intervene in Busi's life.

Late one evening, Busi was drinking beer with some friends at the backpacker Lodge bar when she decided to show them a "magic trick" involving a raw egg. The alcohol had made her clumsy, however; she fumbled, and the egg fell and broke. The trick was foiled, but the mess was promptly taken care of by a hungry dog, and Busi and her friends went home to be bed shortly afterward.

By early morning, word of Busi's ill-fated magic trick somehow spread through the village, and by afternoon a community meeting was called on the insistence of an older man named Mzoxolo. Seemingly indignant over Busi's irresponsible behavior, Mzoxolo cited an incident where a backpacker lodge employee—an older widow—had been fired for stealing bedsheets for her own use. According to Mzoxolo, these situations were analogous: Busi had stolen backpacker lodge property and must be fired for her transgression.

This accusation sparked a lengthy debate, with many men and elders siding with Mzoxolo. I found the debacle more and more absurd as the meeting wore on: all that was broken was an egg, and it had been dropped by mistake. Eggs were available at nearby shops or could be purchased from neighbors, and Busi had apologized and had offered to replace the egg immediately. Unlike most orders for compensation that arise at community meetings—for young men fined for impregnating their girlfriends, for young men fined for beating their girlfriends excessively, for young men fined for killing other young men in drunken knife fights—the stakes were low, no one had been harmed, and the fine might actually be paid because Busi could easily afford it.

Later, among friends, I voiced vexation at the absurdity of the situation. My local friends laughed. "Oh, Katie, this is obviously not about the egg at all!" they told me. Everyone readily identified other motivations. Several suggested that Mzoxolo was driven by jealousy and, in keeping with his calculating and entrepreneurial character, hoped to turn the situation to his benefit. Knowing how lucrative Busi's job was, friends speculated that Mzozolo hoped Busi would be fired so he could put forward his own daughter (a single, unemployed peer of Busi's age) as a replacement. Someone else added more fuel to the rumor mill: "I'll tell you what is actually happening: Mzoxolo has been trying to get Busi to be his girlfriend, but she is not interested. He likes younger girls, and he's angry because she doesn't love him. And she has a lot of money, *kaloku* [remember], so she doesn't need a man like that."

I saw no reason to doubt these claims. Yet as I pointed out, this did not explain why so many men and elders supported Mzoxolo's position. "Ah," said one friend. "I agree that this thing with the egg, it's not about the egg at all. It's about the old ones not liking girls out at night, drinking beer. You know, because of the way Busi is. A lot of them, they don't like it. But Busi has *imali* (money), so they can't easily stop her." The other young people present readily concurred with this interpretation.[3]

By this point, it should be clear that working women attract scrutiny and judgment in Mhlambini. Both examples that I have provided so far are of women who actively distance themselves from the forms of feminine personhood that locals associate with tradition and Xhosa identity—and thus with a patriarchal gender order. They do this both through explicit reference to their civic freedom and human rights—in particular, their right to earn wages and not marry—and implicitly through their habits of dress, spatial mobility, and consumption. It bears mention here that young women's access to items such as jeans, hair extensions, and commercially produced beer has more do with greater opportunities to travel and consume since the end of Apartheid than with human rights, gender equality, and the rejection of gerontocratic patriarchy per se. The availability of these consumer items (and access to media that promotes them) and employment opportunities that allow some women to participate in this consumption has been concurrent with the transition to rights-based democracy, making it easy for people to connect human rights, gender equality, changes in women's habits of consumption, and the challenges that many rural communities face.

Mandisa and Busi's habit of buying and consuming commercially produced beer warrants particular attention in this regard. A substance with symbolic power in many societies, beer has long been important in Xhosa society, to the point that entire ethnographic monographs have expounded on its significance. Home-brewed beer is regularly produced and consumed in the village (except by Christians, most of whom pointedly abstain) both for recreation and as an integral element of ancestor-related ritual practice. The ritual events where it is consumed, called *umgidi* (beer drink rituals), are events exclusively for mature adults and elders. Alcohol is allocated at *umgidi* according to complex rules that reproduce and reinforce hierarchies of gender and age,[4] making these events "important forums for the ritualized enactment of generational power and respect" (Bank and Qambata 1999, 115). Elder women are welcome to drink and are enthusiastic participants at *umgidi*, although they are often allocated less beer than their elder male peers. Young married men are welcome at *umgidi*, and unmarried men sometimes attend but are marginalized spatially and socially. Although young women usually brew the beer, there is no place for them at all at *umgidi* except in the background, washing dishes and filling drinking vessels. Because beer drinking is a ritualized means of sustaining and reproducing generational privilege, *young* people's drinking practices are a source of consternation and dismay for elders.

At the same time, over the latter half of the twentieth century, beer consumption has become a point of contention between generations of men in Southern Africa,[5] because wage labor allows anyone with a job to purchase commercially produced beer as a commodity or to pay women to brew it for them. Rich ethnographies of men's drinking practices have examined the considerable tension that stems from older men's investment in the notion that beer drinking is an earned privilege of elderhood and young men's repositioning of beer drinking as an integral aspect of masculinity and an achieved privilege earned through wage labor (e.g., van der Drift 2002; Suggs 2001, 1996; Wilson 1977). Indeed, alcohol has become an important mark of distinction that resonates with larger post-Apartheid projects of individualized self-making and wealth.

A tight connection between masculinity and alcohol consumption has been widely documented globally and is pronounced in South Africa.[6] This makes young working women's alcohol consumption contentious both in how it reframes drinking as a privilege accessible to anyone with money and for how it challenges gender norms that link drinking with masculinity and tradition. For men who have no jobs and cannot afford beer, seeing women like Mandisa and Busi enjoying their hard-earned leisure with beer in hand can be a tough pill to swallow and contributes to the judgments and hostility that are sometimes targeted at them.

Finally, the impetus to understand the how alcohol use may elevate the risk of HIV infection in South Africa has led to a sizable body of literature on the meanings that men and communities attach to women's drinking.[7] This literature frames women's drinking within a gift economy wherein men supply women with alcohol (and food or small sums of money) and women are assumed to have consented to sex by accepting men's drinks and other provisions. Unaccompanied women in bars are presumed to be looking for this sort of arrangement. Such assumptions about sexual laxity carry over into Mhlambini, where most young men emphasize that only nondrinkers are suitable candidates for wifehood (more on this later). It is no accident that women like Busi and Mandisa mainly drink at the Lodge in proximity to young Euro-American women who can likewise afford to buy their own beers and who are not assumed to be looking for sex or money.

Despite these pragmatic and conceptual obstacles, a life like Mandisa's and Busi's is one form of womanhood that is available to young women in the rural Eastern Cape—one contingent on the economic power that these women enjoy. The next example offers a slightly different approach to navigating the tensions between being a worker and a good woman according to locally meaningful metrics.

Amahle

Amahle is in her late twenties and is a manager at the Lodge. She is the only person in her household who is employed now that her father has become paraplegic in a mining accident. As her parents' eldest surviving child, she resides at their homestead along with her teenage brother and her late older sister's young son. She also pays school and boarding fees for her teenage sister, who attends secondary school in Cape Town.

I came to know Amahle well over the course of my fieldwork and was struck early on by how she strove to maintain two very different modes of femininity in her daily life: a demure, domestic daughter while at home and a savvy business manager while at work. These divergent roles were apparent in dramatic differences in her dress and comportment: while at work, she sports stylish Western clothes and weaves, and she successfully builds rapport with tourists with her charm, sense of humor, and outgoing personality. Yet at home, she dresses much like young wives do, often with face clay (ocher or yellow clay that is applied to the face for sun protection, and sometimes as decoration) and wearing a kerchief, long skirt, and apron. She is always busy with domestic chores. In contrast with her workplace persona, at home she is remarkably reserved and soft-spoken; if her father is present, she won't raise her eyes, let alone her voice.

Like Mandisa, Amahle uses her income to support her family. Rather than building her own house, however, Amahle turns most of her money over to her father and brother, who have built an attractive thatched-roofed rondavel in a traditional style, which her father uses to hosts elder male friends. With time it became clear to me that Amahle felt her work life and her home life necessitated the successful performance of femininities that were somewhat incommensurate, one rooted in hierarchical *hlonipha* practices, the other associated with liberal forms of personhood that are rewarded in the workplace.

For the first two years of my research, Amahle managed to juggle these roles with a fair degree of success, and she did not attract the negative judgments that are often directed at women like Mandisa. Maintaining this balance became complicated, however, when she became pregnant with the child of a boyfriend from Mthatha, much to her parents' disappointment.

Amahle had met her boyfriend in her last year of secondary school, which she was able to attend by boarding with extended family in Mthatha. By the time I met Amahle, her boyfriend held a job as a security guard in Cape Town, meaning that unlike most young village men, he could perhaps afford to support Amahle and their child. Upon learning of her pregnancy, he began pressuring Amahle to consider marrying him. I initially assumed that she might jump on this offer; they had been together for years at that point, she claimed to really love him, and marriage would confer a certain respectability and spare her the kinds of judgments that are leveled at women like Mandisa. But when I asked Amahle if she planned to marry him, she threw up her arms in dismay, saying, "My God, Katie, I can't get married! Me, I'm the only one working here. Who is going to support my family? I would have to leave my job, to go live in Mthatha to cook and care for his mother! Uh-uh, I can't work and be a wife. It's not possible. I have to stay here and work for my family."

Ultimately, Amahle chose to remain at her parents' home as a single mother, leaving her young son in her mother's care when she is at work. She continues to excel at her job in the tourism industry and strives to improve her image by doubling down on the performance of *hlonipha* and of responsible motherhood when at home.

WORK AND WIVES

I have already explained that the contemporary economic and political moment has constrained the possibility of achieving long-standing normative life trajectories for most young rural Xhosa. Women like Mandisa, Busi, and Amahle, however, demonstrate that new horizons of possibility have also opened up for some young women. The judgments and controls with which they must contend as working women demonstrate that these new possibilities come up against gendered ideas about appropriate comportment and a worthy life course—these are particularly challenging to contest and navigate because they are bound up with tradition. What Amahle's circumstances especially illuminate is that though material provision and married manhood are connected, wifehood and wage labor are largely incompatible.

Employed wives are not the norm in this region, and most husbands forbid their wives from working outside the home. All my women friends who hold jobs have explicitly told me that husbands will demand that their wives stop working and cite this is a key reason why they prefer to remain single. In some instances, this seems to stem from possessive jealousy: on several occasions, young men I know have gotten visibly upset by the idea that a wife might use her job as an opportunity to meet other men unsupervised. And given the long-standing connection between wage labor, masculinity, and the project of building the rural home, many men feel emasculated by the idea of a wife as provider. Nevertheless, I remain struck by the sheer intensity of most men's aversion to wage-earning wives. For example, I have witnessed cases where men used violent discipline to compel their wives to stop working even where the wife's wages were the only source of income in households that included dependent children, where the family went hungry once the wife gave up her job, and where children stopped going to school because the family could no longer afford necessities such as shoes. Men's antipathy to working wives also surfaces regularly in men's descriptions of the kind of women who are suitable for marriage. In the words of Melikhaya (late twenties), his hoped-for wife "must be a girl who's truthful, who doesn't drink. Who works only with a wheelbarrow and a plow. And is a cultivator, who can milk cows, who can do these things, you see. And who doesn't drink alcohol."

Concerns about women outside patriarchal control are a familiar and longstanding locus of anxiety about social change in South Africa (Hickel 2015;

Carton 2000; Posel 1995; Walker 1990; Gaitskell 1982), and anthropological research in the field of human rights and gender equality shows that in many regions, legislative transformations in women's status catalyzes masculine concerns about moral degeneration and loss of male privilege (Taylor 2008; Wyrod 2008; Jolly 1996). Beyond these concerns, however, I contend that the critiques leveled at working women—be they critiques of their character, their clothing, or their habits of consumption—are but the outward manifestation of much deeper anxiety about the gendered meanings attached to social roles, work, and alcohol. On one level, wifehood is bound up with a whole symbolic lexicon of moral femininity, one that is disavowed by Mandisa and Busi, albeit with consequences for them. Employment is typically incompatible with the gendered comportment that is expected of young wives. Recall that in keeping with *hlonipha* customs, young wives are expected to behave meekly, to speak softly and infrequently, to carry themselves submissively, and to remain close to the homestead except when chaperoned. Households are proud of young wives who successfully embody these ideals. Yet the workplace generally requires women to abandon these many of these practices (at least while working), and flouting these restrictions reflects poorly on a husband and his kin.

Furthermore, the home-building activities and wage-earning, breadwinning aspirations of women like Mandisa closely resemble long-standing models of a worthy masculine life course. Through a complex, historically rooted process, these activities have come to constitute at once cornerstones of Xhosa tradition and key components of gender difference for rural Xhosa. As covered in the introduction, migrant labor capitalism in South Africa was both premised on and reproduced a conceptual dichotomy between urban and rural forms of personhood; wage labor in this region has long required men to undertake dangerous journeys to the city as a means of sustaining employment. Scholars have shown that navigating this fraught relationship between the urban workplace and the rural home has long posed pragmatic, personal, and spiritual challenges for South African men, and these challenges persist in profound ways despite the dismantling of segregationist policies and transformations in the nature of work (Steinberg 2013; Ashforth 2005). For example, as Hylton White (2010) has explained, with the decline of the mining industry, some young men suffer a terrible circularity of failure: the inability to secure urban employment is interpreted as an outcome of their failure to maintain rural forms of moral personhood and spiritual rightness, even as successful rural manhood is contingent on achieving success in the urban sphere of paid work. Drawing on critiques of women like Mandisa and Busi, it appears that there is a tension between urban and rural forms of (gendered) worthy personhood that has undertheorized but important implications for women trying to make a respectable life in a context where long-standing patterns of social reproduction have become largely untenable.

Colonial and Apartheid policy was especially concerned with keeping African women in the countryside, for fear that their presence in cities would create opportunity for Africans to settle in town (White 2010). Although this was not a seamless project,[8] the relative absence of African women in the city and their hugely disproportionate presence in the rural homelands resulted in the feminization of the South African countryside, in a literal sense but also in South Africans' social imaginaries. As the rural became the place of women, family, and reproduction, sharply gendered spheres of practice and codes of feminine comportment and self-presentation came to represent Xhosa femininity and authentic Xhosa personhood. *Hlonipha* practices reinforce and reproduce this form of femininity, and the practices through which this gender difference is sustained and produced are held as tradition. The activities and aspirations of girls who earn wages, build their own houses, and provide for their families are readily recognizable as precisely what their male peers are expected to achieve. Indeed, the few young men whose lives most closely resemble those of women like Mandisa and Amahle are well respected in the community. However, it is evident that when young women engage in these practices, it is perceived as a very different kind of activity, one that is morally ambiguous and that undermines their status as good Xhosa women. The fact that it is difficult—if not impossible—for working women to uphold practices of gendered and generational respect reinforces this perception. This places working women in a very difficult position, one characterized by tensions between incommensurate forms of gendered personhood and between obligations and opportunity.

The timbre of anxieties and controversies about working women is disproportionate to the number of young working women in Mhlambini. Although they seem to concentrate ambivalence about social change, such women remain few. To foreground the final discussion of this chapter, I turn now to an example of a young woman whose life followed a more typical path, at least for a while.

Nomvula

Nomvula, a shy, reserved monolingual isiXhosa speaker, was seventeen years old, unmarried, and pregnant when I first met her in 2011. She is the firstborn child at the *umzi* where I lived for sixteen months. Nomvula's family is poor by village standards, and living at their home offered an often sobering window into the daily struggles of impoverished women in rural villages.

The family's poverty apparently began when Nomvula's mother, Nobongile, was abandoned both socially and financially by her labor migrant husband, Thembekile. In the early years of Nobongile's marriage, Thembekile invested heavily in the *umzi*, paying school fees for the children and building, among other things, the three-room square hut that was selected by the community as a suitable home for me.[9] However, at some point in the mid-2000s Thembekile married a second wife, this time a younger woman from a nearby village. Named—fittingly in her case—"mother of beauty," the second wife and her five children are greatly favored by Thembekile. This is apparent from their stylish clothing and well-maintained homestead, which features a solar panel, ample furniture and kitchenware, and a radio. Meanwhile, Nobongile and her children wear old, shabby clothes that are often ill-fitting, and their cramped, run-down *umzi* has virtually no furniture. The difference in affluence between Thembekile's wives' respective households is apparent to all passersby because the homesteads are some hundred meters apart.

Nomvula explained to me that her father's second marriage led to her dropping out of school in eighth grade because he stopped supplying money for her transportation, school uniform, shoes, and books. By the time I met her she had been unemployed at home for four years, and I was witness to her daily routine of chores and childcare. Although we spoke on occasion about her future aspirations, these conversations never got far. Once, she suggested that she would like to work but was pessimistic about her prospects given her lack of experience, limited education, and minimal command of English. Although she told me on several occasions that she does not want to stay in the village, she never shared any concrete plans for where else she would live or what she would do there; she simply wished to be "far away" and "in town." I recall a conversation where, when I asked her about what she wanted in life, she shrugged, adjusted her infant daughter on her lap, and said softly, "*Ndifuna ukuphuma noko ndibuye ndimhle* [I just want to go away and come back beautiful]."

Single unemployed teenaged mothers are ubiquitous in the village, but during the months I lived with her, I found Nomvula's circumstances to be especially heartbreaking. Plain like her mother and radiating an aura of withdrawn calm, she rarely broke from cooking, cleaning, and looking after her daughter and younger siblings. Unlike the teenage girls who roam the village and sit around at the backpacker lodge, Nomvula never ventured far from the *umzi*—even when I offered to treat her, she would not accompany me to the Lodge to share a pack of biscuits. The only times I saw her leave the *umzi* were to fetch firewood, and once to take her daughter to the clinic. She seemed to rest from her work only when she would sit on my porch on Sunday evenings waiting for a phone call from her daughter's father, who lived a half-day's journey away near the district hospital.[10]

Throughout the year and half that I lived with her family, I secretly shared Nomvula's pessimism about her prospects for finding work. The young women I knew with jobs were much better educated than she was and could also speak enough English to get by in the workplace. Given her mother, Nobongile, had no schooling whatsoever, I was not optimistic that the family's fortunes would change. So I was surprised when I returned to Mhlambini a year later to find the *umzi* much improved, with four healthy cows and nearly a dozen goats in the family's formerly empty *kraals* (livestock pens). Nomvula had apparently married her daughter's father and was now living near the hospital at her husband's parents' *umzi*. The family's new wealth was Nomvula's bridewealth.

The lives of most young women in Mhlambini are similar to Nomvula's prior to her marriage. Many have a child young, drop out of school in their teens, and live as dependents at their natal homes. This is the most common but least desirable path available to young village women. Marriage, however, evidently remains an alternative for some of these women.

Ethnographic and demographic data suggest that South African marriage rates have been in decline since the 1960s,[11] but this decline seems to be more recent and less pronounced in and around Mhlambini. Tellingly, the village-wide demographic survey that I conducted for the profiling research (see chap. 1) in 2012 showed that of the 345[12] people between the ages of fifteen and thirty-five, 78 (just over one in four) reported being married or widowed. Women are disproportionately represented among this younger married cohort because there are a number of wives and widows who married older men. Evidently, some young women do marry today.

Significantly, nearly all the young local women who have married in the eleven years that I have worked with this community have been women who are very much like Nomvula: their means are modest, and they closely reproduce long-standing notions of traditional Xhosa femininity. They are meek and dependent, hardworking in the domestic sphere, do not wear trousers, have limited schooling, do not drink alcohol, speak very little English (and thus cannot compete for employment even if they wish to work), and, even before marriage, rarely venture far from their parents' homesteads except to fetch water and firewood.

There are several reasons why it is predominantly these women who marry. First, young women like Nomvula know that they have little hope of finding work, so they may be more inclined to seek a provider through marriage despite concerns about domineering husbands and in-laws. Indeed, men who can afford marriage are generally the most affluent, and the promise of ongoing support from these men is hugely attractive to women who have grown up poor. Relatedly, they are beholden to the demands of both natal and marital families because they are dependent on them for their daily survival—they may be more likely to go along with a marriage proposal that their parents are in support of. Moreover, although unmarried and unemployed adult daughters are usually valued and loved members of their natal households, their singledom is also disappointing to parents and grandparents, especially if those daughters have children. In contrast, young married women who are industrious and embody *hlonipha* are sources of pride and objects of praise—some young women would readily accept a certain degree of unfreedom in exchange for the rewards of pleasing their families and being praised and admired in their communities. Finally, such women are evidently perceived as more capable than women like Mandisa, Busi, and Amahle of realizing the hierarchical complementarity necessary to achieve moral rural personhood. They "fit" with tradition.

Wifehood, therefore, though far from a safe bet for a secure and happy life, *is* still an appealing option for some rural women. And beyond the security that it can provide to poor, poorly educated women, in current times it holds a broader appeal as well—one that sits awkwardly alongside widespread concerns about intense patriarchal control. Indeed, the meaning of wifehood itself is contested and in flux, especially for young people. It has polysemic qualities that contribute toward the broader uncertainties about gendered morality and meaning that are the overarching foci of this book. The next story will further illustrate why some women will accept—even desire—wifehood despite the constraints and sacrifices that it entails.

Wifehood, Freedom, and Value

A couple years ago, I found myself sitting around a table in a village tavern with Busi, Khanyisa (an unmarried local girl in her early twenties), Busi's older brother Bongani, and a young man named Fhulu, whom I had never seen before. I soon learned that Fhulu was temporarily in the area as part of a work team doing maintenance on a nearby reservoir dam. Heralding from faraway Limpopo province, he was Venda (a South African ethnocultural group), and his work took him all over the country. This was his first visit to the rural Eastern Cape.

The discussion turned to marriage because Busi and Bongani's sister Cebisa had recently moved a few villages over to live with her new husband and his family. I was surprised by this news because I would not have believed her to be a good candidate for marriage. Although she was hardworking, modest, and traditional in comportment and dress; lacked formal education; and spoke almost no English, Cebisa was also well into her thirties and was the mother of three children born out of wedlock. I asked for more details about the marriage, and Busi explained that Cebisa had finally married her longtime boyfriend, the father of her two youngest children. Busi, Bongani, and Cebisa's parents, Busi reported, were "very, *very* happy" to see Cebisa wed.

This made sense to me, especially given that many young men who marry today choose women with whom they have already had a child. Busi then continued by reporting Cebisa was also very happy especially because her new husband loved her so much that he allowed her to bring her eldest child—a son by a different father—with her when she relocated to his natal home. Knowing that premarital childbearing is usually reflected in smaller bridewealth at marriage, I asked, "How many cows?"

"Nine!" said Bongani.

"Nine?" repeated Fhulu from Limpopo, and he whistled, seemingly taken aback. "It's too much!" He then shot the young and exceptionally pretty Khanyisa a flirtatious grin and said, "And how much for this one?"

"Thirteen cows!" she chirped with a mischievous smile.

"What?" Fhulu squawked dramatically. "No, it's too much! And what about you?" he said, turning to Busi.

Given Busi's strongly critical views on marriage and bridewealth, I was surprised to hear her state imperiously, "Twenty."

"*Aie!*" Fhulu moaned theatrically. "This is way too much. The only person here who can [should] cost twenty cows is this lady," he said, gesturing toward me. "You know why? Because if I marry this lady, she is educated, and she can do something for me [being educated and employable, she will help me generate wealth]. You see, with her, she can help grow my home. But you two, what can you do for me, really?"

Not liking how Fhulu had devalued my friends, I quickly countered this reasoning by pointing out my education offered no training in the skills that village wifehood requires: if Fhulu wanted someone to fetch firewood, cook on a wood fire, re-dung the floor, take good care of his parents, and make mud bricks, he'd be far better off marrying Busi or Khanyisa. What's more, a younger woman than I would be a much better choice for a man who wants to grow his family. Fhulu snorted and dismissively waived my arguments aside.

This banter about bridewealth and value continued as I retreated into a thoughtful silence. This conversation had been lighthearted, of course. Everyone knew that twenty cows would be a farcical sum for a village marriage and that no one would be rounding up their livestock for any of us anytime soon. Yet this disagreement about which woman is "worth" more—the youngest, prettiest, as yet childless one; the wealthiest and most educated one (also childless at the time, but well into my thirties as well); the one whose family is large, influential, and well-connected—offers important insight into certain ambiguities surrounding what wifehood means today, and into the ambivalent feelings that many young women have about it. It speaks to a tension between the fundamentally hierarchical gendered relations that wifehood traditionally entails and the ways that young people—women especially—attempt to reconcile modern discourses of romantic love and egalitarian gender politics that are promoted through post-Apartheid public discourses and state practices.

Although bridewealth remains vital to legitimizing marriage and connecting extended families with one another, colonialism and the intrusion of capitalist notions of value into ever broader domains of public life have brought bridewealth practices increasingly into alignment with notions of property rights.[13] As one example among many, when I asked Sipho (a married male Lodge manager) how bridewealth works, he bluntly stated, "It's like you sell your daughter." When I suggested that there must be more to it, he argued, "Listen, I give you cows, and you give me your daughter. Isn't it like you are selling her?" Framed in such economic-rationalist terms, men like Sipho assume they are entitled to a return on their investment. Studies (Shope 2006; Ansell 2001) have found, and my own research affirms, that most men assume that what they are paying for is gendered privilege. Accordingly, men struggle to reconcile the obligation to pay bridewealth with prominent discourses of gender equality. This is captured eloquently in the following statement by Mbeko:

> In the old days, we as the men were leaders in the family. But now we are told that the control in the marriage must be fifty-fifty, and that the wife and the husband must have equal authority, so I as the husband am no longer able to tell my wife, "Do this! Do that!" What I don't like is that it would seem reasonable for a woman to *lobola* me with R5,000, and I *lobola* her with R5,000, so that it can be fifty-fifty and we can be equal. But no, I have to lobola her with R10,000, and then after that she comes to me and tells me that we must be equal! No, it's not right, you see? There is just a free-for-all going on now, because we [men and women] are [supposedly] equal now.[14]

Virtually every young man in Mhlambini would concur with Mbeko that bridewealth payment and gender equality are not compatible. And though young men are certainly the most vociferous proponents of this interpretation of bridewealth, virtually all older people equate bridewealth payment with gaining privilege and authority over the wife. For instance, I documented one case where the parents of a young wife harshly chastised the wife's husband for disciplining her with violence after she took issue with his infidelity, explicitly pointing out that he had little authority to discipline her in this way because he had paid very little bridewealth upfront (this is not uncommon) and had thus not yet secured the authority to do so.

Conceptual links between bridewealth payment and gender hierarchy are thus deeply entrenched in the rural Eastern Cape, and the interpersonal dynamics of most marriages reflect this. Yet for young women, bridewealth today is taking on other meanings that sit in tension with the hierarchy and gender privileged just described, and these meanings further explain why some women marry (or hope to) despite the sacrifices that it usually entails in practice. First, like many young people all over the world, most young women consider romantic love to be a desirable attribute of modern personhood, and they believe if a man truly loves you, he should want to marry you. Similar to what has been documented elsewhere, young women associate romantic love with more companionate conjugal partnership and more egalitarian gender relations.[15] They share an assumption—widespread globally but confounded by research—that people are unlikely to dominate and mistreat those whom they love. In other words, young women trust that in a love marriage, gender relations will be more egalitarian and that their husband will be more helpful, will be less inclined to excessive drinking and wife beating, and will protect the wife from the domineering overtures of his kin. Furthermore, as South African scholar Danai Mupotsa (2015) notes, in the social imaginaries of many Black South African women, love marriage has a particular, affective allure in the post-Apartheid context given "romantic love . . . stands to stage marriage as a conquered site upon and through which the free can perform romance as freedom and choice" (185). The convictions that romantic love leads to gender equality and that love marriage is a desirable component of modern, post-Apartheid free personhood are, I argue, crucial for understanding how young women who marry today feel about an institution that, in practice, continues to be characterized by patriarchal power and domination. Indeed, interpreting bridewealth as evidence of love and freedom rather than as a payment that secures and legitimates male privilege means bridewealth can sit alongside the gender rights in which young women are heavily invested, albeit uneasily much of the time.

It is significant that although some young women are critical of bridewealth, the vast majority are profoundly attached to it, and even its harshest critics would not marry without it. Everyone concedes that bridewealth can trap women in bad relationships, but most young women nevertheless staunchly defend the practice, framing it not as a mechanism that enables gendered privilege but rather as the paramount manifestation of a man's love and regard. Although bridewealth payment can be conceived of as a means of securing gendered privilege, it can also be reframed as a reflection of the intensity of a man's love—especially if accompanied by other evidence of that love, such as acts of kindness and generosity, verbal declarations of love, and permission to bring prior children born to different fathers into the marital home. As one example among many, the sixteen cows that were rumored to have been paid for a young woman named Nandipha from the next village over held almost mythic appeal among my young women friends. When I asked why a man would pay so much, without exception my friends firmly stated that he paid big bridewealth because he really loved her. Like Cebisa mentioned earlier, this was evident, my friends claimed, because Nandipha already had a child by a different father, and this ought to have *lowered* her value in bridewealth terms. Her large bridewealth payment, therefore, made sense only if her worth was determined solely by the metric of her husband's love.

Despite their reservations about gendered subordination in marriage, many young village women would therefore be keen to marry if they were confident in the groom's love, even as the staunchest supporters of bridewealth concede that it is difficult to leave an abusive relationship, to request condom use, or to refuse sex once bridewealth has been paid. Many young women nevertheless hope and believe that a relationship based on love is unlikely to be characterized by precisely these sorts of gendered inequities: a man who loves you wouldn't put you at risk of STDs and would share your goals for fertility control. He wouldn't force sex upon you and would give you no cause for wanting to escape the relationship. Unfortunately, young women's overemphasis on love and equality in marriage seems to amplify rather than diminish gendered tensions about rural village marriage, because men assume that women know that marriage is actually about authority, and that by deflecting the meaning of bridewealth into the domain of love, romance, and freedom, they are trying to have their cake and eat it too. Yet despite these ongoing tensions, beyond the material security that it can offer, marriage also holds ample appeal in the contemporary era for the promise of love and freedom that it can entail, even amid circumstances that constantly confound this interpretation of the institution.

Having explained both the reasons why some women eschew wifehood and the reasons why others would readily choose it, I turn now to my final story, which brings together many threads discussed above to illustrate the complementarity between the divergent forms of feminine moral personhood discussed above.

Fezeka

During my most recent sojourn in Mhlambini, I paid a visit to Fezeka, the young woman whose words introduced this chapter. When we first met, she had recently been awarded a rare scholarship to complete secondary school in Cape Town. However, she managed only a few months at school before illness forced her to return to Mhlambini to be cared for by her family. I came to know her better during that time because she had great energy to talk but could not walk far on the steep village trails. Bored and housebound, she seemed to welcome my company and my many questions about village life.

In the intervening years Fezeka has made a great recovery and has secured a job at the NGO. But she has also lost both her mother and her beloved elder sister. The purpose of my most recent visit to Fezeka's home, therefore, was threefold: I wanted to congratulate her on her job, to express my condolences for her recent losses, and, if she seemed up to it, to ask if she would be interested in assisting me with my research again.

When I arrived at Fekeza's home, we exchanged greetings and then sat in the shade of her family's kitchen hut to catch up. Fezeka looked well compared to the last time I had seen her, and I saw this improvement mirrored in the condition of the *umzi*. A fat mother pig rooted around the yard trailed by energetic piglets, hens scratched industriously in the dirt, and three small children (Fezeka's daughter, her niece, and a neighbor) played in the dust with sticks and a toy car. A warm, late-summer breeze fluttered the laundry and rustled through the maize stalks in the large vegetable garden. Yet I noticed most of all how quiet and empty the homestead seemed without her mother and elder sister, both warm, active women who were always bustling about doing domestic chores.

As if reading my thoughts, Fezeka broke the silence. "Thank you for sending money for the funerals. It was a big help for us."

"Of course," I said. "I'm sorry that I was not here."

After a pause, Fezeka added, "Katie, I want to help you, but things are different for me now. I have my job, and then I come home and cook and look after my father, and my child, and my sister's child. All those house chores of my mother and my sister. All the time now I am working."

I felt ashamed to have sought her help in the first place. I should have known how busy she must be since their deaths. But I was also concerned for her given her history of poor health. "Is your [other] sister not able to help you?" I asked.

"No" responded Fezeka. "She's schooling now, grade 11, so she's staying near where she studies. And I am paying for that. You know I cannot abandon the children of my mother."

After a long pause, I asked, "Will you just stay living here, then, at your father's home?"

"Yes, of course!" she exclaimed. "Because, *kaloku* [remember], I don't want to get married. Anyways, I have a job now, so I can build my house! You can see that I have already started." She gestured toward a pile of concrete bricks stacked on a patch of cleared ground. Her somber mood was abruptly gone; her eyes lit up with a familiar energy as she spoke of building her own home. "And," she continued breathlessly, "did you did you know that my brother is working now too, on the fruit farm at Grabou?[16] So I am just waiting for the day that he can get married! Me, I am saving for that also, to pay the *lobola*! Then he can bring his wife here, and my work will be less. When she is doing all the work of this home, then my life will be much, much easier. Then, I can just do my job!"

I had known since that initial interview years prior that Fezeka had long aspired to find work and build a home, but this was the first time she mentioned mobilizing another woman's domestic labor as an element of that plan. I certainly sympathized with Fezeka's heavy workload, and I had no doubt that having a young wife in the home would alleviate this. Yet I also recalled how critical she was of marriage, and how often she reiterated the virtues of employment and financial autonomy. It therefore struck me as somewhat disingenuous that securing her own well-being entailed compelling another (almost certainly poorer, less educated, and therefore more vulnerable) woman into taking on a role that she herself so strongly disavowed.

This conversation stayed with me over the coming weeks and prompted me to consider more closely how the single working women I knew were dependent on the domestic labor of other women. Reminiscent of middle-class and affluent working women in North America and Europe who rely on the labor of poorer, often racialized women, it became clear that all of them were able to earn wages, enjoy relatively unrestricted mobility, and pursue leisure activities like visiting taverns and going to town to shop because other women—usually sisters-in-law, but sometimes their mothers or unemployed sisters—took on domestic responsibilities that would have otherwise been theirs. Moreover, those with sisters-in-law clearly expected those women to adhere to standards of married femininity that align with the traditional gender order. For example, although Mandisa's sister-in-law was our age peer and was always present—usually cooking or cleaning in the same hut—when I visited Mandisa's family home, in all the years of our friendship, Mandisa has never invited her to join us in conversation. She does, however, always expect her sister-in-law to bring us food and drink and to look after the children while we socialize. Similarly, the headmistress of the local school (aloof, unmarried, and the only village-born woman over forty who goes bareheaded) has two young daughters-in-law in her household. She financed their bridewealth herself, both directly, through her own monetary contributions, and indirectly, through purchasing the *bakkie* (pickup truck) that her sons use to earn income as taxi drivers. These young women do all the domestic work of the headmistress's home and treat her with great respect and deference.

Furthermore, with some probing, it became clear that my working friends hoped to acquire a daughter-in-law of their own one day—and investing in their sons' education could only help toward this goal. As further evidence that this is an acknowledged strategy for alleviating excessive workload for wage-earning women, in the backpacker Lodge kitchen, Amahle once aimed the flashlight of her cell phone onto an old photo of Fezeka that was mounted on the wall and commented, "[It's a] shame, that one. Imagine, so much work that she has to do. It's too much. I think her father must marry again."[17]

"I was talking to her about that," I said. "I think she is hoping her brother will get married."

"Hmm," said Amahle thoughtfully. "Yes, maybe her father is too old. So yes, now I am thinking maybe the brother is the best option."

Much scholarly attention has been devoted to exploring what widespread unemployment and the unfeasibility of marriage and provider masculinity mean for young South African men and for those who are harmed through acts of frustrated male power.[18] Less attention has been paid to the impact of political and economic transformations on women's lives,[19] especially in rural areas. Yet young women too must navigate these challenges and changes as they forge new lives in the post-Apartheid era of rights-based democracy, economic transformation, and industrial decline.

With the diminished availability of migrant labor jobs, new life trajectories are necessary as long-standing models of social reproduction and moral personhood are becoming unattainable for most young people. This poses great challenges for young people because the practices and things that have long been constitutive of gendered moral personhood are at once central to sociality and increasingly decoupled with the realities of daily life.

Amid this uncertainty, young women's prospects for securing a male provider and realizing long-standing models of feminine life course have diminished. The examples I have provided show that there are several paths available to young Eastern Cape women today. Accordingly, some young women with the means to do so are diverging from established norms of womanhood by earning wages, building homes, and supporting their kin. Some succeed in finding jobs. The nature of the employment opportunities available in the rural Eastern Cape means that access to these jobs is largely restricted to those who can speak, read, and write in English—in this community, it means that they are available to women who have spent some time in more urban areas to complete the necessary schooling. At the same time, some young women—almost invariably uneducated and less widely traveled women—adhere more closely to established standards of gendered propriety. Although doing so is no guarantee of securing a husband and provider, a minority of these women *do* marry. What this means is shifting, and young men and women negotiate among themselves the relative value and relevance of authority, patriarchy, discipline, gender equality, and romantic love. In many ways, it seems that these divergent femininities represent an either-or situation for young women: attempting to pursue one path precludes the possibility of future success on the other. Moreover, there is a price attached to either approach, and neither option guarantees happiness and security.

However, Fezeka's story illustrates that there is both contradiction and possibility inherent in this difficult position. Most young working women dismiss hierarchical, relational forms of feminine personhood, drawing instead on autonomous, independent, and egalitarian moral frames that resonate with the constitution and with post-Apartheid imaginaries of consumption and self-crafting. Doing so protects them from the critiques and judgments of men and elders and gives moral force to their aspirational goals. Moreover, they refuse marriage in part because they believe that it would enmesh them in a patriarchal and gerontocratic social hierarchy, and they find that prospect unappealing. Yet unlike working men, even when they are the sole breadwinners in their families, they are not free of gendered expectations about domestic reproduction.

Some villagers claim otherwise, but the interrelated phenomena of limited employment opportunities for men; the presence of working, unmarried women; and the instability of patriarchal authority are not entirely novel in the former Bantustans.[20] What *is* recent and powerful is new human-rights-based discourses and their associated idioms of equality as frameworks through which to experience and understand work, gender roles, and social life. These proffer new, potent language through which to explain and justify young women's behavior and with which to resist male efforts to reassert patriarchal privilege. Women's embrace of paid work and rejection of marriage on rights-based grounds is especially powerful here because of the way the right to refuse an unwanted marriage resonates with notions of freedom, control, and choice that are fundamental to South African human-rights culture. At the same time, as Danai Mupotsa (2015, 185) notes, in post-Apartheid social imaginaries, rural traditional marriages are especially emblematic of "the 'past,' the communal and unfreedoms."

The weight of obligations to others is also a common tension in the stories above. For all their desire for autonomy and independence, the working women I have discussed here believe it is extremely important to provide for their families. Despite their deployment of human rights to reject certain obligations grounded in relational and hierarchical forms of personhood—obligations to marry in accordance with their parents' wishes, for example—they evidently feel obliged to support their families and are willing to suffer criticism and personal sacrifice to do so. Although these responsibilities can be demanding and burdensome, working women are also proud of their ability to provide.

Working women are also evidently dependent on the domestic labor of un-employed, usually married young women, and thus on the continuation of patriarchal and gerontocratic femininities that they vociferously reject. At pres-ent, they can truly realize their vision of post-Apartheid freedom only if other women will take on the domestic portion of their "double shift." Although working women could, in theory, simply pay unemployed women to take on their responsibilities in the home, I know of no examples of this happening in and around Mhlambini. I suspect that this approach would be seen as shirking kinship obligations and would reflect poorly on both these women and their kin.[21] Instead, either they or their parents or brothers (or some cooperative combination of all of these) work through institutions such as bridewealth and marriage to mobilize traditional forms of feminine moral personhood as a means of securing this labor through kinship.

The opposite side of the coin is that working women in Mhlambini are also often the only employed people in their households; most support a large net-work of dependent kin. As such, young wives whose domestic labor and gen-dered submission and servitude support working women are, in turn, able to survive precisely because some women reject gerontocratic patriarchy in favor of work. This shows that navigating the contradictions inherent in living with multiple incommensurate forms of feminine personhood is both simply a way of being amid economic and political transformations and also a resource for mobilization. As we have already seen with other dimensions of life (e.g., social security grants), this kind of strategic mobilization of contradictory moralities is a survival strategy for many in Mhlambini.

Furthermore, working women's strategies for building viable lives for them-selves and their children dovetail with men's widely discussed frustrations about the loss of patriarchal authority and privilege associated with being the heads of households. Although ample literature documents this in the context of male unemployment generally,[22] focusing on working *women* exposes the possibility that young men are also frustrated because working women unmask them as largely irrelevant for social reproduction. As we have seen, a working woman can support her parents and children on her own, and the economic contributions that she brings to her natal household afford her leverage to live on her own terms. Moreover, as we see with Fezeka and women like her, working women can mobilize their economic power to harness the domestic and reproductive labor of *other* women, leaving them free to focus on earning wages, providing for their families, and setting up homes independent of men. Men's anxieties about working women likely stem in part from the perception that they are usurping patriarchal power—ironically by mobilizing institutions grounded in hierarchical, deeply patriarchal modes of social reproduction.

Finally, the stories I have shared about Mandisa, Amahle, Busi, Fezeka, Cebisa, and Nomvula also have implications for the theorization of life course and social change. That meaning is created through practice is a fundamental tenet of anthropology, and anthropological work on life course demonstrates this by showing how certain societal changes are grounded in the actions of individuals who aspire to futures in conditions of contingency, uncertainty, and constraint.[23] In rural South Africa, circumstances force this kind of life-shaping endeavor: as established forms of female life course become unreliable, young women have a strong impetus to envision and pursue futures that are not contingent upon marriage and spousal support.

Anthropological studies of social change also demonstrate that envisioned futures are created from existing cultural categories that are at once inseparable from the historical conditions of their emergence but also not simple reflections of past cultural forms (Cole 2010; White 2010). As Jennifer Cole (2010) has demonstrated with respect to young Malagasy women, established cultural categories shape young women's efforts to create futures for themselves in times of rapid globalization and economic reform, yet in so doing they create new, hybrid cultural meanings that can reorient relations of power between actors and institutions. Social change, then, occurs as people mobilize cultural categories that are both products of historical circumstances and also changes in response to their deployment in the present. This kind of productive hybridity is evident in the case of working women in Mhlambini. Through the activities of women like Mandisa, we see long-standing male cultural scripts being taken up and transformed by young women providers who mold these scripts with practices and discourses characteristic of rights-based democracy to create new yet not wholly unfamiliar forms of womanhood.

FIVE

THE MORAL AMBIGUITY OF *UKUTHWALA*

ONE SUNNY DAY IN 2011, a fifteen-year-old girl named Bomkazi was walking home from school down a wide dirt road when a young man in a car pulled over and asked for directions to a nearby trading store. When Bomkazi approached the vehicle, several other young men jumped out and pulled her into the back-seat. Ignoring her protests, the young men refused to stop the vehicle to let her out. Instead, they drove for roughly an hour before pulling into a homestead that Bomkazi had never seen before. There, in the presence of the young men and several older men and women, she was informed that she had been taken through *ukuthwala*: abducted with the intention of making her a wife. Word would soon be sent to her family informing them of the abduction and asking that they consent to the union by entering into *lobola* (bridewealth) negotiations with the abductor and his kin. If they consented, she would stay at this homestead as a bride.

Bomkazi was familiar with *ukuthwala*; although her widowed mother, Nomthandazo, personally disapproved of the practice, in the past members of her extended family had acquired wives in this way. Certain that she did not want to marry a stranger, Bomkazi waited until the dead of night and then crept past several sleeping elders, snuck out of the hut and into the forest, and began running as soon as she reached the road. Near dawn, she managed to hitch a ride to the small town where her mother's sister lived, and from there she managed to phone her mother. As Bomkazi had hoped, Nomthandazo was furious about the abduction. Nomthandazo left Mhlambini immediately to fetch Bomkazi and refused all further negotiations with the abductor's family.

Bomkazi lived just down the hill from me at the time of this abduction, and her *ukuthwala* quickly became the talk of the village. Before she had even returned home, rumor reached me that the abduction had been organized by her grandmother, Nonikele. Nonikele was a woman I knew moderately well. Although she had a reputation for being ill-tempered, she had always been kind to me, and I sympathized with her difficult circumstances. She lived in two run-down rondavels on her family's ancestral land. Although she had received an old-age pension for many years and could afford to pay someone to fix her leaking roofs, she refused to do so because she felt that this work should be done for her by younger, more able members of her kinship network, and her pride prevented her from paying someone else to do this work. She lacked these human resources because her eldest son had died several years ago, and his widow (Bomkazi's mother, Nomthandazo) had subsequently built her own homestead across the village after quarreling repeatedly with Nonikele. Nomthandazo's two daughters lived with Nomthandazo (the eldest being Bomkazi), and her teenage son resided sometimes with his mother and sometimes in Nonikele's spare hut. Nonikele's younger son is a migrant mine worker. Like many young people, he is of the opinion that modern relationships require cohabitation as an integral component of conjugal intimacy.[1] Accordingly, rather than leaving his wife in the village to care for his elderly mother, he broke with convention by bringing his wife to faraway Rustenberg[2] so they could live together near the mine where he worked. Nonikele felt betrayed by her son's priorities and told me of the sadness, pain, and loneliness that she suffered because of his neglect.

Although I was initially surprised and skeptical that Nonikele would orchestrate her own granddaughter's abduction, friends in the village explained that she was by far the most likely culprit. "She wanted the bridewealth cows, can't you see? With these cows, she could pay the *lobola* [bridewealth] for Bomkazi's brother, meaning the family could acquire a new daughter-in-law." Given Nonikele had a spare rondavel and given Nomthandazo's homestead consists of one crowded two-room hut, the new couple would almost certainly reside with Nonikele, where the new wife would provide both companionship and labor. This failed *ukuthwala* stained an already tarnished relationship between Nonikele on the one hand and her daughter-in-law and granddaughter on the other. After the fact, Nonikele frequently complained that she had raised Bomkazi since infancy only to have her grow wayward and disrespectful of elders. For her part, Bomkazi was angry about what she perceived as a profound betrayal on her grandmother's part and vented to me that she wanted to beat her grandmother for her greediness.

In many ways, Bomkazi's experience is typical of *ukuthwala*, which is practiced primarily in rural Xhosa and Zulu communities.[3] Her abduction from a public space, her young age at the time, and the premediated nature of the abduction are all typical of the seventeen *ukuthwala* that I have personally documented through in-depth, first-person accounts.

My research suggests that *ukuthwala* occurs frequently in the rural Eastern Cape today, thereby supporting a claim made by the government, advocacy organizations, popular media, and lawyers that incidences of *ukuthwala* have risen in recent years.[4] Although recent demographic studies do not exist to my knowledge, earlier survey data suggest that incidence of *ukuthwala* have been rising since at least the 1950s (see Manona 1980; Wilson et al. 1952). It is noteworthy that this apparent rise in *ukuthwala* coincides with a reduction in marriage rates throughout South Africa as a whole (recall that marriage is now the exception rather than the norm in most low-income communities). The reasons for this decline in marriage rates are the subject of ongoing analysis and discussion, but it is widely acknowledged that widespread and worsening unemployment has placed bridewealth payment and provision for family beyond the reach of most young men.

Ukuthwala became a major research focus for me because people in Mhlambini identified it as a significant locus of conflict between men and women, youth and elders, state and community, and law and culture. Early on in my research, people frequently presumed that my open-ended queries about gendered and generational conflicts and disagreements were queries about *ukuthwala* specifically. Through examining local critiques of, justifications for, and opinions about *ukuthwala*, it became clear that it is a case-in-point example of the ways in which state laws and liberal public discourse are perceived to clash with long-standing networks of obligation and authority. As a site where divergent moral frames come into conflict and where different gendered and generational subjectivities are strategically deployed for reasons that are rarely transparent, *ukuthwala* is an especially lucid example of divergent moral frameworks in action. Through a close examination of why and how people instigate, negotiate, avoid, prevent, and sometimes escape from *ukuthwala* in this chapter, it will become evident that moral uncertainty is sustained and produced as people attempt to create meaningful, viable futures for themselves and their kin in a time of great economic and political transformation.

BACKGROUND: *UKUTHWALA* IN HISTORICAL CONTEXT

Historical records and contemporary cultural authorities agree that *ukuthwala* is a long-standing albeit irregular form of marriage, usually deployed to kick-start marriage negotiations that have either broken down or proven difficult to initiate.[5] As exemplified by Bomkazi's experience, a prospective groom and his male allies will typically seize an unmarried girl or woman and will forcibly bring her to the groom's family home. Although the woman will almost certainly fight to escape, the odds are always stacked against her. This is because the men will have waited until she is either alone or in the company of others who are in collusion with the abductors, all of whom will use force and intimidation to overcome her resistance. Once the young woman has been brought to the abductor's home, word will be sent to her family, who may choose to either begin negotiating bridewealth with the abductor's elder kin or demand the woman's return.

Historical sources suggest that many *ukuthwala* are staged elopements, where the show of male force and feminine resistance serve to sustain and reproduce dominant scripts of masculine assertiveness and feminine submission and modesty. Monica Hunter ([1936] 1961, 187) writes, "It is seemly that she should make a great show of resistance, even though she is pleased to marry the man who has taken her, and sometimes girls lie down and are dragged along the ground, getting their limbs grazed before they will submit to going with their captor."[6] Although early sources do acknowledge that some *ukuthwala* are "real cases of forcible abduction" (Soga [1933] 2013, 271), and although recent historiographical research confirms that violent, forcible abduction is not new (Karimakwenda 2020; Thornberry et al. 2016), early scholarly sources claim that in the past genuine abductions were the exception rather than the norm.

Drawing on these sources and on the advice of traditional leaders, contemporary South African law recognizes *ukuthwala* as a legitimate form of marriage (CRL Rights Commission 2014; Seymour 1982; Koyana 1980). The assumption underlying this law is that marriage by abduction may be consensual even where it appears otherwise—a woman may pretend to resist an abduction that she in fact wants because the performance of resistance is expected of her. Although the South African constitution and bill of rights entitle South Africans to live according to their custom and to marry under Customary Law if desired, constitutional rights to gender equality trump Customary Law in situations where Customary Law is in violation of these rights. In practice, this means that *ukuthwala* is illegal in South Africa for all people under eighteen (the legal age of majority) and is permitted for adults only where a woman genuinely wants to marry her abductor. A high-profile South African court ruling has unambiguously clarified that *ukuthwala* of a genuinely unwilling girl or woman of any age constitutes human trafficking, which is illegal under both South African and international law.[7] Despite the legal accommodation of *ukuthwala* in some circumstances, recent research suggests that it often involves girls too young to legally consent (Rice 2017, 2014; Kheswa and Hoho 2014) and that many *uku-thwala* entail considerable violence and genuine unwanted kidnapping (Smit and Notermans 2015; Rice 2017, 2014).

UKUTHWALA IN THE EASTERN CAPE TODAY

Ukuthwala is contentious in Mhlambini both because villagers hold deeply divergent opinions about it and because individuals understand the practice in different ways. These viewpoints tend to diverge along gendered and genera-tional lines, and it is partially for this reason that so many people identify *uku-thwala* as emblematic of the problems that accompany recent societal change. In my experience, all young women oppose *ukuthwala*. For example, though NomaIndia (early twenties) had never been abducted herself, when I asked her if she felt there were any problems in her community, she immediately re-sponded, "Oh, there's that thing when you're married! Maybe you're just going to town or going to the *spaza* [informal shop], and they just take you like that! I think it's not good." Similarly, Nosapho, a twenty-five-year-old woman who had "married for love," wrung her hands in dismay while stating, "*Yhu*, I don't feel good about *ukuthwala*. It's not right. It's not right! To marry a guy that you've never seen before! It's not right. But it's happening, even in these days." These sentiments are typical of young village women.

A few young men also find *ukuthwala* outdated (more on this below), but most young men consider *ukuthwala* to be a long-standing cultural practice that continues to have some merit. Recall, for instance, Unathi's reflections about village life as discussed in the introduction. When I asked him how Mhlambini differs from his original home, he compared the village favorably with urban ar-eas, which he considered "less traditional." He offered *ukuthwala* as an example of the differences between urban and rural Xhosa society:

> This place is more traditional, and more peaceful. You see, in places like near town, you know, there's always violence and stuff like that. But here, it's quiet and peaceful. Yeah, people are doing their own traditions. They've got the *strong* beliefs. You know, like just grabbing a girl. If you want to marry a girl, you don't have to talk to her or anything. If you want her, you just talk to the parents, and then you just grab the girl. Even if she doesn't want you. Yeah, here, they are still walking exactly on the culture. Which is a good thing!

Mature and elderly village residents are not always in agreement about the value of *ukuthwala* either. Although most share Unathi's view, some mature vil-lagers oppose the practice, especially if they are Christian, because the church advocates for companionate marriage based on mutual choice. Indeed, most abducted women who return to their families do so because their parents refuse to marry their daughters in this way. Elders—and especially elder women—situate *ukuthwala* as gerontocratic obligation, however, emphasizing the importance of suppressing one's personal preference to accommodate the wishes of their seniors. Consider the following excerpt from an interview with an elderly woman whose daughter had married through *ukuthwala*:

> Kate: Is *ukuthwala* a good thing?
> Nophikele: Yes, among us Xhosa people. It's our tradition, yes, it's our way of doing things. Even me, I come from far away, from the Dwala clan,[8] and I was abducted, and here I am now, and I'll spend my old age here. I'm submitting to my parents' wishes.

Similarly, Nokhumbulele, a middle-aged woman who described herself as "traditional," reflected, "In the old days, when you were wanted by a young man or an old man who has been widowed, and you are wanted by his parents, then you settle with him. Something like marriage, you understand? You are married when you are still a child, but you were just obeying your parents' way of doing things. You would just put up with it in the old days, because your parents would say 'Stay with this person.' And you'd eventually become used to your husband."

Nokhumbulele went on to sympathize with men who abduct and are then deserted by their abducted wives, and to express distain for these new "rights" that young women now possess. When I asked her what she would think of a woman who reported her parents or husband to the police, Nokhumbulele quickly turned to my research assistant and asked her incredulously, "Is that woman [Kate] telling me that she would be able to live in her home after having her husband locked away in jail?" She then turned back to me and said accusingly, "[If you went to the police,] you'd be left having to explain yourself to your husband's mother and father!" This emphasis on the importance of submission to parental authority, combined with genuine puzzlement over young women's legal right to refuse arranged marriage, is widespread among elderly men and women.

ELDER WOMEN, *UKUTHWALA*, AND CHANGING IDEALS OF GERONTOCRACY

South African society is notorious for its antagonistic gender politics, especially with regard to sex, intimacy, and domestic life.[9] Stemming from an impetus to respond to the HIV/AIDS epidemic, much research that has sought to explain these interpersonal politics has focused on understanding how social inequality plays out between women and men, given male power is recognized as a key driver of the HIV/AIDS epidemic. Much of the best of this work has examined how the economic and social issues outlined in earlier chapters are catalysts for violence initiated by men and boys (more on this later).[10]

This emphasis on male power and female vulnerability has carried into popular perceptions of *ukuthwala*; most media coverage frames the issue as one of violent, frustrated men exercising power over young women. This chapter will show that this interpretation is well-founded, but it is generally inattentive to the ways in which violence is legitimized by men *and* women as a form of gendered discipline that is appropriate in some circumstances. It also fails to consider how transformations in work and marriage affect groups besides young men. In so doing, it obscures the powerful role that elders—primarily elder women—play in instigating *ukuthwala*. The error of this omission is evident from Bomkazi's abovementioned abduction story.

In Bomkazi's case, young men carried out the actual abduction, but the individuals with the power to plan, organize, and ultimately impede this abduction were all mature or elderly women. Fully half of the in-depth accounts of *ukuthwala* that I collected were much like Bomkazi's in that respect: orchestrated solely or in part by elder women who stood to benefit greatly from the companionship, labor, and status that the acquisition of a daughter-in-law would bring. In most cases, these were women whose sons or grandsons were unable to secure the bridewealth necessary for marriage, meaning these elder women were deprived of the status and leisure that they had looked forward to in their old age, and that they themselves had paid a heavy price for in their youth.

Although men tend to be the focus of conversations about who stands to lose through the concurrent downsizing and the legislation of gender equality, scholars have long known that elder women also have powerful stakes in the maintenance of patriarchy (Hunter 2011; Redding 2006; Kandiyoti 1988). As Deniz Kandiyoti (1988, 279) explains, deeply patriarchal communities are typically characterized by a patriarchal bargain, whereby "the deprivation and hardship [a woman] experiences as a young bride is eventually superseded by the control and authority she will have over her own subservient daughters-in-law." This describes normative hierarchies in Mhlambini, yet, as explained in the introduction, such patriarchal bargains are destabilized under both capitalism and conditions of poverty. Under such conditions, "women escape the control of mothers-in-law . . . at a much younger age, but it also means that they themselves can no longer look forward to a future surrounded by subservient daughters-in-law. For the generation of women caught in between, this trans-formation may represent genuine personal tragedy, since they have paid the heavy price of an earlier patriarchal bargain, but are not able to cash in on its promised benefits" (Kandiyoti 1988, 282). Many elder women in this village are caught in precisely this position, and their suffering is often compounded by heavy childrearing responsibilities in cases where their adult offspring have died or have vanished into the city in search of work. The limited economic opportunities available to young men means that men cannot afford to marry and establish independent households, but their poverty also means that their mothers are deprived of the companionship and labor that daughters-in-law provide. As was the case with Nonikele, this example suggests that it is often elder women who are decisive actors in planning *ukuthwala*, invested as they are in either acquiring a daughter-in-law in this way, or in acquiring the bride-wealth to obtain one.[11]

UKUTHWALA, ELOPEMENT, AND CHANGING CONJUGAL IDEALS

Many elder women struggle because of young men's unemployment, but their isolation and heavy domestic burden cannot solely be attributed to the implica-tions of economic transformations for marriage practices. Rather, my research on *ukuthwala* shows that changing conjugal ideals also impede their access to the companionship and labor that daughters-in-law provide, in turn generating impetus to acquire a daughter-in-law through abduction marriage.

Recall that younger people in Mhlambini increasingly hold the opinion that romantic love is requisite for marriage. Although love marriages remain rare, most young people aspire to a partnership premised on companionate compatibility rather than fulfillment of filial obligations to elder kin. And, as documented elsewhere, most consider cohabitation and autonomy and privacy from kin to be conducive—if not integral—to achieving this goal. Consider the following excerpt from an interview with Unathi, the young man who grew up near town. In this excerpt, he juxtaposes convention in Mhlambini with more "modern" (his wording) practices of conjugality:

> In my village now, the only person you marry is the person you agree with
> [the person you choose for their personal qualities, and who likewise chooses
> you over others]. You agree that *I* am going to marry *you*. And in my village,
> if I marry you, I must go to my place of work with you. You must go and stay
> where I'm working. I don't just marry you and go and work in Jo'burg [where
> the mines are], leaving you there with my parents. No! Because my wife can't

just stay here in the village, look, I'm married here! But when it comes here in *this* village, if you marry, you marry for your parents. *Ja*. Because really, long time ago, when you were marrying, you were marrying for your parents. You see? Your wife, her work is for your parents. Not for you.

In Mhlambini, young married couples who share Unathi's values have recently begun to establish their own homesteads at a distance from their elders, and as with Nonikele's younger daughter-in-law, some wives whose husbands are labor migrants are leaving the village entirely to live at their husbands' places of work.

The desire for love marriage is also, in some cases, cause for *ukuthwala* in and of itself. I became aware that some contemporary *ukuthwala* are staged elopements while walking with my friend Tandiswa past the homestead of a young wife who had been married by *ukuthwala* some six years before. Tandiswa informed me that the young wife was pregnant again. I expressed sympathy for the wife because she had told me of her violent abduction. Tandiswa laughed and corrected me: "No, in the end, that *thwala* [sic] is not a bad *thwala* [sic], because she loves her husband. I know. The *thwala* [sic] is very bad, but sometimes, if they love the man, it's not bad at all." This conversation came back to me a few months later, when I became acquainted with a young woman named Phakama. When we met, Phakama was living with her parents after being banished by her mother-in-law. Phakama states that she was married by *ukuthwala* and describes *ukuthwala* as "terrible." From her narrative, however, it is difficult to conclude that her marriage took place entirely against her will. Initially she was vague about the nature of her relationship with her husband prior to the abduction, before eventually explaining that he had been her boyfriend. When I asked her how she came to be married, she told me that she had requested to marry (*ndicela* ["I asked/requested"]) but had not expected her husband to take her by force. She recalled being taken by surprise when he accosted her with his posse and dragged her to his home in a neighboring village. Although she emphasized that she had been terrified during the abduction, she also reiterated that her marriage had been a happy one, that she truly loves her husband, and that she misses him very much now that they are separated.

Phakama continued her story by explaining that her marriage became intolerable because although her mother-in-law Nobomi had been pleased to acquire a daughter-in-law, Nobomi had anticipated complete control over Phakama's time and resources and had expected to control any income that Phakama's husband brought into the household. Moreover, Nobomi had certainly not intended for the emotional bond between Phakama and her son to interfere with her authority over Phakama's time and her claim to her son's money. In keeping with the close connection between material provision and emotional intimacy in this region, when he had money, Phakama's husband circumvented his mother by giving spending money to Phakama directly, and occasionally he gave her gifts.[12] According to Phakama, this enraged her mother-in-law, who abused and tormented Phakama mercilessly as punishment. When Nobomi's efforts to limit Phakama's access to resources continued to fail, she eventually banished Phakama, threatening to kill her should she return.

I remember being confused by Phakama's story as she recounted it to me, especially as she alternated between emphasizing her unwillingness to be married and remain with her husband, his kindness and her happiness with the quality of their relationship, a guarded admission that she had *asked* to marry, and her continued desire to be with her husband again. At the time, I attributed my confusion to a combination of my imperfect language skills and to the much broader scope of attraction and intimacy encompassed by the verb *ukuthanda* compared with the English term *to love*. Now, however, I suspect that Phakama may be one of potentially numerous *ukuthwala* that transpire between established couples who want to be together but may disagree about how to achieve that objective.

Recall that most young people in Mhlambini, like their peers in many parts of the world, desire love marriage based on mutual choice. Of course, records of *ukuthwala* as elopement suggest that young rural Xhosa have long exercised choice of spouse. Nevertheless, young people in Mhlambini repeatedly emphasize that their desire for love marriage and spousal choice is novel and maintain that their elders neither comprehend nor respect this. My young women friends frequently discussed with me their apprehensions about marriage, all of which dovetailed with trepidation about domineering husbands and despotic in-laws. Mandisa, for example, had this to say about "control" in marriage:

> I don't want the man that wants to control me. I don't want anyone to control me. It's good to control myself. I need the man who is just equally [who will treat me as an equal]. You see, in my village, most of them, the men, they will control you. The women they want are that ones that they will get a good answer [from]. You know? Like he can say to her, "You can do that, you can do that, but you don't get to do that," and she doesn't say anything. Yeah, most of them, they need someone to under them.

Such statements emphasizing self-possession, an idealized egalitarian partnership, and despondence about the possibility of ever finding this were echoed over and over to me by young, unmarried women. Virtually all young women aspired to intimate partnerships characterized by less domineering gender relations, with more egalitarian social relations presumed to follow from a relationship premised on love rather than force or parental arrangement.

Such concerns over control in marriage thus complicate the advantages that marriage confers to women, presenting them with a conundrum. Although marriage usually enmeshes women deeply into kinship relations character- ized by gendered and generational inequalities, marriage is also attractive in that wifehood is a feminine role of great value in Xhosa society. As previously discussed, through marriage, a woman can obtain a certain kind of respectable adulthood and, one day, the status and autonomy of an elder wife or widow. Moreover, through marriage, she will gain a legitimate claim to ongoing support for herself and her children. And finally, as explained in the previous chapter, though young women hope to avoid the gendered subordination that characterizes rural Xhosa marriages, they value a loving partnership and see marriage as the ultimate expression of a man's love. Remaining unmarried is therefore undesirable in many ways, but so is a marriage characterized by gendered domination and domestic servitude, and there is no guarantee that a relationship that starts out happy will remain so after marriage. Both mar- riage and remaining unattached thus potentially entail sacrifice and reward for rural women—especially for those with poor employment prospects—and for some of them the idea of choosing between two risky options can be para- lyzing. This is relevant to some cases of *ukuthwala*, because for some women, marrying a lover through *ukuthwala* may render marriage attainable if her boy- friend and her family cannot afford formal marriage, while simultaneously relieving her of the responsibility of making the difficult choice to marry or to stay single.

UKUTHWALA, MASCULINITY, AND VIOLENCE

Although some *ukuthwala* do appear to be a form of elopement, this possibil- ity should not detract from the violence that *ukuthwala* frequently entail. The violent, forcible abductions that feature in popular media and in courts of law today are grounded in the experiences of many abducted women, as the fol- lowing two examples will show. Both are abridged versions of first-person nar- rative interviews that I carried out with women who had experienced violent abductions.

ABDUCTED AND TAKEN TO RUSTENBERG

Nomandla (early twenties) had been abducted roughly a year prior to our in- terview by a man she had seen in passing but had never spoken with. He ap- proached her with some male friends and accosted her on the road in broad daylight. Although she tried to run away, he beat her into submission and dragged her to his home village. He promptly left her there, locking her in a hut and going drinking with friends. The next day, she was informed that word had been sent to her parents' home. Although Nomandla did not want to marry the man, and although her mother supported her resistance, her father consented to the abduction. Nomandla's mother, who was present for one of our meetings, emphasized that his actions were bound up with gerontocratic kinship obligations: more senior men in his lineage had made the decision. Nomandla, however, offered an economic explanation: her father could not resist the promise of bridewealth cows.

Already unhappy with her new family, things became worse when Nomandla's husband returned to his home in Rustenberg, taking her with him. He regularly beat her, left her alone at home all day, punished her if she left their shack or spoke to neighbors, forced her to sit quietly next to him while he spoke with his girlfriends on the phone, and made her beg him for money to meet her basic needs. Nomandla emphasized repeatedly that her husband had several girlfriends, and that she feared he might infect her with HIV. Mercifully, her misery was eventually relieved when neighbors became so concerned for her welfare that they helped her escape by breaking her out of her husband's house while he was working and paying her mini-bus taxi fare back to the Eastern Cape. Dismayed at the abuse that she had evidently suffered, her parents took her back.

A TEENAGER IS ABDUCTED WITH HER PARENTS' CONSENT

Aphiwe grew up in a village a few kilometers from Mhlambini and was a fifteen-year-old schoolgirl when she was married by *ukuthwala*. Although she rarely leaves her in-laws' homestead, I interacted with her regularly throughout my fieldwork because their homestead is near the NGO office, and I often saw her working in the yard on my way to and from my volunteer job. At the time that I interviewed her, she had been married for several years.

Unlike most young women I interviewed, she knew ahead of time that her parents had been approached about her by a family with two unmarried sons, and she understood that because her family was poor, *ukuthwala* would be attractive to them because it would save them all wedding costs while still ensuring that they would receive some bridewealth. She is a compelling speaker, so I have included an abridged narration of her abduction, in her own words:

> Aphiwe: When I listened to the conversation [between my father and that family] on the phone, I cried. I cried a lot. I knew that my heart was small, that I was anxious, and I couldn't even eat at school, because I was worried. The teachers asked me what my problem was, because they saw that I was

worried all the time, they perhaps saw that I was dreading what was going to happen. Meanwhile I was afraid to tell them. When I arrived home my mother wasn't friendly, and I ended up sulking and didn't even want to eat. I took a pen to the river, and I scratched around in the gravel on the riverbank, while I thought about the problems at home. I fell asleep only at 12 [a.m.], [because I was] imagining the people from Mhlambini that would carry me off. I work up early in the morning, bathed, and put the iron on the stove. I hurried so that if they arrived, they would arrive when I had already left, and I would be at school. I ironed my shirt and put on my school skirt. When I was putting on my shirt (I hadn't even put my panty on), a boy came to block me from leaving. He came immediately, wanting to fight. He took a stick and said, "Aphiwe, let's go." I said, "I'm not going to do that." He hit me. I took another stick and fought for myself. A boy from an adjacent homestead came, and I hit him. I intimidated him. I fought with my older brother. He is older than me. I sat down on the floor. They dragged me, they hit me. My mother went and disappeared. I left not wearing any shoes, and not even having put my panty on. When we arrived here, I sat over there in that chair and cried and cried and cried and cried. The mother arrived, she took out the clothes, and I was dressed in a skirt. I cried. I wanted to die.[13] I thought about going to the police, but I couldn't report my parents.

Kate: So, what is it like now, being a married woman?

Aphiwe: It's bad. If you are a married woman, you are ordered around a lot. You can't just do what you like. If you are told you're not going to school, you're not going. That's it. You even stop going to church. If you were a believer before, you are told, "Sit down! You aren't going to go to church. We don't attend church here." ... My husband is a cruel man ... For a long time now, my husband has been going to hang out with the girls and leaving me here wearing my headdress. He still isn't working. He's looking for work.

These stories are not the only accounts of *ukuthwala* that I collected that entailed genuine abduction, violence, and neglect, nor are they the most graphically violent. In making sense of this violence, I draw on theories of masculinity and violence, and of violence as gendered discipline in South Africa, as well as research on bride abduction elsewhere in the world. In so doing, I contribute toward explaining gendered violence in South Africa today, with broader implications for understanding the relationship between gender and violence in similar conditions of patriarchy.

UKUTHWALA: IMPLICATIONS FOR THEORY

Variously termed bride "abduction," "capture," "theft," and "kidnapping," taking wives by force has a long history in many societies. It is practiced today in some form in several world regions, most prominently in rural central Asia (especially Kyrgyzstan and Kazakhstan), but also Indonesia, Ethiopia, Vietnam, and within living memory in rural Greece, Bosnia, Mexico, Turkey, and China, among others. The literature suggests that bride abduction mainly occurs in patriarchal societies where extended kinship relations are integral to status and personhood and where successfully reaping the benefits of the patriarchal bargain is important for married women's status, security, and comfort in later life (e.g., Kim and Karioris 2020; Werner et al. 2018; Rice 2017, 2014; Werner 2009). Societies that practice bride capture today also share a recent history of social and political upheaval (e.g., dramatic transformations in central Asia following the collapse of the Soviet Union, transformations in South Africa following the end of Apartheid) followed by economic decline, the failure of prior forms of subsistence, a lack of opportunity for young people, and a confluence of these factors that threaten valued forms of masculine dignity, identity, and achievement (e.g., Kim and Karioris 2020; Rice 2017, 2014).[14]

In South Africa since the 1980s, for example, economic and political changes have resulted in a dramatic decline in employment opportunities for "unskilled" South Africans, leading to unemployment rates that place marriage and support of family beyond the reach of most young men. In Mhlambini, as in many rural villages, there is now a large cohort of unemployed young men who are dependent on kin. This was less the case a decade or two ago, when mine work was more available. Yet marriage and support of family remain cornerstones of masculine dignity. Disappointment over this change was apparent to me through many conversations with young men in Mhlambini and has been richly captured in ethnography from across South Africa.[15] Furthermore, a close association between material provision, sex, and emotional intimacy—what Mark Hunter (2002) has termed the "materiality" of sex and intimacy—means that poor men struggle to attract women. This too featured repeatedly in conversations with young men, variously expressed as a crestfallen conviction that they had no chance with the women they desired, or as bitter claims that *all* women are shallow gold diggers. As formal marriage becomes increasingly unaffordable to a large cohort of young men, these disenfranchised young men may have greater impetus than their forefathers to try to gain status as married men through the abduction of women whom they would otherwise have little chance of attracting as girlfriends, let alone obtaining as wives. Moreover, the poverty of many parents—most of whom are well aware that they are unlikely to receive much, if any, bridewealth for their daughters—may provide some impetus for their collusion in *ukuthwala* marriages. In broad strokes, this resonates with current analyses of bride abduction elsewhere.

Yet despite these similarities, *ukuthwala* also differs in important ways from bride capture in other regions even as it resonates with violent forms of gendered practice in South Africa. Analyzing these differences can help us understand something about patriarchy, gender, and violence, especially in this region. First, in other societies that currently practice bride abduction—central Asia certainly (Kim and Karioris 2020; Borbieva 2012), but also Indonesia (Salenda 2016)—social norms limit opportunities for young men and women to meet and socialize, and thus to identify and court potential spouses. Relatedly, in those societies female virginity holds extremely high value; premarital virginity loss—even the suspicion of it, which abduction entails—has tragic and long-lasting consequences for abducted women and their families. In rural central Asia, for example, returning home following abduction usually means a tarnished reputation and a future characterized by shame, childlessness, and spinsterhood in a place where such women are rare exceptions and have limited opportunities for other forms of status and fulfillment. There is thus strong impetus for abducted women to remain with their abductors, and for parents to encourage their daughters to do so.

This does not accurately describe rural South Africa. Rather, ample opportunities exist for unmarried people to meet and socialize in the rural Eastern Cape, whether at school, at church, at shops and *shebeens*, or out and about in the village. Furthermore, although it would be inaccurate to say that virginity has no value in rural South Africa, the social ramifications of premarital sex and virginity loss are minimal in comparison with other regions where bride abduction is practiced today. Virginity is not truly expected of *anyone* unless they are very young. Even premarital childbearing attracts little stigma and does not preclude marriage in the longer term—indeed, sometimes the opposite is true, given that men who *do* marry frequently marry the mothers of their children both because they care for those women and their children and because they want the rights and status that married fatherhood confers.

A further difference from other societies that practice bride abduction is that at the family and community level, the concerns people have about the condition of abducted women are not about abducted women's sexual purity per se. People operate under the assumption that sex will not happen without parental consent,[16] and virtually everyone is horrified by the idea that someone would have sex with an abducted woman without—or prior to—formal assent to marriage from her kin. It is no exaggeration to say that the most vociferous critics of *ukuthwala* consider bride abduction to be an acute problem in their community yet view sex with an abducted woman without family consent as an altogether different and more serious moral breach. Consent is central to the moral legitimacy of sex following abduction, but in keeping with a relational notion of personhood and kinship, it is the consent of elder (usually male) kin that is considered most relevant at the local level. Thus, though forced sex may well occur during short-lived failed abductions, everyone assumes that no sex transpired. And in any case, women and girls who return home are viewed no differently than women who have never been abducted, even in cases where the parents initially consented and it is widely known that sex did indeed occur.[17] Certain social norms and pressures that are central to *ukuthwala* are thus different from other regions where women marry by abduction today.

Importantly, *Ukuthwala* in South Africa also differs from similar practices elsewhere in the degree of violence that it regularly entails. Although bride abduction is framed as an act of violence by international governing bodies everywhere (e.g., Sultanalieva 2021; UNHROHC 2018), no recent studies of bride abduction from elsewhere in the world document the degree of overt physical violence—sexual and otherwise—that South African sources regularly do.[18] My own research certainly suggests that many *ukuthwala* involve intense violence, including beating, isolation and intimidation, rape, and in some cases even gang rape. Given bride abduction is an act of patriarchal power that is exercised under particular social, political, and economic circumstances, analyzing the violence that *ukuthwala* entails can tell us something about violence and patriarchy in South Africa more broadly.

At the level of Xhosa cultural practice, it seems that *ukuthwala* has long been violent (see Karimakwenda 2020, 2013; Thornberry et al. 2016) and has long been practiced by rural Xhosa. Many elders either were violent abductors or were abducted violently themselves in their youth, meaning the violence of contemporary *ukuthwala* seems normal and unremarkable to them. More broadly, South African society has long been violent, with the violence of colonization followed by an era of segregation in which a white minority consolidated and maintained their dominance through both structural and overt forms of violent repression.

Furthermore, both white colonial society and the African societies that were subject to colonialism were deeply patriarchal, meaning the violence and conflict of these eras took gendered forms (Gqola 2007). Historical and ethnographic evidence shows that gendered violence and antagonism increased greatly during the colonial and Apartheid era. As Anne Kelk Mager (1999) demonstrates with respect to the Ciskei (the other Xhosa former Bantustan), the migrant labor system and the various ways in which rural African households were drawn into the racist capitalist colonial and Apartheid-era economy more generally meant that rural women's fertility became a burden more so than an asset. At the same time, access to wages dramatically diminished the hold that elder men had over younger men, meaning control of women became the most powerful hold that elder men retained over their juniors.[19] As Cheryl Walker (1990, 180) remarks, "As the efficacy of internalized social sanctions began to break down, chiefs, fathers, and husbands felt compelled to turn to more overt forms of control over women's mobility." Historians suggest that physical and sexual violence was a key method through his which was achieved: "Sexually violent behavior can be seen as stemming from men's (and boys') investing in masculinities constructed as power over women. For many sexually violent men manhood was given expression in a context where they felt thwarted in their ability to fulfil masculine ideas. Nor were they a small, pathological fringe. Those who invested in aggressive masculine identities and brutalized women were often 'ordinary men' acting out their sexuality as a relation of dominance" (Mager 1999, 183–84).

Violence against women was thus mobilized to bolster patriarchal and gerontocratic authority against social and economic transformations that fundamentally undermined the stability of the rural patriarchal homestead under conditions of conflict and racist colonial violence. Although most people alive in South Africa today did not live under Apartheid, the heritage of violence and gendered antagonism that colonialism and Apartheid entailed has influenced the socialization of many South Africans, in Mhlambini and beyond, thus further normalizing the antagonistic gender relations that characterize *ukuthwala* both as a practice and as an issue of community disagreement. Indeed, broad evidence suggests that in South Africa, violence is widely normalized as a form of discipline aimed at shaping the moral person generally, by encouraging appropriate behavior and punishing transgression.[20] This normalization of violence came up frequently in my own research in statements by older women who blandly explained that violence is really the only tool that men have for teaching appropriate comportment to children and for educating a wife of about his likes and dislikes.

More recent work on gendered and generational contests and violence in South Africa has focused on the ways in which recent transformations in work and economy have marginalized young men. Placing violent *ukuthwala* in conversation with the literature on South African masculinities suggests that there is a connection between the rise in *ukuthwala*, widespread gendered violence, and men's frustrations over economic transformations. Much has already been written about the relationship between the frustrations and humiliations experienced by these young men and widespread gendered antagonism and violence (see note 14 of this chapter). This literature suggests that with few other prospects for achieving socially valued markers of masculinity, young men increasingly emphasize sexual prowess and power over women as the primary expression of their masculinity, with violence being a defining characteristic of intimacy and the frequent outcome in situations where men's authority over women is questioned (Hunter 2010; Wood and Jewkes 2001; Mager 1999; Campbell 1992). Women's rights to equality as enshrined in the constitution are perceived to add further fuel to this fire, with many men perceiving gender relations to be a sum-zero equation in which women's empowerment comes at men's expense (du Toit 2014). Within this analytic frame, gendered violence serves as a tool for putting women back in their (subordinate) place. In alignment with this analysis, I collected several stories of truly extreme gendered and sexual violence following the initial violence of the abduction itself, where sexual violence was deployed as punishment in response to women's attempts to escape. Such examples suggest that some men, like Nomandla's husband, deploy this practice as a means of exercising violent gendered power and of reinforcing a gendered hierarchy in situations where women defy them. That Nomandla's husband was employed as a mine worker and could perhaps have afforded formal marriage (although her family could not) further indicates that his violent behavior toward her was motivated by more than just the goal of acquiring a wife.[21]

Understanding contemporary *ukuthwala* as a mechanism for reasserting patriarchal dominance also makes sense within the broader tensions between conflicting modes of gendered personhood. From the perspective of individual human rights—*irhayti*—sexuality is an individually possessed erotic capacity that can be enjoyed, deployed, withheld, and violated at the level of the individual. From the perspective of relational personhood, sexuality is encompassed by kin and exceeds—indeed, elides—individuals' desires. This is apparent in bridewealth, where rights to a woman's sexuality are transferred from her natal lineage to that of her husband, and from related, emergent research into marriage and subjectivity in South Africa. As Memory Mphaphuli and Letitia Smuts (2021, 453, 460) note in their recent narrative study of sexual violence in the relationships of Black married South African women, "the payment of *ilobolo* can be seen as decriminalizing the rape and converting it into a sexual right and entitlement... marriage is an important turning point because it dictates the nature of the sexual relationship going forward." Their study illustrates that many African women themselves view sex in marriage as categorically different—more obligational—than sex in other contexts; they draw on the narratives of Black wives to argue, "The experiences of married Black women need to be understood as occurring within this specific ontology of what it means to be a person, especially a Black woman in a community. . . . Rights-based gender messages, particularly the right to say no to one's husband, are turned on their head and rejected in defense of an ontology of womanhood that resonates with the project of building Black families" (457, 461). This is why parental consent is key to the legitimacy of *ukuthwala* at the local level. Keeping a woman against her family's will is a violation of sexuality that is, from their perspective, more theirs than hers. With respect to *ukuthwala*, although the South African legal system places primary emphasis on the will of the abducted woman, the dominant perception among elders and some men in rural Eastern Cape is that her will is tangential and that all sex is legitimate provided it occurs in the context of a marriage condoned by her kin.

Furthermore, drawing on South African men's narratives of rape, Helen Moffett notes that some men believe that by resorting to sexual violence, they are "participating in a socially approved project to keep women *within certain boundaries and categories*" (2006, 140; emphasis added). She argues that sexual violence is "an ordeal visited on women in order to keep them . . . compliant with social 'norms' determined by hegemonic, powerful, yet threatened patriarchal structures . . . [and is] related to the project of not only refusing to '*recognise [women's] independent subjectivity*,' but *actively punishing such 'independent subjectivity*'" (2006, 138–39; emphasis added). Also writing on rape, Louise du Toit (2014, 116) states, "Raping a woman and being known to have done so can earn a man many gratifications, such as higher status and standing within a group of men and easy access to women's resources, including female sexuality but also female labor and female-generated income (the 'goodies' secured for men by patriarchies everywhere)." This list of benefits could easily be re-phrased to describe the impetus and rewards of *ukuthwala*, because *ukuthwala* reinstates contested boundaries and categories, pulls women back into a more interdependent subjectivity, and, if successful, bestows all the above mentioned "goodies" of patriarchy but with much greater success than could be achieved through rape alone.

As explained in chapter 3, rights and equality, which many women draw on to refuse marriage and justify a way of life outside the parameters of tra-dition and reproductive domesticity, are problematic for men and elders on pragmatic, emotional, and ontological levels. Laws forbidding forcible bride abduction are encompassed within laws prohibiting gendered discrimination and violence more generally (as well as laws prohibiting human trafficking and child marriage). They are thus a component of the sociolegal structure that puts the entire rural Xhosa system of gender under pressure. The boundaries and categories that are upended—and, potentially, resolved through successful abductions—are not just hierarchical ones between men and women. Rather, they are the building blocks of reality for many. This is why women like No-kumulele are bewildered by my questions about going to the police, and why young women cannot go to the police despite knowing that *ukuthwala* is wrong.

Furthermore, *ukuthwala* makes a special kind of sense within this broader logic of gendered violence and personhood because it resolves ontological con-flicts *through marriage*, which is at once the sine qua non of women's place within the rural patriarchal gender hierarchy and the crowning achievement of a relational form of worthy feminine personhood. It achieves what the abovementioned theorists of sexual violence have shown that sexual violence achieves, but with far more efficacy. *Ukuthwala* is thus revealed here as an in-credibly potent site for the consolidation of patriarchy.

Finally, in her analysis of bride abduction in Kyrgystan, Cynthia Werner (2009) shows how post-Soviet discourses of tradition intersect with cultural discourses of shame to give men greater patriarchal power over women by controlling their sexuality and harnessing them to marriage. In that context, shame serves as a kind of structural violence, achieving similar work to what *ukuthwala* accomplishes but without the need for excessive physical force. In light of the history of violence outlined above—and in particular, of evidence indicating that overt physical violence has long been employed as a means of maintaining power over women when other tools are unavailable—I venture that one reason for the extreme violence of contemporary *ukthwala*, and for the exceptional violence of gendered relations in South Africa more broadly, is the relative lack of *structurally* violent means at men's disposal to achieve an out-come that remains hugely important for many in the community. *Ukuthwala* is by no means foolproof, but it remains a widespread and widely condoned method for wedging young women into a position where their sexuality and labor advance the status and interests of men and elder kin.[22]

CONCLUSION

As the genuine abduction of an unwilling young woman, *ukuthwala* is a clear violation of state-sanctioned rights to autonomy and bodily integrity. From the perspective of South African law (not to mention the moral sensibilities of most urban-dwelling South Africans), *ukuthwala* is unambiguously wrong except in rare cases. Virtually everyone in Mhlambini is aware of this, but opinions diverge dramatically along fault lines of gender and generation. Young women seem unanimously in support of these laws and readily reference their human rights to justify their position. Most younger men support human rights in some respects yet feel that the laws go too far when they are perceived to impede the achievement of masculine goals and ambitions. Elders, especially elder women, are frankly bewildered by a legal system that they find foreign, arbitrary, and punitive of elders. These perceptions all shape *ukuthwala* practices.

Meanwhile, young women are the most adamant critics of *ukuthwala*, and many are fearful that they will experience it firsthand. Such apprehensions partially stem from a pragmatic awareness that their families might consent to the abduction and the knowledge that by calling in the police, they would lose support of their families and face poverty and isolation. Yet these fears also stem from a complex moral conundrum about respectability, obligation, and ultimately personhood: young women know that abduction is wrong, but they also know that it is wrong to defy your people—that in doing so, you are in some ways less worthy as a person. Beyond conceding that *ukuthwala* is Xhosa tradition, women friends who fear *ukuthwala* also speak about their feelings of guilt about unmarried brothers who would benefit greatly from their bridewealth, and of their sympathy for overworked and disappointed elderly mothers. Without exception, all admit that they could never turn to the police for protection, because doing so would be "so, so wrong." They struggle to reconcile two very different forms of morality and obligation.

Furthermore, *ukuthwala* brings together complex questions about morality, obligation, and personhood in large part because is so difficult to evaluate consent and complicity where genuine force and staged elopement appear indistinguishable. Indeed, where ideas of social reproduction and femininity are bound up with a bridewealth system, both elopement and genuine abduction are analogous to the extent that they involve the appropriation of a woman's productive and reproductive capacity from her kin (Wardlow 2006). Here again we see dissonance between different moral frames laid bare: according to state law and its accompanying liberal values, the only salient questions are whether a woman herself consents to the abduction, and whether she has the maturity and intellectual capacity to do so. Consent is crucial for rural Xhosa too, but for most, the meaningful consent is that of a woman's elder kin.

There is thus an irony to *ukuthwala*, in that abduction marriage can be a mechanism though which young people can mobilize a so-called traditional practice to exercise considerable spousal choice as well as an institution through which women's capacity to exercise choice can be most constrained. Any given abduction may be a calculated act of violence or a creative mobilization of tradition by young people or elders in response to highly contemporary pressures, and the distinction may be unclear to both the individuals involved and to the wider community. In virtually all cases, financial constraints are a significant motivating factor for why people choose *ukuthwala* over other ways of making marriage happen. *Ukuthwala* is thus a strong example of shifting, incommensurate moral meanings in action.

As a final note, except for Aphiwe, the *ukuthwala* stories I have presented here are all examples where the union ultimately dissolved, and where the young women ended up back at their natal homes. This does not accurately reflect the outcomes of most *ukuthwala* that I documented. Rather, exactly half of the women I spoke with remained with their abductors' families at the time of interview. In some cases, these women had been wives for many years. I have primarily discussed examples of failed *ukuthwala* because these are characterized by the most overt negotiation and conflict, meaning they are examples where divergent interests and values are most laid bare. With nearly all *ukuthwala* that end in long-term partnership, the very ambiguities discussed here make it difficult to determine who instigated what, and to what end. This ambiguity is precisely why *ukuthwala* can be so effective in a time and place where established forms of family and modes of social reproduction are undergoing massive transformation concurrent with ideological transformations that call long-standing notions of morality into question.

—〜—

CONCLUSION

Rights and Responsibilities Revisited

THIS BOOK'S CENTRAL ARGUMENT IS that in the rural Eastern Cape today, domestic life entails deep moral ambiguity about gender, age, status, and moral personhood, which manifests in gendered and generational conflict and is characterized by deep uncertainty about what it means to be a good person who knows their place in the world. This ambiguity exists in part because people are interpellated in incommensurate ways—as autonomous, rights-bearing subjects whose intrinsic value and social power should be equal, and as relational persons for whom identity and moral action are grounded in patriarchal and gerontocratic kin-based social hierarchies. Although the coexistence of competing social orders and subjectivities is by no means unique to this region, it poses particular challenges in the rural Eastern Cape because of how difficult it is for people to get by together amid widespread poverty, weak infrastructure, and conditions of rapid social change. Moreover, though networks have long been crucial for survival in this region, economic, social, and political changes mean that relationships of dependency are being reconfigured in ways that challenge established gendered and generational hierarchies while leaving interpersonal obligations of care—"responsibilities"—unfulfilled. Rights-based laws and public discourse promote discrete, independent, and responsible individuals, but worsening poverty combined with ongoing demands for care mean that people rely on one another arguably more than ever before.

In such uncertain circumstances, patriarchal authority, gerontocracy, and the idiom of tradition are resources available for mobilization at the same time that *irhayti* and attendant practices of consumption, personhood, and so on provide the language through which to articulate and allocate responsibility for unfulfilled obligations and to present alternatives to a hierarchical social order. For those individuals who *can* fulfill their obligations and responsibilities to others, this can often be achieved only by selectively mobilizing modes of personhood rooted in incommensurate moral frames, rendering moral action uncertain and situational. It is for this reason that I view South Africa's crisis of social reproduction as one of moral ambiguity over the meaning of fundamental identity categories, practices, and cultural forms. I now consider the broader implications of this argument and of the ethnography in which it is grounded, as well as how we might respond to this interpersonal, moral, and ontological crisis. In so doing, I expand current scholarly understandings of gendered and generational politics in Southern Africa. Finally, I explain how we might rethink the idiom of human rights to bridge the distance between rights as *irhayti* and rights as *amalungelo*, thereby contributing to broader theory on how human rights can be reconciled with relational modes of personhood.

GENDER AND GENERATION IN SOUTHERN AFRICANIST SCHOLARSHIP

My arguments in this book draw on a large body of scholarship that provides historical and political context for South Africa's fractious gendered and generational politics, as well as its current crisis of social reproduction. Although many scholars have explored what this history and these politics mean for contemporary South African society, the overwhelming bulk of recent social research in this domain has focused on men and masculinity. Although not always explicitly stated, the quantity and, in some cases, tone of this work imparts the perception that it is men—and young men in particular—who are most affected, victimized, and rendered insecure by these societal transformations. This, in turn, gives the impression that appreciating how these changes affect men is the keystone to understanding South African gendered and generational politics more broadly, and that addressing the emotional and practical challenges that men face is the linchpin to resolving a broad range of problems that impact Southern African society today.[1]

There is no question that men are affected by recent political and economic transformations in South African society: they are, for instance, interpellated as criminals (e.g., Langa et al. 2020; Jensen 2008; Posel 2005), scapegoated for failing to uphold models of provider masculinity (Hickel 2015; Hunter 2010; Ashforth 2005), and galvanized by feelings of lost authority when faced with the egalitarian ethos of South African human rights culture (Hickel 2015; Dworkin et al. 2012; Shefer et al. 2008; Sideris 2004; Morrell 2002). Nevertheless, the comparatively limited focus on Southern African women—and rural women in particular—remains puzzling given that gendered and generational subject positions are mutually constitutive (Connell 2005), given that one in three South Africans are rural-dwelling (Parliamentary Monitoring Group 2018), and given the long-standing interconnection between urban and rural regions. This review's focus on domains such as domesticity and intimate social relationships and foregrounding of women's experience provides compelling evidence that arguments about insecurity and transformed life courses extend to women as well. There are several important insights to be taken from having refocused the ethnographic lens in this way.

First, through paying attention to women's lives, this book shows that political, legislative, economic, and ideological transformations have produced considerable generational tension and conflict among women. Although this likely characterizes urban domestic life as well, generational conflicts among women are prominent in rural areas because the state's legislative, economic, and ideological reach is so weak in the countryside. In their milder form, these tensions manifest in a sense of generational rift between older women who feel bewildered by human rights and state bureaucracy and younger women who resent their elders' attempts to recenter gerontocracy and wifehood as feminine ideals. Yet we have also seen that such conflicts can have quite dramatic effects on domestic life, for instance in cases where elder women's deep investment in the companionship and labor of their juniors is a key motivating factor in instigating *ukuthwala*. An important broader implication here is that generational tensions among women evidently play a meaningful but underacknowledged role in shaping South African women's well-documented experiences of violence and subjugation. Further attention to generational politics among women would likely deepen understandings of regionalist gender politics, including in domains such as gendered violence and HIV.

Second, focusing on women has shed light on the interrelationship between young women's ambitions to work and set up independent households, and widely documented masculine frustrations about the loss of patriarchal authority and privilege associated with heading a household. Although ample literature documents this in the context of male unemployment, focusing on working women illuminates the possibility that young men are also frustrated because working women render them largely irrelevant for social reproduction. As we have seen, a working woman can support her parents and children on her own, and the economic contributions that she brings to her natal household afford her considerable leverage to live on her own terms. Moreover, working women can mobilize their economic power to harness the domestic and reproductive labor of other women, leaving them free to focus on earning wages, providing for their families, and setting up homes independent of men.

Third, foregrounding women's perspectives builds on and contributes to contemporary understandings about gender, power, and popular ambivalence about rights and democracy that have implications for understanding South African gender politics and that extend to other regions characterized by similar controversy about women's rights, men's status, and societal wellbeing (e.g., Chowdhury 2014; Coston and Kimmel 2013; Taylor 2008; Jolly 1996). For instance, in a recent ethnography, Jason Hickel (2015, 3) explores the "cultural logic" of antidemocratic sentiment among migrants living in labor hostels around Durban. Although the political and historical context of peri-urban KwaZulu-Natal differs in important ways from that of the rural Eastern Cape, Hickel's predominantly male, middle-aged Zulu interlocutors express ambivalence about human rights and democracy that resonates closely with that expressed by men and elders in Mhlambini, as well as by men in widely differing regions who grapple with similar anxieties about women's status and human rights. The similarities prompt Hickel (2015, 199) to write that South Africa is experiencing "an ontological crisis—a crisis of being. The institutions that the architects of neoliberal capitalism sought to dismantle for the sake of more flexible patterns of production, consumption, and accumulation are now coming back in fashion, as if in resistance to neoliberal modes of governmentality. People want their hierarchies back; they long for a bygone era of domestic social order and of predictable gender relations."

As I read it, Hickel's overarching objective is to probe the limits of liberal politics and democracy in a broad sense, exposing the violence inherent in how these institutions and ideologies privilege the autonomous individual. This serves as his springboard for the important task of rethinking motivation and agency independent of the cultural categories that underpin normative Western ideas about personhood and political motivation. He achieves this goal admirably, and I commend the work that he has done to advance a model of politics not predetermined by colonial categories. However, Hickel also clearly argues that his interlocutors call for hierarchy *not* "to retain their grip on power over women and minors but to defend an overarching moral order that . . . is regarded as crucial to collective wellbeing" (23).

It is difficult to believe that the desire for patriarchy and gerontocracy is truly independent of the desire for power. First, men who resort to gendered and sexual violence most often do so to assert control (e.g., Hunnicutt 2009; Mager 1999; Dobash and Dobash 1979), and the extraordinary pervasiveness of gendered and sexual violence across South Africa is consequently difficult to explain without acknowledging widespread male desire for power over women (Lake 2018; Abrahams et al. 2012). But beyond this critique, I take issue with this claim because my own ethnography confounds it: as preceding chapters have shown, young women perceive men and elders' critiques of rights and of the maintenance of patriarchy to be *very much* about control. And they certainly do not call for the consolidation of patriarchy and gerontocracy as a solution to the many challenges they face. Instead, they desire a less authoritarian social order—admittedly while living lives fraught with contradiction about the merit of more autonomous, egalitarian identities relative to hierarchical and relational forms of personhood and while benefiting from patriarchal and gerontocratic hierarchy in some respects. Although I concur with Hickel that most of those who call for illiberal politics and the reconsolidation of hierarchy do sincerely feel that a hierarchal moral order is best for everyone, I have clearly shown that reinstating hierarchies to achieve more stable moral order will leave many unsatisfied. Young women, at the least, overwhelmingly reject it, and young men do too in some respects. This alone should be sufficient grounds to consider other options.

In closing, I offer preliminary steps down an alternative path forward from the many challenges that I have featured throughout this book. Rather than reconsolidating fragile hierarchies, I instead propose we might begin envisioning a moral order that both maintains a sense of rights as *amalungelo*—and is thus attentive to the desirability and necessity of interdependent social life in conditions of economic insecurity—and diminishes the aspects of the gerontocratic and patriarchal social order that some find harmful and repugnant. Put differently, could people in the rural Eastern Cape live well together without resorting to practices such as violent *ukuthwala*? I believe it is possible, but achieving this will not be easy.

RIGHTS AND RESPONSIBILITIES REVISITED

The oscillating tension and accommodation between *amalungelo* and *irhayti* have been explored and elaborated throughout this book. Previous chapters have shown that young people—especially women—do mobilize *irhayti* in their efforts to defend their lifestyle, consolidate their economic security, and resist coercion and violence. But while many of them are indeed critical of a hierarchical social order, a close look at the content of their concerns about authority and power suggests that at the crux of their grievances lie with men's *techniques* of enforcing the social order alongside men and elders' unfulfilled obligations vis a vis those in socially subordinate positions. We can see this illustrated in the following narratives by Busi, Fundumi, and Mandisa as they reflect on why they prefer not to marry:

> Busi: When you're married in my culture, your work, it's a lot. [People] just say, "Cook now! And after that wash the dishes, and just clean the house, all that house!" And just go to do the washing, and also go to the garden, you know? And also go to the river to fetch the water, and also go to the bushes to look for firewood there. And carry [it back]. It's a lot of work, so I don't want to do this. And your husband, sometimes [he is] just going to party, he needs to go to a party, and when you say, "Me, also I'm going there [with you,]" [he says,] "No! You just sit there until I come back!" And then usually your husband is lazy. He doesn't help you, you know. [He says,] "I don't do this [work]." And then he just lies on the bed after that, and needs [you to bring him] food, needs a lot of things, needs [you to bring him] water.
>
> Fundumi: Among those who are married, some men want money to go and drink, but there's no food for the family to eat, no one to satisfy the children's needs at home, but he just takes all the income, and then he will go and drink alcohol, and stay at his girlfriend's house, eating this income, and then after the money is over, he will come back home, and the violence, it will be starting there in that home. [And the wife,] she's just sleeping! Just sleeping and crying every day because of what is happening in her life. It is not good, because you just *belong* to that other person [your husband], then when he is getting income, he runs away from you, then after the money is over, he will come [back] to you and say, "I love you." After all, you are struggling alone with his children.
>
> Mandisa: It's hard for us, because . . . if you just sit on the bed, you feel comfortable, when [the husband] enters the house, there are some dirty dishes, no food, they just cross you [they get angry and are aggressive with you], and say, "You must do this, and this, and this, and this!" That's what I hate. Because . . . men, they go to the *shebeen* to drink, and when they're drunk, they come in the house, and they just wake [the wife] up and say, "I need my food!" And she has to make the food to give it to him. Even if it's nighttime. Whenever.

For women like Busi, Fundumi, and Mandisa, *irhatyi* are a tool that can be mobilized to abstain from hierarchical arrangements such as these, which they describe in disheartening terms. I invite the reader to now consider these statements with an eye to responsibilities, both fulfilled and unfulfilled, and considering young women's experiences and conduct as explained in previous chapters. Yes, young women complain about how hard young wives work compared to others in the home, and they question the merit of a system that places disproportionate responsibility on wives to labor for the well-being of household and community. But previous chapters have shown that women work hard anyway, whether married or not. They work hard to hustle the means to support their children, they work hard at domestic chores, and in some instances they work double hard as wage-earning providers *and* domestic laborers in their natal homes. Working mothers and providers like Mandisa are among the most assiduous people in Mhlambini. So, I think the primary concern expressed by my interlocutors is not that work itself is distasteful; it is rather the lack of care and support from others—husbands especially—that they perceive village marriages to frequently entail. What these young women take issue with is less hierarchy itself than how that hierarchy is deployed by others to disempower them while nevertheless affording men power and authority *even when* men behave in ways that everyone agrees are reprehensible: by drinking away the child support money that a wife receives because she is poor, by coming home drunk and beating her and her children because he is frustrated by the rift between his aspirations and his circumstances, and by contributing little to the household yet demanding that the wife serve him because, although he has not fulfilled his responsibilities to her, she is still obligated, no matter what, to care for him and his people. *Irhayti* are tools to challenge this.

It is also important to recognize that *irhayti* are not the only tools that serve these ends. Kinship, for example, can also be deployed to challenge neglected responsibilities, as we have seen with women who return to their families following mistreatment at their marital homes. Although they regularly mobilize *irhayti* at the level of discourse, in practice women deploy kinship to protect themselves from mistreatment far more often than they resort to civil courts and law enforcement. This is partly because this latter strategy is more likely to garner community support and therefore to succeed. But it is also a preferred strategy because it makes more coherent moral sense: it mobilizes a relational—and, not incidentally, hierarchical—form of moral personhood to compel the proper fulfillment of responsibility and care. With this in mind, I now propose how we might rethink rights in a way that foregrounds care and the mutual fulfillment of responsibilities as paramount moral imperatives, instead of the twin dichotomies of autonomy/relationality and equality/hierarchy. That is, I am interested in how to bridge what people in Mhlambini view as a conceptual chasm between *irhayti* and *amalungelo.*

RESPONSIBILITIES AND RELATIONAL RIGHTS

As touched on in chapter 3, people in Mhlambini identify (at least) two problems with *irhayti*, and thus with the mainstream idiom of human rights. First, *irhatyi* is premised on an autonomous individual who stands alone and who can do as they wish (skip school, smoke marijuana, marry a person of the same gender, and so forth) independent and regardless of their relation and obligations to others. Second, *irhayti* positions everyone as equal regardless of gender, age, ability, or any other quality that is constitutive of identity. Taken together, people in Mhlambini find these notions of rights problematic on the grounds that equality and autonomy turn communal life into a kind of free-for-all, where everyone can put themselves first no matter the cost to others and where people are no longer obligated to treat anyone with respect.

Since the transition to democracy, theorists and leaders in South Africa and across the continent more broadly have proposed alternatives that are truer to African life and thus more suitable for African society. Importantly, these focus on a different notion of personhood—one rooted in the concept of *ubuntu.*

Scholarly debates are ongoing in terms of the meaning of *ubuntu* and its implications for politics and morality, but a common definition is as follows: an *ubuntu* moral philosophy is one where community takes precedence over the individual (Molefe 2018; Menkiti 1984). Often summarized by the Xhosa proverb *umntu ngumnu ngabantu* (a person is a person through other persons) and in alignment with *amalungelo*, an *ubuntu* philosophy assumes that all individuals are enmeshed with others through relations of mutual obligation, and these relations are constitutive of personhood.[2] In contrast with notions of the person in mainstream human rights discourse, within an *ubuntu* philosophy, personhood and dignity are not qualities that are possessed inherently and equally by all people but are rather acquired slowly over the life course through moral behavior and through fulfilling one's interpersonal responsibilities and obligations. Personhood and dignity, therefore, are individual attributes "to the extent that they exhibit a sense of ethical maturity and confirm to social rules of behavior appropriate to one's position in the community" (Oyowe and Yurkivska 2014, 90). This sounds a lot like *irhayti*; a social order founded on *ubuntu* as described here would likely satisfy most men and elders in Mhlambini.

However, in its mainstream conceptualization, *ubuntu* is not egalitarian—a point of ongoing contention to many African feminists, for instance, who critique *ubuntu* on grounds that the person in *ubuntu* is presented as gender neutral but is in fact a man (Okyere-Manu and Konyana 2018; Oyowe and Yurkivska 2014; Keevy 2009). That is to say, the person in *ubuntu* is located ontologically within relationships that are gendered and patriarchal, and who gains dignity and personhood by acting in and through these patriarchal structures. From this perspective, *ubuntu* philosophy is insidious in that it *advances* patriarchy while claiming to promote equality (Mangena 2009), and it convinces many of its effectiveness as a path to justice precisely because patriarchy and gender discrimination are so deeply embedded and culturally normative that they are rendered invisible in theory (Keevy 2009).

I agree with these critiques, but I nevertheless contend that *ubuntu* philosophy can go some way toward resolving the tension between *irhayti* and *amalungelo*. I turn now to several theorists whose work provides guidance in that regard: law scholar Jennifer Nedelsky, and political philosopher Thaddeus Metz.

Nedelsky, a North American scholar of law, does not consider *ubuntu*. However, she does take issue with mainstream concepts of human rights in ways that would resonate with many in South Africa and argues for a relational concept of rights that goes some way to bringing *amalungelo* closer to *irhayti*. First, Nedelsky (2011) objects to mainstream human rights' focus on protecting and advancing individual autonomy against intrusions from others with whom they are understood to be in competition. For Nedelsky, these assumptions of personal autonomy and interpersonal antagonism reflect a poor understanding of both what rights should do and what they already are—one that is unlikely to foster harmony in society. As opposed to conceiving of rights as a series of trump cards that protect one interest against another, Nedelsky proposes that rights should be viewed as "evolving commitments that societies make to their core values" (233)—values here being what "society sees as essential to humanity or to the good life for its members" (241) and thus open to change. In organizing society to realize those core values for its constitutive members Nedelsky asks us to begin from the collective and to think about rights in terms of how they shape social relations within society. In alignment with *ubuntu*, she agrees that we are all constituted by our relations with others, and that individuals' abilities to enjoy values such as security, peace, and friendship are contingent on relationships that enable or limit our capacity to do so. Therefore, rather than thinking of rights as tools to protect individual interests against the competing claims of others, we should view them something that structures relationships. Our concerns about rights, then, should be about how they enable or foreclose our ability to live according to agreed-upon societal values. Although she is does not focus on African philosophy, *amalungelo* and *irhayi* nevertheless come together in her model of rights in the way she creates space both for the individual and the collective. In her words, "The relational approach [to rights] is not some sort of collective *alternative* to protecting and enforcing individual rights. It is, rather, a means of doing so. When I say that a right structures relationships, that also means that those relationships make possible the enjoyment of the right. . . . The human actions to be governed are not seen primarily in terms of the clashing of rights and interests, but in terms of the way patterns of relationship can develop and sustain both an enriching collective life and the scope for genuine individual autonomy" (2011, 238, 245; emphasis in original).

Interpreting rights in the manner she proposes would, for many in South Africa, be more palatable than *irhayti* as lived and experienced, would be recognizable to those committed to *ubuntu*, and would likely lead to welcome forms of socioeconomic justice, but it does not go far enough in resolving the conflicts that I have presented here. Although Nedelsky acknowledges that values change and vary both cross-culturally and within societies, she makes assumptions about equality and autonomy, for example, being core human values. We have seen that these values are highly contested in South Africa and are misaligned both with *amalungelo* and with mainstream interpretations of *ubuntu*. If core values are fundamentally gerontocratic and patriarchal, questions remain as to how a relational approach to rights will lead to equality for women and youth, for example. And yet Nedelsky's approach remains helpful in showing both that it is possible to decenter an individualistic notion of personhood within human rights discourse and that individual rights are inseparable from the collective because the enjoyment of individual rights is only enabled collectively.

This process of exposing individual rights and collective well-being as co-constitutive is taken one step further by South Africanist philosopher Thaddeus Metz (2014, 2011), who explicitly argues that an *ubuntu*-based moral philosophy is, in fact, a *foundation* for human rights. In alignment with liberal notions of rights, Metz maintains that human rights depend on a core concept of human dignity. However, he takes issue with national and international human rights bodies' definition of dignity *as autonomy*. Drawing on African philosophy and in harmony with Nedelsky, Metz suggests that behaving in alignment with *ubuntu* entails people acting in ways that foster friendly and harmonious communal life. For Metz, the desire for these kinds of communal relationships, and what is required to achieve and maintain them, is what should guide politics and dominant social norms (2011). Yet as explained earlier, within mainstream *ubuntu* theory, this dignity (or personhood, or humanness) is not equally possessed by all people but is rather gained over the life course, meaning some people—especially older people—have more of it. Arguing that this cannot be a premise for human rights, Metz offers instead a notion of human dignity not as autonomy or *earned* personhood but rather as the capacity to "develop one's humanness by communing with those who have dignity in virtue of their capacity for communing" (2011, 544), and where human rights can be defined as "ways of treating people as special by virtue of their capacity to commune" (2014, 307). For Metz, people have rights because we can "exhibit friendliness and be treated in a friendly way" (2014, 311). Thus, one is morally required: "To develop one's humanness by honouring friendly relationships (of identity and solidarity) with others who have dignity by virtue of their inherent capacity to engage in such relationships, and human rights violations are serious degradations of this capacity, often taking the form of very unfriendly behaviour that is not a proportionate, counteractive response to another's unfriendliness" (547).

This, I think, may be a better model of rights, one that emphasizes the communal nature of social life (and indeed the desirability) (as in *irhayti* and *ubuntu*) and the equal entitlement of all people to safety, harmony, and well-being (as in *amalungelo* and global human rights discourse) and that places emphasis on treating those with whom one lives in a community in ways that will allow them to thrive.

Unfortunately, important questions remain unanswered in terms of what this would actually mean for gendered social relationships and with respect to how people will know what is in others' best interests in situations of ambiguity and disagreement. For example, parents and daughters may genuinely disagree about whether marriage is in their daughter's best interest. Metz and Nedelsky offer a promising path toward reconciling *irhayti* and *amalungelo*—for reenvisioning a framework for rights that values the dignity of the individual while foregrounding both their embeddedness in social relations and the importance of acting ethically within those relationships. But if certain patriarchal structures are viewed as traditional (and thus partially constitutive of gender difference) and if acts like men beating women are bound up with these structures (and, I believe, both Nedelsky and Metz would not condone this), even Metz's concept of *ubuntu* cannot work without dramatic transformation of gender relations in South Africa unless we are willing to accept that beating women is compatible with treating them in a friendly way. Absurd as it sounds when worded this way, some men and older women in Mhlambini, for example, might well argue that this sort of violence is kind if it pushes a wayward and inexperienced young woman or child toward something that will serve them well in the long run. Metz (2011, 548) writes, "What genocide, torture, slavery, systemic rape, human trafficking, and apartheid have in common, by the present theory, is that they are instances of substantial division and ill-will directed to those how have not acted in this way themselves, thereby denigrating their special capacity to exhibit the opposite traits of identity and solidarity."

I agree. But what about a practice like marriage? Metz is clear that genuinely sharing a way of life and living communally in friendship requires that people come to communal life of their own accord. But we have seen, for instance with some *ukuthwala*, that even agency itself can be ambiguous.

So, is gendered and generational conflict inevitable in rural South Africa? No, I don't believe so. As with all identities, the categories that organize human experience in the rural Eastern Cape are ongoing discursive practices that are open to reinterpretation. However, achieving a different social order will entail a lot of uphill work because of how human rights intervene in practices and things that are constitutive of identities and selves. Change will not be possible without a close engagement with tradition as active and dynamic—as living in the sense of living Customary Law (see Himonga et al. 2015; Mnisi Weeks and Claassens 2011; Mnisi Weeks 2011). This is evident most of all in how, as I have shown, male violence against women is bound up with how gendered subject positions are sustained and produced even as these subject positions are constitutive of tradition as it is currently evoked. This can change because, as we have seen, in practice people already selectively draw on multiple, incommensurate cultural categories, so we know that they are not fixed and that people are open to alternatives if those alternatives serve them. As Kopano Ratele (2018) reminds us in a reflection on the widespread misuse of tradition in masculinity studies, tradition should be best thought of as a polysemic resource. It can be mobilized in service of a less antagonistic gendered and generational order, but only if circumstances are such that people feel genuinely compelled to do so. I hope others—ideally closer to these communities culturally, philosophically, and affectively—will point the way forward in this regard.

Finally, there is also a profound socioeconomic dimension to the antagonisms and conflicts that I have explored. Although economic transformations alone will not resolve the moral ambiguity that characterizes contemporary life in the rural Eastern Cape, the interpersonal conflicts that have featured in preceding chapters are indisputably amplified by poverty. For example, people in Mhlambini do not engage in *ukuthwala* simply because they are poor; some poor households firmly refuse the practice, and some men with means acquire wives in this way. But the previous chapter has clearly shown that for many people, the lack of opportunities to secure care, dignity, status, companionship, and so forth provides impetus to opt for *ukuthwala* as a means of securing these goods. And although tensions and uncertainties about the meaning of old age and disability are not caused by poverty, the content of these categories matters to people in Mhlambini in large part because being recognized by the state as "elderly" or "disabled" is a gateway to financial security. And importantly, people are usually failing to uphold their responsibilities to one another not because they do not want to uphold them, but rather because they cannot fulfill them despite strong desire to do so.

Independent of how the state—or any other institution—might intervene in rural domestic life through the promotion or enforcement of an egalitarian social order, the state could do more to meet the widespread need for better socioeconomic security. Indeed, alleviating poverty would likely ease the frustrations of poor men who suffer due to their inability to achieve masculine ideals tied to employment and the ability to provide for their families—a state that is likely a barrier to mobilizing men in favor of more caring, less hierarchical gender relations (Ratele 2013; Silberschmidt 2011). Although the interpersonal conflicts and crises that arise from moral ambiguity in the rural Eastern Cape are not resolvable solely through economic intervention, addressing socioeconomic needs remains a pragmatic place to start.

GLOSSARY

abafazi abadala: elder women
amadoda: men
amalungelo: [relational] rights; rightness
irhayti: a Xhosaization of "human rights"
isiduko: clan
isithethe: ritual; tradition; custom
hlonipha: respect
kraal: a livestock pen
lobola: bridewealth
shebeen: informal tavern/bar
spaza: informal shop (usually selling a broad range of basic food and household
    items)
ukuthwala: bride abduction (literally, to carry [off])

NOTES

1. The name Mbeko is a pseudonym, as are the names of all individuals (except my own) who are discussed in ethnographic portions of this book. The name Mhlambini is also a pseudonym; I have concealed the name of the village because the book discusses practices that are widespread and widely condoned in this region but are illegal under South African and international law.

2. To know more about how human rights are contentious in contemporary South Africa because of how they are felt to privilege the individual in ways that decenter interpersonal obligations, see Rice 2017; Hickel 2015; Englund 2004; Nyamnjoh 2004; Oomen 2004; Posel 2004.

3. Apartheid (*apartness* in Afrikaans) was a social and political system of segregation in South Africa. It was officially implemented in 1948 and ended with the election of Nelson Mandela as president on April 27, 1994. Although Apartheid developed out of colonial political forms, it exceeded earlier systems of segregation in its systematic breadth and depth (see Davenport and Saunders 2000; Mamdani 1996).

4. On crises of youth in Africa, see Honwana 2012; Hansen 2005, among many others. On related crises of masculinity, see, among others, Hickel 2015; Hunter 2010; Morrell 2002; Campbell 1994.

5. For relevant ethnographic work focused on rural South African men, see White 2015, 2004; Steinberg 2013; Ngwane 2001.

6. Social reproduction was initially a Marxist concept referring to the perpetuation of modes of production and the relations of inequality that capitalist production entailed. Feminist scholars have demonstrated that it entails a range of fundamentally gendered activities, emotions, practices, and

relationships that are essential to the maintenance of day-to-day lives and the production of generations through time (Bezanson 2006; Katz 2001; Laslett and Brenner 1989). Although the concept has long appealed to scholars of African social organization (e.g., Guy 1990; Bozzoli 1983; Meillassoux 1981), there is renewed interest in the concept today because the maintenance of day-to-day life and the reproduction of society seem to be increasingly problematic across the continent (e.g., Hunter 2011; Makhulu, Buggenhagen, and Jackson 2010; Fakier and Cock 2006; Weiss 2004).

7. See, for example, Ferguson 2006, 1999; Weiss 2004; Auslander 1993; Comaroff and Comaroff 1993.

8. On the implications declining economic opportunities for masculinity in South Africa, see, among others, Steinberg 2013; Hunter 2010, 2006; Ashforth 2005; White 2001, 2010; Morrell 2002; Campbell 1992.

9. The Eastern Cape is the poorest of South Africa's nine provinces (Statistics South Africa 2016), and the predominantly rural district where Mhlambini is located is the second-poorest district in South Africa, with a poverty rate of 89.5 percent (Business Tech South Africa 2016).

10. This is a reference to *ukuthwala* (bride abduction); see the penultimate chapter.

11. On plural modernity, see, among many others, Knauft 2002; Comaroff and Comaroff 1993. On tradition and modernity as coconstitutive, see Hobsbawm 1983; Williams 1973. For literature that engages critically with the tradition/modernity dichotomy in Africa, see Newell 2012; Piot 2010, 1999; Ferguson 2006, 1999; Comaroff and Comaroff 1993. On the modernity of witchcraft in Africa, see Ashforth 2005; Moore and Sanders 2003; Comaroff and Comaroff 1999; Geschiere 1997; Auslander 1993.

12. I refer to tradition without scare quotes from this point onward, with the clarifier that I use this term as an emic concept and not as my own analytic.

13. Contemporary gerontocratic patriarchies in Southern Africa arose out of a complex interplay of resistance and accommodation between African patriarchs and colonial administrators, with both sides deploying essentialized and inflexible notions of African tradition in ways that constrained women and youth (Carton 2000; McKittrick 1996; Walker 1990; Chanock 1982). This hierarchal social structure was ossified, sustained, and produced through a legal system for Africans known as Customary Law, which, was a result "of a process not only of selective understanding by colonial officials but also of selective presentation of claims by African witnesses who were invariably male elders—chiefs and married men" (Walker 1990, 182, citing Chanock 1982, 66). On the ensuing gender order and its emphasis on the "traditional" gender relations which men and elders frequently reference, Walker (1990, 192) continues: "the reinvented ideology of female deference to men that characterized the new 'traditionalism'

was reinforced by the assumptions of female inferiority and domesticity that informed gender ideology in white society." Because the colonization of the region was intimately bound up with the exploitation of minerals, contemporary gerontocratic patriarchies have also long been connected to resource capitalism.

14. See especially Ferguson 1999, 82–122; also see Hickel 2015; White 2010; Piot 1999; Thomas 2002; Rebhun 1999.

15. For an impressively succinct summary of this history and its ongoing debates, see Worden 2011.

16. For in-depth discussion of *hlonipha* in Southern Africa, see Rudwick and Shange 2009; Herbert 1990. A system of restrictions and imperatives pertaining to comportment, spatial mobility, speech, bodily carriage, and dress, *hlonipha* practices apply to all people according to their age and gender but are most proscriptive for young wives.

17. Others have already done this well; see especially Bank 2011, 35–59. Also see Piot 1999 for a sophisticated critique in the West African context. For works that exemplify this kind of category thinking in Xhosa communities, see Mayer and Mayer 1980, (1960) 1971. For further critical analyses of it by Xhosa scholars, see Magubane 1973; Mafeje 1971.

18. For important African scholarly critiques of and contributions to Northern gender theories, see Mfecane 2020, 2018, 2016; Ratele 2018; Everitt-Penhale and Ratele 2015; Oyěwùmí 2002; Okome 2001.

19. In contrast to urban areas, cohabitation outside marriage is not possible in Mhlambini. In this particular case, low bridewealth payment backfired for the groom. His young wife left him after a bitter dispute during which he hit her (she had taken issue with his infidelity), and her family cited the low bridewealth as a reason why he was out of line for doing so, as well as why they would not compel her to return to him despite his apologies and pleas.

20. Young men sometimes attend these meetings but sit at a distance from elders. Young women never attend these meetings, even when they themselves are subjects of discussion.

21. Dangerous roads, working conditions, lifestyles (e.g., heavy drinking), and violent masculinities all contribute to men's higher mortality rates relative to women (Hosegood, Vanneste, and Timaeus 2004). Moreover, South African men are less likely than women to know their HIV status and to be on treatment; this is also thought to contribute to the gendered disparities in mortality rates (Shisana et al. 2014).

22. Although the cultural ideal is for children to be born within marriage, out of wedlock childbearing is extremely common. Many women have a child by age twenty, and remaining childless beyond age twenty-five is rare.

23. On the South African countryside as a place of feminized dependency, see also Liebenberg 1997; Moodie and Ndatshe 1994; Mayer 1980.

24. Scholars (e.g., Ngwane 2001; Bozzoli 1983) have noted that the restrictions of the migrant labor system made possible the continuation and ossification of structures and hierarchies that people associate with long-standing tradition.

25. On South Africa's very low rates of marriage relative to global norms, see Pauli and van Dijk 2016; Posel, Rudwick, and Casale 2011; Hosegood, McGrath, and Moultrie 2009. A vast body of literature on African youth expands on the topic of thwarted adulthood, much of it relevant to the circumstances of young people in Mhlambini (e.g., Mains, Hadley, Tessema 2013; Masquelier 2013; Honwana 2012; Hunter 2010; Christiansen, Utas, and Vigh 2006; Hansen 2005; Weiss 2004). On working women's decision to remain unmarried, see James 2017; Pauli and van Dijk 2016; van der Vliet 1991.

26. Unlike elsewhere in Africa (e.g., Piot 2010), local employers do not preferentially seek women to fill these jobs. Rather, local girls tend to stay in school longer than boys and are consequently more likely to possess the literacy, numeracy, and English language skills that are necessary for jobs in tourism and development. For example, when I tried to hire an assistant apiece from each of three neighboring villages to support data collection for an NGO-sponsored demographic survey (see chap. 2), I was only able to hire women because I could not find a single man who could read and write well enough to fill in the survey form.

27. As elaborated in chapter 2, the CWP state-funded make-work programs pay low wages for eight days of work per month. In Mhlambini, community leaders (who are elderly men) were given responsibility for allocating these coveted jobs, and they reserved them for those they deemed most deserving: fellow elders who were not receiving old-age pensions due to bureaucratic error, and widows with children. All low-income South Africans receive old-age pensions from the age of sixty. The politics of pensions is a major focus of chapter 3.

28. Even those born in the late 1980s and the early decades of democracy speak confidently of the democratic transition as a time of great sociocultural rupture, whereby traditional (gerontocratic and patriarchal) forms of social organization were upended by "rights" and "freedom." This demonstrates that tradition, rights, and equality are moral frames through which people understand emergent social forms.

29. During the colonial era and under Apartheid, rural Black communities were governed by a legal system known as Customary Law, a colonial product reflecting essentialized ideas about African practices and social norms. Recourse to this gerontocratic and patriarchal legal system is protected as a cultural right in post-Apartheid South Africa (albeit trumped by civil law in cases where Customary Law and civil law are in conflict), and it is an important legal system

in former Bantustans. On the content of South African Customary Law, see Seymour 1982. On the status of Customary Law in post-Apartheid South Africa, see (Mnisi Weeks 2010; Himonga and Bosch 2000).

30. Most young men wish to marry because married life entails many advantages and few drawbacks for men. However, several young husbands have complained to me about how much pressure their elder kin placed on them either to marry a specific woman, or even to marry in general. Although most young husbands that I know were happy for their parents' support, one young man whom I knew quite well flatly refused to marry, and his widowed mother ultimately sought out a wife for him. Having recently received a financial settlement from the mine where her husband had died in a workplace accident, the mother was keen to use that money to pay bridewealth for her son before other kin laid claim to it, and she organized a marriage for her son despite his great reluctance.

31. About half of the older wives whom I have spoken to report having married men who were strangers to them, whereas the other half married men with whom they had already established a romantic relationship. Several older men also told me in formal interviews that they married women with whom they had no prior relationship. The penultimate chapter, which focuses on abduction marriage, demonstrates that some recent marriages were arranged entirely by elder kin.

32. Fundile could, in theory, have married both women because polygyny (a form of polygamous marriage in which one man may have more than one wife) is legal in South Africa and is socially acceptable in rural Xhosa society (Mabaso, Malope, and Simbayi 2018). Historically, it was the preferred form of marriage for wealthy men (Wilson 1981; Cook 1931), but it has long been on the decline and is rare in Mhlambini today. Young local men have told me that polygyny is unappealing because of its prohibitive expense (supporting multiple wives and their children is costly indeed) and the potential for jealousy and antagonism between wives.

33. On love and modern personhood, see Collier (1997) 2020; Yan 2003; Ahearn 2001; Rebhun 1999; Giddens 1992. On the connection between the primacy of romantic love and patterns of individualized consumption under capitalism, see Cole and Thomas 2009; Wardlow and Hirsch 2006; Zelizer 2000; Illouz 1997. On romantic love in post-Apartheid popular discourse, see James 2017; Mupotsa 2015. On love marriage and spousal choice as a means of asserting a modern identity, see Cole and Thomas 2009; Wardlow and Hirsch 2006; Hirsch 2003.

34. As Mark Hunter (2010) explains, contemporary ideals of love and marriage in South Africa came about through a complex interplay between missionary influence, colonial policy, labor migration, and precolonial

conventions of social reproduction. Although church and school played pivotal roles, the concurrent appropriation of land, labor migration, and integration into the cash economy meant that control over wealth was increasingly transferred from patriarchs, who had historically paid bridewealth for their sons, toward young men who paid bridewealth with their own earnings. This afforded young men greater independence in their choice of spouse: as they became less beholden to elders to finance their marriages, they became more able to choose a spouse based on her personal qualities (Carton 2000).

35. As the person in the village with the most formal education, I encounter this kind of thinking a lot, with people referencing my education (interestingly, never the fact that I am white) as the reason why I sometimes struggled to understand aspects of village life.

36. Among rural Xhosa, girls have apparently accessed more formal education than boys for many decades (see Whooley 1975; Hunter [1936] 1961). That this is still the case was confirmed through the demographic profiling survey that I conducted in my capacity as an NGO volunteer. I found that among the cohort of people under age forty who have no schooling, roughly two-thirds are men. Moreover, males make up only a third of those who have continued beyond the eighth grade. People tell me that boys are needed for herding livestock and are overall less interested in schooling.

1. THE LODGE AND THE NGO

1. The cottage had been built and used by white South Africans on fishing holidays. There are many such structures along the scenic former Transkei coast, all of them built illegally during the Apartheid era. Most of them were used as holiday homes by white residents of Mthatha and East London, many of whom are now locked in drawn-out legal battles with a government that has slated these structures for demolition.

2. Most of the information in this section is drawn from the NGO's website, from their annual reports, and from my own observations as an NGO volunteer from February 2011 to May 2012. The overview that follows is undoubtedly already out of date; inaccuracies and insufficiencies in this overview reflect my own errors and limitations.

3. The hope is that a local secondary school will allow all local children to continue their education beyond eighth grade. The secondary school opened as I finished writing this book. It may have profound impacts on many topics and issues discussed in here.

4. The health point was established after my fieldwork was complete. It is staffed by a local woman with basic first aid training who provides services such as wound care and condom distribution and directs more serious ailments and injuries to clinic or hospital as appropriate.

5. Apart from composting pit toilets at the Lodge, there are no sanitation systems in the village. At the time of my fieldwork, the nearest source of piped water was forty kilometers away, and the local springs were contaminated. As such, the NGO was instrumental in ensuring that all local households have at least one large water tank for collecting rainwater and have drilled boreholes for communal taps. Two of these boreholes produce water suitable for drinking, and the remaining two are too saline for drinking due to their proximity of the ocean. However, as of June 2013 (one year after I completed my primary stretch of fieldwork), the Eastern Cape provincial government installed communal water taps in Mhlambini. During both my most recent visits the taps had been turned off for months, ostensibly to conserve water during a prolonged drought.

6. The CWP is a job-creation program. An organization that has a need for low-skilled workers can get government funds to pay these workers minimum wage for eight days per month. During my time at the NGO, they managed one team of CWP workers in each of the four villages. These teams were assigned tasks such as road maintenance, beach cleanup, erecting fences around community gardens, and painting community buildings. The NGO also hired the occasional skilled worker under the CWP program but paid them full-time minimum wage for half-time work. Although the low pay is much grumbled about, there is nonetheless considerable competition for these jobs.

7. The coast around Mhlambini is famous for shipwrecks due to strong ocean currents and intense storms, and local oral histories speak of integrating shipwreck survivors into local communities. The largest *isiduko* (clan) in Mhlambini claim descent from shipwrecked European seafarers, and it was this history that the professor from Rhodes University aimed to capture with her interviews. Nevertheless, her transcripts contain some documentation of local gender politics as articulated to elder villagers at that time which have been useful for me.

8. Guma is the only person I have ever met from this part of the rural Eastern Cape who has successfully completed a university degree. Guma's younger sister also has a law degree. Apparently through their church, the sisters learned of a bursary program to support university education for promising students from low-income rural households, and both applied successfully.

9. Although the NGO had hoped to hire someone from Mhlambini, they were not able to find anyone local who had the necessary skills (literacy, numeracy, English-isiXhosa translation) and was not already employed through the Lodge or NGO.

10. Guma and I trained the data collectors, and three mornings per week, I went out into the neighboring villages with them to collect profile data. After several weeks of visiting with me, the data collectors worked without me an additional two days per week. All of the data collectors were young women

who had at least grade nine education. The intention was not to hire women exclusively, however we found no literate men in any of the villages.

A Cape Town–based statistician was hired to analyze the quantitative data, and her analysis was submitted to me in June 2012. I analyzed the qualitative data and submitted a final report to the NGO in August 2012. Since completing the project, the NGO has used this data in their campaigns to attract government infrastructure and funding for their projects. I continue to draw on the profiling data in my own work.

11. Senior people in these organizations have shown genuine openness to my opinions and insights into the impacts of their work. At the same time, unlike most NGO personnel, I am not local and not even South African. In the end, my approval is unwarranted for the work that they do.

12. I use the term *wealth* here in relative terms. Although some families have livestock and modest income and savings that allow them to pay for medicine for their livestock, school fees for children, and funerals as needed, none except the school headmistress afford luxuries like holidays and consumer items like cars. Most people in South Africa and internationally would find all households in the village materially poor.

13. This perception is almost certainly an expression of internalized racism, which is itself an outcome of South Africa's history. As Adam and Moodley (1993, np) write, "The oppression of apartheid society was overt and blatant: all opposition had been silenced, and institutionalized racism flourished triumphant. Centuries of exclusionary practices led to what might be described as the 'inferiorization' of blacks [in South Africa]: Blacks were portrayed as innately inferior, accustomed to dehumanized living, sexually promiscuous, intellectually limited, and prone to violence; blackness symbolized evil, demise, chaos, corruption, and uncleanliness, in contrast to whiteness, which equaled order, wealth, purity, goodness, cleanliness, and the epitome of beauty." Several decades into democracy, this internalized racism is further complicated by the continued marginalization of many Black communities despite the legislation of equality; rather than understanding their situation as both historically rooted and entangled with neoliberal capitalist economies, many people individualize their situation and blame themselves and their own communities for their continued marginalization.

14. Legal protections notwithstanding, many South African communities are intolerant toward gender and sexual minorities. No local person is "out" in Mhlambini, but same-sex or gender-queer couples who visit the Lodge as tourists or NGO volunteers are viewed with amusement and mild fascination rather than hostility. During her residency in the village, for instance, Janet's home was apparently included on the Lodge's village tour. To her wry bemusement, Janet

belatedly learned that tourists were being invited to view "the home of Janet, who is married to a woman!"

2. RIGHTS AND RESPONSIBILITIES

1. See, for instance, Smith 2019; Hickel 2015; Makhulu, Buggenhagen and Jackson 2010; Nyamnjoh 2004.

2. For illustrative examples of the tension between human rights and gendered and gerontocratic sensibilities in South Africa, see Smith 2019; Hickel 2015; Oomen 2004; Posel 2004. For international examples, see Taylor 2008; Wyrod 2008; Jolly 1996.

3. The African National Congress is a South African political party that historically advocated for voting rights for non-white South Africans and was instrumental in ending Apartheid. They have won every election since 1994.

4. On rural women's weak access to both state and traditional courts, see Osman 2020; Higgins and Fenrich 2011; Claassens 2009.

5. The Traditional Courts Bill (TCB), which may soon be implemented, directly challenges this. It allows traditional (usually male) leaders to "unilaterally define the content of custom within ethnically delineated tribal boundaries" (Claassens 2009, 10; see also Mnisi Weeks and Claassens 2011; Mnisi Weeks 2010), forbids anyone living in a former Bantustan from opting out of the Customary legal system, and stipulates that anyone living in a former Bantustan has no right to refuse a summons to traditional court (Claassens 2021).

6. Partially to resolve this conundrum, in recent years there has been a move toward approaching Customary Law as "living"—that is, as adaptive by nature (see Himonga et al. 2015, Himonga 2011; Mnisi Weeks 2011). Living Customary Law interprets culture in a more anthropological way, arguing that culture is never static. Customary Law, therefore, must likewise be adaptive—it should change as culture does. Traditional courts should thus function as discussion forums rather than despotic patriarchal institutions (Himonga 2011; Weeks 2011). While this model is promising, Customary Law remains predicated on the idiom of tradition, which is itself connected to an inegalitarian social order.

7. For anthropological discussions of relational personhood, see Boddy 2007; Comaroff and Comaroff 2001; La Fontaine 1985; Nyamnjoh 2004; Riesman 1986.

8. On the nonequivalency of "human rights" and local terminology in South Africa, see Smith 2019; Hickel 2015; Hunter 2010; Nyatsanza 2000. It is difficult to establish exactly why such an imperfect translation is so widely used in South Africa, but it seems that the instrumentality of the idiom of human rights for emancipatory and social development-orientated initiatives offered a strong impetus to find and deploy a local approximation.

9. For example, some young wives are now choosing to live with mine-worker husbands at their husbands' place of work, rather than remaining at rural homes with their mothers-in-law. These young couples argue that contemporary marriages require this form of cohabitation as a component of conjugal intimacy.

10. The data from Profiling Research is replete with such statements made by older people in Mhlambini and the three neighboring villages in which the NGO carries out its work.

11. For literature on the social functions of elders' complaints, see van der Geest 2007; Sanger 2002; Cattell 1999; Rosenberg 1990.

12. This can also mean "oppression."

13. Although human rights regimes may offer some women new tools for circumventing patriarchal authority, critiques of women who resist or subvert patriarchal control are far from new in this region. A rich body of scholarship demonstrates long-standing anxieties on the part of African patriarchs and colonial authorities about women who allegedly exercised wayward habits of reproduction beyond the purview of patriarchal control (e.g., Cockerton 2002; Mager 1999; Bonner 1990; Gaitskell 1982).

3. SOCIAL GRANTS AND THE MORAL BUREAUCRACY OF MERIT

1. The Eastern Cape is one of the two poorest provinces in South Africa, with an adult poverty rate of 67.3% (Statistics South Africa 2019). This poverty is most extreme in rural areas within former Bantustans.

2. The monetary value of old-age pension payments has slowly increased over time. Most recipients received R1,500 per month at the time of writing, although individuals whose identity documents indicate that they are seventy-five or older receive an additional R20 per month. Very few people in Mhlambini qualify for this top-up.

3. Government investigations suggest that such forms of fraud are widespread (SA News 2015; Reddy and Sokomani 2008).

4. On the nonneutrality of bureaucratic artifacts, see Hull 2012.

5. There is an important implicit conceptual and moral distinction to being made here between the notion that a person deserves state support because they are too old to work and the notion that a person deserves state support because they cannot find a job. Until the recent implementation of South Africa's temporary COVID-19 relief grant—launched long after this research was completed—the state never acknowledged or implied responsibility for the millions of South Africans who are working-aged and able-bodied but unemployed. These grants both topped-up preexisting social security grants (e.g., old-age pensions and child support grants), and provided R350 per month

(approximately 25 US dollars) to unemployed individuals who did not have access to other forms of social security.

6. For evidence of the efficacy of Disability Grants in South Africa, see OECD 2020; Phaswana-Mafuya, Peltzer, and Petros 2009; Nattrass 2006.

7. Disability grants are available to HIV-positive individuals who are debilitated because of low immune function. Because antiretroviral drugs (ARVs) are available at no cost to all HIV-positive South Africans who require them, individuals who receive DGs due to HIV-related debility can, through ARV therapy, improve to a point where they no longer qualify for a DG (see Nattrass 2006). I do not know whether this applied in Sibabalwe's case, but it seemed plausible to me at the time.

8. This is apparent, for instance, in American cultural myths about "welfare queens" (e.g., Cassiman 2008; Edin and Lein 1997).

9. On the social construction of disability, see Staples and Mehrotra 2016; Reid-Cunningham 2009; Ginsburg and Rapp 2013; Kasnitz and Shuttleworth 2001.

10. In her ethnographic research in the Cape Town, area, Kelly (2016a) has found that many physicians chastise young DG applicants for seeking grants when they should be seeking work and are particularly sympathetic to older applicants, especially those who are a few years shy of receiving an old-age pension. An individual cannot receive both a DG and an old-age pension concurrently.

11. This is not unexpected given ambiguity is a widespread feature of how laws actually operate, regardless of their design (see, e.g., Schane 2002).

12. In understanding their health, ability, and well-being as inseparable from their poverty, across these various studies interlocutors are arguably calling on physicians to acknowledge what medical anthropology has long argued: that many diseases should be seen as manifestations of social suffering (Kleinman, Das, and Lock, 1997). Moreover, in framing poverty as grounds for deserving a disability grant, people are calling for a broader definition of disability, one that acknowledges that poverty is deeply limiting. For Southern African research on popular perceptions of disability grant merit, see Kelly 2017; 2016b; Hansen and Sait 2011; Steele 2006; Segar 1994.

13. Bernard Dubbeld (2021) has recently made similar arguments based on fieldwork in rural KwaZulu-Natal. Beyond highlighting the high moral value that rural South Africans continue to place on paid work as opposed to social security, Dubbeld argues that wage work is valued more highly in part because grants provide insufficient funds to enable investment in future projects (e.g., paying for children's education). The example of Sibabalwe suggests that grants can be viewed as a means of investing in future security, provided the grant is fairly large and the recipient is perceived as someone able to work.

14. The COVID-19 pandemic, and the launch of the temporary COVID-19 relief grants in particular, have reinvigorated debates about BIG in South Africa. At the time of writing, these debates remain preliminary and inconclusive.

4. WORKING WOMEN, WIVES, AND RURAL FEMININE PERSONHOOD

1. See, for instance, Allerton 2007; Chamlee-Wright 2002; Hodgson and McCurdy 1996; Clark 1994.

2. For in-depth ethnographic engagement with this issue, see Bank 2011; Hunter 2010.

3. In the end, a backpacker Lodge manager pointed out that technically, Busi could not be fired from the Lodge because she was a self-employed business owner and not a Lodge employee. Instead, it was decided that she would be banned from the Lodge for one month as punishment for the broken egg, meaning she would not be able to drink at its bar and would not be able to solicit clients there.

4. On beer in Xhosa culture, see McAllister 2006, 2001, 1993; Davies 1927. On the beer drinking and the reproduction of gender and age hierarchies, see McAllister 2006, 2001.

5. See Bryceson 2002, van der Drift 2002; Suggs 2001; Wilson 1977.

6. On alcohol and masculinity, see Lindsay and Lyons 2018; Kirkby 2003. On masculinity and alcohol in South Africa specifically, see Mfecane 2011; Mager 2010; Kaminer and Dixon 1995.

7. On attitudes toward women's alcohol consumption in South Africa, see Watt et al. 2012; Wolff, Busuza, Bufumbo, and Whitworth 2006; Wojcicki 2002.

8. On South Africa women in town during the Apartheid era, see Bozzoli and Nkotsoe 1991; Bonner 1990.

9. The family received rental income from the NGO for housing me; the community had selected Nobongile's household because they had a spare hut and were in dire need of the rental income.

10. Nomvula's boyfriend never came to the village the entire time I lived there—at least not that I witnessed—and I never learned how Nomvula met her daughter's father or how she found the privacy to get pregnant. When I once asked her, she merely responded that it happened "at Christmas" (a time of great festivity).

11. On marriage rates in South Africa, see Hosegood, McGrath, and Moultrie 2009, Pauli and van Dijk 2016; Posel, Rudwick, and Casale 2011.

12. Sixteen people were not included in this count because they were not home when I profiled their homes, and no one present knew their ages.

13. On bridewealth and capitalist logics, see Ansell 2001; Posel, Rudwick, and Casale 2011.

14. R5,000 and R10,000 refer to sums of money in South African Rand (local currency).

15. On the perception that romantic love, companionate marriage, and aspirations of gender equality, see Cole and Thomas 2009; Spronk 2009; Hirsch and Wardlow 2006.

16. Located in the Western Cape, Grabou is the commercial hub of South Africa's largest fruit-producing region. Some people from Mhlambini find seasonal work there as fruit pickers.

17. The implication here is that Fezeka's widowed father's new wife could take over Fezeka's domestic chores.

18. See, among many others, Steinberg 2013; Hunter 2010.

19. For notable exceptions, see James 2017; Fakier and Cock 2009; Bezuidenhout and Fakier 2006.

20. Leslie Bank (1994), for example, analyzed similar gender politics in the former Bantustan of QwaQwa in the 1990s.

21. Some women (both married and single) *do* pay other women to help them make mud bricks for building. This practice, however, seems driven by the need to form and dry bricks quickly. Because mud bricks need to bake in the sun for some time and because they dissolve when it rains, mobilizing the labor of many women is the best strategy for ensuring that a hut gets built during a stretch of dry weather. This is most often achieved by mobilizing kinship obligations and negotiating reciprocal agreements ("You help me build now, and I'll help you next year"), but for wealthier households, paying non-kin can be the most efficient way of gathering many women for a few days of intense work.

22. See, for example, Hunter 2010; Morrell 1998; Campbell 1992.

23. See Cole 2010; Johnson-Hanks 2006; Bledsoe 2002.

5. THE MORAL AMBIGUITY OF *UKUTHWALA*

1. For anthropological engages with the notion that cohabitation is an essential component of conjugal intimacy, see Cole and Thomas 2009; Hirsch and Wardlow 2006.

2. Rustenberg is a mining town northwest of Johannesburg. It is the primary destination for labor migrants from Mhlambini.

3. For an exhaustive overview of contemporary literature on *ukuthwala*, see Karimakwenda 2020, 2013; Thornberry et al. 2016; Rice 2017, 2014; Smit and Notermans 2015; Nkosi and Wassermann 2014; Monyane 2013; Mwambene and Sloth-Nielsen 2011.

4. For government coverage of rising rates of *ukuthwala*, see DOJ and CD 2021. For the perspective of advocacy organizations, see Gasa 2014; Fabricius 2010. For media coverage, see Malan 2011, among many others.

5. For a discussion of *ukuthwala* in historical context, see Thornberry 2019, 2016; Hunter (1933) 1961; Cook 1934; Soga 1933 (2013). For the perspective of contemporary cultural authorities who argue for its long-standing authenticity as cultural practice, see Mashaba 2015; CRL Rights Commission 2014; *Daily News* 2013. On the argument that it serves primarily to kick-start stalled marriage negotiations, see Mashaba 2015; Nkosi and Wasserman 2014.

6. See also Soga (1933) 2013; Hunter (1933) 1961; Cook 1934.

7. For further information about this court ruling, see Jezile v. the State and Others (2014). For further information on *ukuthwala* in relation to South African law, see Monyane 2013; Mwambene and Sloth-Neilsen 2011; Bennet 2010.

8. There are no Dwala families in Mhlambini.

9. The literature that seeks to document and explain the degree of gendered violence and antagonism in South Africa is enormous. A few solid examples include *Mail and Guardian* 2020, United Nations 2015; Hunter 2010; Moffett 2006; Wood 2005.

10. The literature on gender power and HIV in South Africa is also vast. See, among others, Hunter 2010; Jewkes and Morrell 2010; Wood 2005; Dunkle et al. 2004.

11. I do not suggest that women who arrange or collude in *ukuthwala* are simply cold-hearted and calculating. Although self-interest is often one motivation for such collusion, most elder women hope their daughters will marry for selfless reasons as well. Elder women generally believe that the most complete, happy, and respectable form of womanhood is married womanhood, and that children born and reared in wedlock are better off than those of single mothers. Women who had no vested interest in my own marriage often went out of their way to create opportunities for me to meet a suitable marriage partner; my host mother, for instance, asked me several times—only half in jest—if I wanted her to help in arranging an *ukuthwala* for me.

12. On the materiality of intimacy in sub-Saharan Africa, see Hunter 2010, 2002; Cole and Thomas 2009.

13. The act of having one's old clothes removed and replaced by the garb of a married woman, including a head covering, featured in nearly every *ukuthwala* story that I collected and was framed as one of the more traumatic aspects of the abduction.

14. For an overview of anthropological research on bride abduction globally, see, among others, Conor 2013; Barnes 1999; Ayres 1974; Bates, Conant, and Kudat 1974. On contemporary bride abduction in Central Asia, see Kim and Karioris 2020; Becker and Steiner 2018; Werner et al. 2018; Borbieva 2012;

Werner 2009; Handrahan 2004. On Indonesia, see Salenda 2016. For Ethiopia, see Peveri 2014. For Vietnam, see Nguyen, Oosterhoff, and White 2013. On bride abduction in the recent past, see Herzfeld 1988 for Greece, Lockwood 1974 for Bosnia, Stross 1974 for Mexico, Bates 1974 for Turkey, and McLaren 2001 for China.

15. For excellent analyses on wounded masculinity in contemporary South Africa, see Bank 2011; Hunter 2010; Morrell 2002; Ngwane 2001, Mager 1999.

16. This is not to say that sex never occurs as part of an abduction, but rather that people behave as through it did not unless confronted with strong, unconcealable evidence otherwise (e.g., pregnancy).

17. For example, one young local woman was abducted with parental consent by a man who abused her terribly. The abuse was so severe that she managed to have him arrested and taken to court, where he was convicted of gang rape and subsequently jailed. The woman in question had been back at home in Mhlambini for several years by the time I met her. She lived as most other unmarried women live: at her family's home, with a baby conceived out of wedlock with a boyfriend sometime after her marriage ended, and with considerable autonomy. She seemed to suffer no shame or stigma because of her experience.

18. Admittedly, this alone does not confirm that abductions elsewhere are indeed less violent. Elsewhere, the stigma associated with abduction would likely prevent women from speaking candidly about their experiences of violence.

19. On increasing gendered violence and antagonism during the colonial era, see Mager 1999; Beinart 1991; Walker 1990. On wage labor and elder men's increased authority over younger men, see Cockerton 2002; McClendon 2002. On control over access to women as a form of control exercised between elder and younger men, see Cockerton 2002; Walker 1990.

20. For example, literature from the healthcare sector shows that nurses often use violence to encourage compliance among women patients (for instance, during childbirth; see Chadwick 2017, Jewkes, Abrahams, and Mvo 1998) and often assume that if women patients have been beaten by their male partners, they must have done something to deserve it (e.g., Kim and Motsei 2002). For recent research on the normalization of gendered violence as discipline in South Africa, see Mazibuko 2017; Mesatywa 2014.

21. That said, the few men I know who openly disavow *ukuthwala* are affluent by village standards—all of them work at either the Lodge or the NGO. Employed, married, and well-educated in comparison to their peers, they are among the few who have succeeded in achieving increasingly illusive masculine ideals. It is significant, I think, that these men felt themselves to be in the minority in their disavowal of *ukuthwala*. For example, when Lonwabo and I were discussing *ukuthwala*, he shook his head emphatically and spat out, "*Aie*, it's

not right at all, the *thwala* [*sic*]. It's *irape* [rape]! I'm always telling the guys, the *thwala* [*sic*] is a rape! But most of them, *haibo* [wow], they aren't listening."

22. It is perhaps also relevant that working women are seemingly not targeted for *ukuthwala*, presumably because they cannot easily be harnessed to men and elders' interests in this way. Parents who depend on working daughters may be less likely to consent to an *ukuthwala* because they benefit from their daughters' support, but there is also a general consensus that some women are simply not good candidates for abduction. For instance, at one point during my fieldwork, a man from a neighboring village tried (and failed) to abduct a quiet and attractive young teacher from the NGO nursery school. The teacher was Xhosa but was well educated, was employed, and had grown up in an urban part of the former Ciskei. The entire Mhlambini community sided with the teacher and chased away the man. Village elders apparently informed him that he could not abduct the teacher because she was not, in the teacher's words, "his *type*"—being too educated and too urbanized for *ukuthwala*.

CONCLUSION

1. This is not a unique to South Africanist scholarship—although youth, social reproduction, and transformations in life course have recently attracted great scholarly attention across Africa (e.g., Mbembe [2001] 2008; Christiansen, Utas, and Vigh 2006; Hansen 2005; Honwana and de Boeck 2005; Durham 2000), the default "youth" in this literature is generally male (Vasconcelos 2010). For exceptions, see Cole 2010; Boehm 2006; Bastian 2001. For literature specific to South Africa, see Jewkes and Morrell 2018; Hickel 2015; Ratele 2015; Steinberg 2013; Morrell, Jewkes, and Lindegger 2012; Hunter 2010; Vincent 2008; Posel 2005; Sideris 2004; McClendon 2002; Morrell 1998; Ngwane 2001; Carton 2000; Mager 1998; Campbell 1994. 1992; Moodie and Ndatshe 1994.

2. For an overview of this topic, see Molefe 2018; Shutte 2001; Mokgoro 1998; Gyeke 1992; Wiredu 1992; Menkiti 1984.

REFERENCES

Abrahams, Naeemah, Shanaaz Mathews, Rachel Jewkes, Lorna J. Martin, and
Carl Lombard. 2012. *Every Eight Hours: Intimate Femicide in South Africa 10 Years
Later.* Pretoria: South African Medical Research Council.

Adam, Heribert, and Kogila Moodley. 1993. *The Opening of the Apartheid Mind:
Options for the New South Africa.* Berkeley: University of California Press.

Aguilar, Mario I., ed. 1998. *The Politics of Age and Gerontocracy in Africa:
Ethnographies of the Past and Memories of the Present.* Trenton: Africa World.

———. 2007. *Rethinking Age in Africa: Colonial, Post-colonial, and Contemporary
Interpretations of Cultural Representations.* Trenton, NJ: Africa World.

Ahearn, Laura. 2001. *Invitations to Love: Literacy, Love Letters, and Social Change in
Nepal.* Ann Arbor: University of Michigan Press.

Allerton, Catherine. 2007. "What Does It Mean to Be Alone?" In *Questions of
Anthropology*: *London School of Economics Monographs on Social Anthropology,*
edited by Rita Astuti, Jonathan Parry, and Charles Stafford, 1–28. Oxford: Berg.

Ansell, Nicola. 2001. "'Because It's Our Culture!' (Re)negotiating the Meaning
of Lobola in Southern African Secondary Schools." *Journal of Southern African
Studies* 27 (4): 697–716.

Ashforth, Adam. 2005. *Witchcraft, Violence and Democracy in South Africa.*
Chicago: University of Chicago Press.

Auslander, Mark. 1993. "'Open the Wombs': The Symbolic Politics of Modern
Ngoni Witch-Finding." In *Modernity and Its Malcontents: Ritual and Power in
Postcolonial Africa,* edited by John L. Comaroff and Jean Comaroff, 167–91.
Chicago: University of Chicago Press.

Ayres, Barbara. 1974. "Bride Theft and Raiding for Wives in Cross-cultural
Perspective." *Anthropological Quarterly* 47, no. 3: 238–52.

Bank, Leslie. 1994. "Angry Men and Working Women: Gender, Violence and Economic Change in QwaQwa in the 1980s." *African Studies* 53, no. 1: 89–113.

———. 2002. "Beyond Red and School: Gender, Tradition and Identity in the Rural Eastern Cape." *Journal of Southern African Studies* 28, no. 3: 631–49.

———. 2011. *Home Spaces, Street Styles: Contesting Power and Identity in a South African City.* London: Pluto.

———. 2015. "City Slums, Rural Homesteads: Migrant Culture, Displaced Urbanism and the Citizenship of the Serviced House." *Journal of Southern African Studies* 41, no. 5: 1067–81.

Bank, Leslie, and Linda Qambata. 1999. *No Visible Means of Subsistence: Rural Livelihoods, Gender and Social Change in Mooiplas, Eastern Cape 1950–1998.* Leiden: African Studies Centre.

Barchiesi, Franco. 2008. "Wage Labor, Precarious Employment, and Social Inclusion in the Making of South Africa's Postapartheid Transition." *African Studies Review* 51, no. 2: 119–42.

Barnes, Robert H. 1999. "Marriage by Capture." *Journal of the Royal Anthropological Institute* 5, no. 1: 57–73.

Baron, Geoff. 1992. "The Long and Winding Road. A Look at Applications for Disability Grants in South Africa." *South African Family Practice* 13, no. 9: 422–28.

Bastian, Misty L. 2001. "Acadas and Fertilizer Girls: Young Nigerian Women and the Romance of Middle-Class Modernity." In *Gendered Modernities: Ethnographic Perspectives,* edited by Dorothy L. Hodgson, 53–76. New York: Palgrave.

Bates, Daniel G. 1974. "Normative and Alternative Systems of Marriage among the Yoruk of Southeastern Turkey." *Anthropological Quarterly* 47, no. 3: 270–86.

Bates, Daniel G., Francis Conant, and Ayse Kudat. 1974. "Introduction: Kidnapping and Elopement as Alternative Systems of Marriage." *Anthropological Quarterly* 47, no. 3: 233–37.

Becker, Charles, and Susan Steiner. 2018. "How Forced Marriages Differ: Evidence on Assortative Mating in Kyrgyzstani Marriages." Working Paper 45, University of Central Asia—Institute of Public Policy and Administration.

Beinart, William. 1991. "The Origins of the Indlavini." *African Studies* 50, no. 1: 103–28.

Bennett, Tom W. 2010. "The Cultural Defence and the Custom of *Thwala* in South African Law." *University of Botswana Law Journal* 10, no. 3: 3–26.

Bezanson, Kate. 2006. *Gender, the State, and Social Reproduction: Household Insecurity in Neo-liberal Times.* Toronto: University of Toronto Press.

Bezuidenhout, Andries, and Khayaat Fakier. 2006. "Maria's Burden: Contract Cleaning and the Crisis of Social Reproduction in Post-apartheid South Africa." *Antipode* 38, no. 3: 462–85.

Bledsoe, Caroline H. 2002. *Contingent Lives: Fertility, Time, and Aging in West Africa.* Chicago: University of Chicago Press.

Boddy, Janice. 2007. "Clash of Selves: Gender, Personhood, and Human Rights Discourse in Colonial Sudan." *Canadian Journal of African Studies/ Revue Canadienne des Études Africaines* 41, no. 3: 402–26.

Boehm, Christian. 2006. "Industrial Labour, Marital Strategy and Changing Livelihood Trajectories among Young Women." In *Navigating Youth, Generating Adulthood: Social Becoming in an African Context,* edited by Catrine Christiansen, Mats Utas, and Henrik E. Vigh, 153–82. Uppsala: Nordiska Afrikainstitutet.

Bonner, Philip. 1990. "Desirable or Undesirable Sotho Women? Liquor, Prostitution and the Migration of Sotho Women to the Rand, 1920–1945." In *Women and Gender in South Africa to 1945,* edited by Cherryl Walker, 122–50. London: James Currey.

Borbieva, Noor O'Neill. 2012. "Kidnapping Women: Discourses of Emotion and Social Change in the Kyrgyz Republic." *Anthropological Quarterly* 85, no. 1: 141–69.

Boyd, Lydia. 2013. "The Problem with Freedom: Homosexuality and Human Rights in Uganda." *Anthropological Quarterly* 86, no. 3: 697–724.

Bozzoli, Belinda. 1983. "Marxism, Feminism and South African Studies." *Journal of Southern African Studies* 9, no. 2: 139–71.

Bozzoli, Belinda, and Mmantho Nkotsoe. 1991. *Women of Phokeng: Consciousness, Life Strategy, and Migrancy in South Africa, 1900–1983.* London: James Currey.

Brand, Danie, and Christof H. Heyns, eds. 2005. *Socio-economic Rights in South Africa.* Pretoria: Pretoria University Law Press.

Bryceson, Deborah, ed. 2002. *Alcohol in Africa.* Portsmouth: Heinemann.

Business Tech South Africa. 2016. "Richest and Poorest Municipalities in South Africa, 2016." https://businesstech.co.za/news/wealth/127213/the-richest -and-poorest-municipalities-in-south-africa/.

Butler, Judith. 1990. *Gender Trouble.* London: Routledge.

Campbell, Catherine. 1992. "Learning to Kill? Masculinity, the Family and Violence in Natal." *Journal of Southern African Studies* 18, no. 3: 614–28.

———. 1994. "Intergenerational Conflict in Township Families: Transforming Notions of 'Respect' and Changing Power Relations." *Southern African Journal of Gerontology* 3, no. 2: 37–42.

Carton, Benedict. 2000. *Blood from Your Children: The Colonial Origins of Generational Conflict in South Africa.* Charlottesville: University of Virginia Press.

Cassiman, Shawn A. 2008. "Resisting the Neo-liberal Poverty Discourse: On Constructing Deadbeat Dads and Welfare Queens." *Sociology Compass* 2, no. 5: 1690–1700.

Cattell, Maria G. 1999. "Elders' Complaints: Discourses on Old Age and Social Change in Rural Kenya and Urban Philadelphia." In *Language and Communication in Old Age: Multidisciplinary Perspectives,* edited by Heidi E. Hamilton, 295–317. New York: Garland.

Chadwick, Rachelle. 2017. "Ambiguous Subjects: Obstetric Violence, Assemblage and South African Birth Narratives." *Feminism and Psychology* 27, no. 4: 489–509.

Chamlee-Wright, Emily. 2002. "Savings and Accumulation Strategies of Urban Market Women in Harare, Zimbabwe." *Economic Development and Cultural Change* 50, no. 4: 979–1005.

Chanock, Martin. 1982. "Making Customary Law: Men, Women, and Courts in Colonial Northern Rhodesia." In *African Women and the Law: Historical Perspectives,* edited by Margaret Jean Hay and Marcia Wright, 53–67. Boston: Boston University, African Studies Center.

Chowdhury, Romit. 2014. "Conditions of Emergence: The Formation of Men's Rights Groups in Contemporary India." *Indian Journal of Gender Studies* 21:27–53.

Christiansen, Christian, Mats Utas, and Henrik E. Vigh, eds. 2006. *Navigating Youth, Generating Adulthood: Social Becoming in an African Context.* Uppsala: Nordiska Afrikainstitutet.

Claassens, Aninka. 2009. "Who Told Them We Want This Bill? The Traditional Courts Bill and Rural Women." *Agenda* 23, no. 82: 9–22.

———. 2021. "Traditional Courts Bill: How to Entrench Inequality and a Parallel Reality for 18 million Marginalised South Africans." *Daily Maverick,* February 4, 2021. https://www.dailymaverick.co.za/article/2021-02-04-traditional -courts-bill-how-to-entrench-inequality-and-a-parallel-reality-for-18-million -marginalised-south-africans/.

Clark, Gracia. 1994. *Onions Are My Husband: Survival and Accumulation by West African Market Women.* Chicago: University of Chicago Press.

Cockerton, Camilla. 2002. "Slipping through Their Fingers: Women's Migration and Tswana Patriarchy." *Botswana Notes and Records* 34:37–53.

Cole, Jennifer. 2010. *Sex and Salvation: Imagining the Future in Madagascar.* Chicago: University of Chicago Press.

Cole, Jennifer, and Lynn M. Thomas, eds. 2009. *Love in Africa.* Chicago: University of Chicago Press.

Collier, Jane Fishburne. [1997] 2020. *From Duty to Desire.* Princeton: Princeton University Press.

Comaroff, Jean, and John Comaroff. 2001. "On Personhood: An Anthropological Perspective from Africa." *Social Identities* 7, no. 2 (2001): 267–83.

———. 2005. "The Struggle between the Constitution and 'Things African.'" *Interventions* 7, no. 3: 299–303.

Comaroff, John L., and Jean Comaroff. 1987. "The Madman and the Migrant: Work and Labor in the Historical Consciousness of a South African People." *American Ethnologist* 14, no. 2: 191–209.

———. 1993. "Introduction." In *Modernity and Its Malcontents: Ritual and Power in Postcolonial Africa*, edited by John L. Comaroff and Jean Comaroff, ix–xxxvii. Chicago: University of Chicago Press.

———. 1999. Occult Economies and the Violence of Abstraction: Notes from the South African Postcolony. *American Ethnologist* 26, no. 2: 279–303.

Connell, Robert. 2005. *Masculinities*. Berkeley: University of California Press.

———. 2012. "Gender, Health and Theory: Conceptualizing the Issue, in Local and World Perspective." *Social Science and Medicine* 74, no. 11: 1675–83.

Connell, Robert W., and James W. Messerschmidt. 2005. "Hegemonic Masculinity: Rethinking the Concept." *Gender and Society* 19, no. 6: 829–59.

Conor, Liz. 2013. "'A Species of Rough Gallantry': Bride Capture and Settler-Colonial Print on Australian Aboriginal Gender Relations." *Settler Colonial Studies* 3, no. 1: 6–26.

Constitution of the Republic of South Africa. 1996. Government of the Republic of South Africa.

Cook, Peter Alan Wilson. 1931. *Social Organisation and Ceremonial Institutions of the Bomvana*. Cape Town: Juta.

———. 1934. *The Education of a South African Tribe*. Cape Town: Juta.

Coston, Bethany M., and Michael Kimmel. 2013. "White Men as the New Victims: Reverse Discrimination Cases and the Men's Rights Movement." *Nevada Law Journal* 13:368–85.

CRL Rights Commission. 2014. *Public Hearings and Research on Ukuthwala: Views and Perspectives Emerging from South African Communities*. CRL Rights Commission. www.crlcommission.org.za/docs/ukuthwala-booklet.pdf.

Daily News. 2013. "Romantic Origins Cruelly Distorted." December 5.

Davenport, Thomas, and Christopher Saunders. 2000. *South Africa: A Modern History*. 5th ed. London: Macmillan.

Davies, C. S. 1927. "Customs Governing Beer-Drinking among the Ama Bomvana." *South African Journal of Science* 24:521–24.

Decoteau, Claire Laurier.2013. *Ancestors and Antiretrovirals: The Biopolitics of HIV/AIDS in Post-apartheid South Africa*. Chicago: University of Chicago Press.

De Paoli, Marina Manuela, Elizabeth Anne Mills, and Arne Backer Grønningsæter. 2012. "The ARV Roll Out and the Disability Grant: A South African Dilemma?" *Journal of the International AIDS Society* 15, no. 6: 1–10.

Deumert, Ana. 2010. "'It Would Be Nice if They Could Give Us More Language'– Serving South Africa's Multilingual Patient Base." *Social Science and Medicine* 71, no.1: 53–61.

Dobash, R. Emerson, and Russell Dobash. 1979. *Violence against Wives: A Case against the Patriarchy.* New York: Free.

DOJ and CD (Department of Justice and Constitutional Development Gender Directorate). 2021. "*Ukuthwala*: Let's Stop Stolen Childhoods." https://www .justice.gov.za/brochure/ukuthwala/ukuthwala.html (site discontinued).

DSD, SASSA, and UNICEF (Department of Social Development, South African Social Security Agency, and United Nations International Children's Emergency Fund). 2012. *The South African Child Support Grant Impact Assessment: Evidence from a Survey of Children, Adolescents, and Their Households.* Pretoria: UNICEF South Africa.

Dubbeld, Bernard. 2021. "Granting the Future? The Temporality of Cash Transfers in the South African Countryside." *Revista de Antropologia* 64, no. 2: 1–19.

Dunkle, Kristin L., Rachel K. Jewkes, Heather C. Brown, Glenda E. Gray, James A. McIntryre, and Siobán D. Harlow. 2004. "Gender-Based Violence, Relationship Power, and Risk of HIV Infection in Women Attending Antenatal Clinics in South Africa." *The Lancet* 363, no. 9419: 1415–21.

Durham, Deborah. 2000. "Youth and the Social Imagination in Africa: Introduction to Parts 1 and 2." *Anthropological Quarterly* 73, no. 3: 113–20.

Du Toit, Louise. 2014. "Shifting Meanings of Postconflict Sexual Violence in South Africa." *Signs: Journal of Women in Culture and Society* 40, no 1: 101–23.

Dworkin, Shari L., Christopher Colvin, Abbey Hatcher, and Dean Peacock. 2012. "Men's Perceptions of Women's Rights and Changing Gender Relations in South Africa: Lessons for Working with Men and Boys in HIV and Antiviolence Programs." *Gender and Society* 26, no. 1: 97–120.

Edin, Katherine, and Laura Lein. 1997. "Work, Welfare, and Single Mothers' Economic Survival Strategies." *American Sociological Review* 62, no. 2: 253–66.

Englund, Harri. 2004. "Introduction: Recognizing Identities, Imagining Alternatives." In *Rights and the Politics of Recognition in Africa,* edited by Harri Englund and Francis Nyamnjoh, 1–29. London: Zed.

Everitt-Penhale, Brittany, and Kopano Ratele. 2015. "Rethinking 'Traditional Masculinity' as Constructed, Multiple, and Hegemonic Masculinity." *South African Review of Sociology* 46, no. 2: 4–22.

Fabricius, Peter. 2010. "President's Babygate Affair a Body Blow for SA Women's Rights Team." *Argus Weekend,* February 28.

Fakier, Khayaat, and Jacklyn Cock. 2009. "A Gendered Analysis of the Crisis of Social Reproduction in Contemporary South Africa." *International Feminist Journal of Politics* 11, no. 3: 353–71.

Ferguson, James. 1990. *The Anti-politics Machine: "Development," Depoliticization and Bureaucratic Power in Lesotho.* Minneapolis: University of Minnesota Press.

———. 1999. *Expectations of Modernity: Myths and Meanings of Urban Life on the Zambian Copperbelt.* Berkeley: University of California Press.

———. 2006. *Global Shadows: Africa in the Neoliberal World Order*. Durham, NC: Duke University Press.

———. 2013. "Declarations of Dependence: Labour, Personhood, and Welfare in Southern Africa." *Journal of the Royal Anthropological Institute* 19, no. 2: 223–42.

———. 2015. *Give a Man a Fish: Reflections on the New Politics of Distribution*. Durham, NC: Duke University Press.

Ferreira, Louise. 2017. "Factsheet: Social Grants in South Africa—Separating Myth from Reality." Africacheck.org. https://africacheck.org/factsheets /separating-myth-from-reality-a-guide-to-social-grants-in-south-africa/.

Fortes, Meyer. 1984. "Age, Generation, and Social Structure." In *Age and Anthropological Theory*, edited by David Kertzer and Jennie Keith, 99–122. Ithaca, NY: Cornell University Press.

Gaitskell, Deborah. 1982. "'Wailing for Purity': Prayer Unions, African Mothers and Adolescent Daughters, 1912–1940." In *Industrialisation and Social Change in South Africa: Africa Class Formation, Culture and Consciousness 1870–1930*, edited by Shula Marks and Richard Rathbone, 338–57. New York: Longman.

Gasa, Nomboniso. 2014. "Girls' Rights Are Being Violated." *Sunday Independent*, February 23.

Geschiere, Peter. 1997. *The Modernity of Witchcraft: Politics and the Occult in Postcolonial Africa*. Charlottesville: University of Virginia Press.

Giddens, Anthony. 1992. *The Transformation of Intimacy*. London: Polity.

Ginsburg, Faith, and Rayna Rapp. 2013. "Disability Worlds." *Annual Review of Anthropology* 42:53–68.

Gqola, Pumla Dineo. 2007. "How the 'Cult of Femininity' and Violent Masculinities Support Endemic Gender Based Violence in Contemporary South Africa." *African Identities* 5, no. 1: 111–24.

Graham, Lauren, Jacqueline Moodley, and Lisa Selipsky. 2013. "The Disability-Poverty Nexus and the Case for a Capabilities Approach: Evidence from Johannesburg, South Africa." *Disability and Society* 28, no. 3: 324–37.

Grant, T. 2006. "Problems of Communicative Competence in Multi-cultural Medical Encounters in South African Health Services." *Curationis* 29, no. 4: 1–7.

Guy, Jeff. 1990. "Gender Oppression in Southern Africa's Precapitalist Societies." In *Women and Gender in South Africa to 1945*, edited by Cherryl Walker, 33–47. Cape Town: New Africa.

Gyeke, Kwame. 1992. Person and Community in African Thought. In *Person and Community: Ghanaian Philosophical Studies*, edited by Kwame Gyeke and Kwasi Wiredu, 1:101–22. Washington, DC: Council for Research in Values and Philosophy.

Handrahan, Lori. 2004. "Hunting for Women: Bride-Kidnapping in Kyrgyzstan." *International Feminist Journal of Politics* 6, no. 2: 207–33.

Hansen, Camilla, and Washeila Sait. 2011. "'We Too Are Disabled': Disability Grants and Poverty Politics in Rural South Africa." In *Disability and Poverty: A*

Global Challenge, edited by Arne H. Eide and Benedicte Ingstad, 93–117. Bristol: Policy.

Hansen, Karen Tranberg. 2005. "Getting Stuck in the Compound: Some Odds against Social Adulthood in Lusaka, Zambia." *Africa Today* 51:3–16.

Herbert, Robert K. 1990. "Hlonipha and the Ambiguous Woman." *Anthropos* 85:455–73.

Herzfeld, Michael. 1988. *The Poetics of Manhood: Contest and Identity in a Cretan Mountain Village.* Princeton, NJ: Princeton University Press.

Hickel, Jason. 2015. *Democracy as Death: The Moral Order of Anti-liberal Politics in South Africa.* Berkeley: University of California Press.

Higgins, Tracy E., and Jeanmarie Fenrich. 2011. "Customary Law, Gender Equality, and the Family." In *The Future of African Customary Law,* edited by Jeanmarie Fenrich, Paolo Galizzi, and Tracy Higgins, 423–45. Cambridge: Cambridge University Press.

Himonga, Chuma. 2011. "Taking the Gap—'Living Law Land Grabbing' in the Context of Customary Succession Laws in Southern Africa." *Acta Juridica* 1:114–39.

Himonga, Chuma, and Craig Bosch. 2000. "The Application of African Customary Law under the Constitution of South Africa: Problems Solved or Just Beginning." *South African Law Journal* 107:307–41.

Himonga, Chuma, Ronald Thandabantu Nhlapo, I. P. Maithufi, Sindiso Mnisi Weeks, Lesala Mofokeng, and Dial Ndima. 2015. *African Customary Law in South Africa: Post-apartheid and Living Law Perspectives.* Edited by Chuma Himonga and Thandabantu Nhlapo. Cape Town: Oxford University Press.

Hirsch, Jennifer. 2003. *A Courtship after Marriage.* Berkeley: University of California Press.

Hobsbawm, Eric. 1983. "Introduction: Inventing Traditions." In *The Invention of Tradition,* edited by Eric Hobsbawm and Terence Ranger, 1–14. Cambridge: Cambridge University Press.

Hodgson, Dorothy L., and Sheryl McCurdy. 1996. "Wayward Wives, Misfit Mothers, and Disobedient Daughters: 'Wicked' Women and the Reconfiguration of Gender in Africa." *Canadian Journal of African Studies* 30, no. 1: 1–9.

Honwana, Alcinda Manuel. 2012. *The Time of Youth: Work, Social Change, and Politics in Africa.* Hartford, CT: Kumarian.

Honwana, Alcinda, and Filip de Boeck, eds. 2005. *Makers and Breakers: Children and Youth in Postcolonial Africa.* Oxford: James Currey.

Hornberger, Julia. 2011. *Policing and Human Rights: The Meaning of Violence and Justice in the Everyday Policing of Johannesburg.* London: Routledge.

Hosegood, Victoria, Nuala McGrath, and Tom Moultrie. 2009. "Dispensing with Marriage: Marital and Partnership Trends in Rural KwaZulu-Natal, South Africa 2000–2006." *Demographic Research* 20:279–312.

Hosegood, Victoria, Anna-Maria Vanneste, and Ian M. Timaeus. 2004. "Levels and Causes of Adult Mortality in Rural South Africa: The Impact of AIDS." *AIDS* 18, no. 4: 663–71.

Hull, Matthew S. 2012. *Government of Paper: The Materiality of Bureaucracy in Urban Pakistan*. Berkeley: University of California Press.

Hunnicutt, Gwen. 2009. "Varieties of Patriarchy and Violence against Women: Resurrecting 'Patriarchy' as a Theoretical Tool." *Violence against Women* 15, no. 5: 553–73.

Hunter, Mark. 2002. "The Materiality of Everyday Sex: Thinking beyond 'Prostitution.'" *African Studies* 61, no. 1: 99–120.

———. 2010. *Love in the Time of AIDS: Inequality, Gender, and Rights in South Africa*. Bloomington: Indiana University Press.

———. 2011. "Beneath the 'Zunami': Jacob Zuma and the Gendered Politics of Social Reproduction in South Africa." *Antipode* 43, no. 4: 1102–26.

Hunter, Monica. [1936] 1961. *Reaction to Conquest*. 2nd ed. London: Oxford University Press.

Illouz, Eva. 1997. *Consuming the Romantic Utopia*. Berkeley: University of California Press.

James, Deborah. 2017. "Not Marrying in South Africa: Consumption, Aspiration and the New Middle Class." *Anthropology Southern Africa* 40, no. 1: 1–14.

Jelsma, Jennifer, Soraya Maart, Arne Eide, Mzolisi Toni, and Mitch Loeb. 2008. "Who Gets the Disability Grant in South Africa? An Analysis of the Characteristics of Recipients in Urban and Rural Areas." *Disability and Rehabilitation* 30, no. 15: 1139–114.

Jensen, Steffen. 2008. *Gangs, Politics and Dignity in Cape Town*. Chicago: University of Chicago Press.

Jewkes, Rachel, Naeemah Abrahams, and Zodumo Mvo. 1998. "Why Do Nurses Abuse Patients? Reflections from South African Obstetric Services." *Social Science and Medicine* 47, no. 11: 1781–95.

Jewkes, Rachel, and Robert Morrell. 2010. "Gender and Sexuality: Emerging Perspectives from the Heterosexual Epidemic in South Africa and Implications for HIV Risk and Prevention." *Journal of the International AIDS Society* 13, no. 1: 6–17.

———. 2018. "Hegemonic Masculinity, Violence, and Gender Equality: Using Latent Class Analysis to Investigate the Origins and Correlates of Differences between Men." *Men and Masculinities* 21, no. 4: 547–71.

Jezile v. the State and Others. 2014. High Court Case No: A 127.

Johnson, Krista, and Sean Jacobs. 2004. "Democratization and the Rhetoric of Rights: Contradictions and Debate in Post-Apartheid South Africa." In *Rights and the Politics of Recognition in Africa*, edited by Harri Englund and Francis Nyamnjoh, 82–102. London: Zed.

Johnson-Hanks, Jennifer. 2006. *Uncertain Honor: Modern Motherhood in an African Crisis.* Chicago: University of Chicago Press.

Jolly, Margaret. 1996. "*'Woman ikat raet long human raet o no?'*: Women's Rights, Human Rights and Domestic Violence in Vanuatu." *Feminist Review* 52, no. 1: 169–90.

Kahn, Marc S., and Kevin J. Kelly. 2001. "Cultural Tensions in Psychiatric Nursing: Managing the Interface between Western Mental Health Care and Xhosa Traditional Healing in South Africa." *Transcultural Psychiatry* 38, no. 1: 35–50.

Kaminer, Debra, and John Dixon. 1995. "The Reproduction of Masculinity: A Discourse Analysis of Men's Drinking Talk." *South African Journal of Psychology* 25, no. 3: 168–74.

Kandiyoti, Deniz. 1988. "Bargaining with Patriarchy." *Gender and Society* 2, no. 3: 274–90.

Karimakwenda, Nyasha. 2013. "'Today It Would Be Called Rape': A Historical and Contextual Examination of Forced Marriage and Violence in the Eastern Cape." *Acta Juridica* 1:339–56.

———. 2020. "Deconstructing Characterizations of Rape, Marriage, and Custom in South Africa: Revisiting the Multi-sectoral Campaign Against *Ukuthwala*." *African Studies Review* 63, no. 4: 763–81.

Kasnitz, Devva, and Philip R. Shuttleworth. 2001. "Anthropology and Disability Studies." In *Semiotics and Dis/ability: Interrogating Categories of Difference*, edited by Linda J. Rogers and Beth Blue Swadener, 19–41. Albany: SUNY Press.

Katz, Cindi. 2001. "Vagabond Capitalism and the Necessity of Social Reproduction." *Antipode* 33, no. 4: 709–28.

Keevy, Ilze. 2009. "Ubuntu versus the Core Values of the South African Constitution." *Journal for Juridical Science* 34, no. 2: 19–58.

Kelly, Gabrielle. 2013. "Regulating Access to the Disability Grant in South Africa, 1990–2013." CSSR Working Paper No. 330, Centre for Social Science Research, University of Cape Town.

———. 2016a. "'We Want Another Doctor!' Citizen Agency and Contested Notions of Disability in Social Assistance Applications in South Africa." CSSR Working Paper No. 383, Centre for Social Science Research, University of Cape Town.

———. 2016b. "Hard and Soft Medicine: Doctors' Framing and Application of the Disability Category in Their Assessments of Grant Claimants' Fitness to Work in South Africa." CSSR Working Paper No. 384, Centre for Social Science Research, University of Cape Town.

———. 2017. "Patient Agency and Contested Notions of Disability in Social Assistance Applications in South Africa." *Social Science and Medicine* 175:109–16.

Kheswa, J. G., and V. N. Hoho. 2014. "'Ukuthwala': The Sexual-Cultural Practice with Negative Effects on the Personality of Adolescent Females in Africa." *Mediterranean Journal of Social Sciences* 5, no. 20: 2808–13.

Kim, Elena, and Frank G. Karioris. 2020. "Bound to Be Grooms: The Imbrication of Economy, Ecology, and Bride Kidnapping in Kyrgyzstan." *Gender, Place and Culture* 28, no. 11: 1–22.

Kim, Julia, and Mmatshilo Motsei. 2002. "'Women Enjoy Punishment': Attitudes and Experiences of Gender-Based Violence among PHC Nurses in Rural South Africa." *Social Science and Medicine* 54, no. 8: 1243–54.

Kirkby, Diane. 2003. "'Beer, Glorious Beer': Gender Politics and Australian Popular Culture." *Journal of Popular Culture* 37, no. 2: 244–56.

Klasen, Stephan, and Ingrid Woolard. 2009. "Surviving Unemployment without State Support: Unemployment and Household Formation in South Africa." *Journal of African Economies* 18, no. 1: 1–51.

Kleinman, Arthur. 2007. *What Really Matters: Living a Moral Life amidst Uncertainty and Danger.* Oxford: Oxford University Press.

Kleinman, Arthur, Veena Das, and Margaret M. Lock. 1997. *Social Suffering.* Berkeley: University of California Press.

Knauft, Bruce M. 2002. "Critically Modern: An Introduction." In *Critically Modern: Alternatives, Alterities, Anthropologies,* edited by Bruce M. Knauft, 1–56. Bloomington: Indiana University Press.

Koyana, Digby Sqhelo. 1980. *Customary Law in a Changing Society.* Cape Town: Juta.

La Fontaine, Jean S. 1985. "Person and Individual: Some Anthropological Reflections." In *The Category of the Person: Anthropology, Philosophy, History,* edited by Michael Carrithers, Steven Collins, and Steven Lukes, 123–40. Cambridge: Cambridge University Press.

Lake, Milli May. 2018. *Strong NGOs and Weak States: Pursuing Gender Justice in the Democratic Republic of Congo and South Africa.* Cambridge: Cambridge University Press.

Langa, Malose, Adele Kirsten, Brett Bowman, Gill Eagle, and Peace Kiguwa. 2020. "Black Masculinities on Trial in Absentia: The Case of Oscar Pistorius in South Africa." *Men and Masculinities* 23, no. 3–4: 499–515.

Laslett, Barbara, and Johanna Brenner. 1989. Gender and Social Reproduction: Historical Perspectives. *Annual Review of Sociology* 15, no. 1: 381–404.

Li, Tania Murray. 2007. *The Will to Improve.* Durham, NC: Duke University Press.

Liebenberg, Alida. 1997. "Dealing with Relations of Inequality: Married Women in a Transkei Village." *African Studies* 56:349–73.

Lindsay, Samuel, and Antonia C. Lyons. 2018. "'Pour It Up, Drink It Up, Live It Up, Give It Up': Masculinity and Alcohol in Pop Music Videos." *Men and Masculinities* 21, no 5: 624–44.

Livermon, Xavier. 2015. "Usable Traditions: Creating Sexual Autonomy in Postapartheid South Africa." *Feminist Studies* 41, no. 1: 14–41.

Livingston, Julie. 2003. "Reconfiguring Old Age: Elderly Women and Concerns over Care in Southeastern Botswana." *Medical Anthropology* 22, no. 3: 205–31.

Lockwood, William G. 1974. "Bride Theft and Social Maneuverability in Western Bosnia." *Anthropological Quarterly* 47, no 3: 253–69.

Lourens, Mariana. 2013. "An Exploration of Xhosa-Speaking Patients' Understanding of Cancer Treatment and Its Influence on Their Treatment Experience." *Journal of Psychosocial Oncology* 31, no. 1: 103–21.

Mabaso, Musawenkosi L. H., Nthabiseng F. Malope, and Leickness C. Simbayi. 2018. "Socio-demographic and Behavioural Profile of Women in Polygamous Relationships in South Africa: A Retrospective Analysis of the 2002 Population-Based Household Survey Data." *BMC Women's Health* 18, no. 1: 1–8.

MacGregor, Haley. 2006. "'The Grant Is What I Eat': The Politics of Social Security and Disability in the Post-Apartheid South African State." *Journal of Biosocial Science* 38, no. 1: 43–55.

Mafeje, Archie. 1971. "The Ideology of 'Tribalism.'" *The Journal of Modern African Studies* 9, no. 2: 253–61.

Mager, Anne Kelk. 1998. "Youth Organisations and the Construction of Masculine Identities in the Ciskei and Transkei, 1945–1960." *Journal of Southern African Studies* 24, no. 4: 653–65.

———. 1999. *Gender and the Making of a South African Bantustan: A Social History of the Ciskei 1945–1959.* Portsmouth, NH: Heinemann.

———. 2010. *Beer, Sociability, and Masculinity in South Africa.* Bloomington: Indiana University Press.

Magubane, Bernard. 1973. "The 'Xhosa' in Town, Revisited Urban Social Anthropology: A Failure of Method and Theory." *American Anthropologist* 75, no. 5: 1701–15.

Mail and Guardian. 2020. "Gender Based Violence: Special Report." December 4. https://mg.co.za/special-reports/2020-12-04-gender-based-violence/.

Mains, Daniel, Craig Hadley, and Fasil Tessema. 2013. "Chewing Over the Future: Khat Consumption, Anxiety, Depression, and Time among Young Men in Jimma, Ethiopia." *Culture, Medicine, and Psychiatry* 37, no. 1: 111–30.

Makhulu, Anne-Maria. 2015. *Making Freedom: Apartheid, Squatter Politics, and the Struggle for Home.* Durham, NC: Duke University Press.

Makhulu, Anne-Maria, Beth A. Buggenhagen and Stephen Jackson. 2010. "Introduction." In *Hard Work, Hard Times: Global Volatility and African Subjectivities,* edited by Anna-Maria Makhulu, Beth A. Buggenhagen, and Stephen Jackson, 1–27. Berkeley: University of California Press.

Malan, Mia. 2011. "Is Today's Ukuthwala a Perversion of an Earlier Tradition?" *Mail and Guardian,* December 15. https://mg.co.za/article/2011-12-15-abduction-a-perversion-of-the-past/.

Mamdani, Mahmood. 1996. *Citizen and Subject: Contemporary Africa and the Legacy of Late Colonialism.* Princeton, NJ: Princeton University Press.

Mangena, Fainos. 2009. "The Search for an African Feminist Ethic: A Zimbabwean Perspective." *Journal of International Women's Studies* 11, no. 2: 18–30.

Manicom, Linzi. 2005. "Constituting 'Women' as Citizens: Ambiguities in the Making of Gendered Political Subjects in Post-Apartheid South Africa." In *(Un)thinking Citizenship: Feminist Debates in Contemporary South Africa*, edited by Amanda Gouws, 21–52. Cape Town: UCT Press.

Manona, Cecil W. 1980. "Marriage, Family Life and Migrancy in a Ciskei Village." In *Black Villagers in Industrial Society*, edited by Philip Mayer, 170–202. Cape Town: Oxford University Press.

Mashaba, Sibongile. 2015. "Ukuthwala Hazard for Traditionalists." *Sowetan*, August 24.

Masquelier, Adeline. 2013. "Teatime: Boredom and the Temporalities of Young Men in Niger." *Africa* 83, no. 3: 385–402.

Mayer, Philip. 1980. *Black Villagers in an Industrial Society: Anthropological Perspectives on Labour Migration in South Africa*. London: Oxford University Press.

Mayer, Philip, and Iona Mayer. [1960] 1971. *Townsmen or Tribesmen: Conservatism and the Process of Urbanization in a South African City*. 2nd ed. Cape Town: Oxford University Press.

Mazibuko, Nokuthula C. 2017. "Checkmating the Mate: Power Relations and Domestic Violence in a South African Township." *South African Review of Sociology* 48, no. 2: 18–31.

Mbembe, Achille. [2001] 2008. *On the Postcolony*. Berkeley: University of California Press.

McAllister, Patrick A. 1993. "Indigenous Beer in Southern Africa: Functions and Fluctuations." *African Studies* 52, no. 1: 71–88.

———. 2001. *Building the Homestead: Agriculture, Labour and Beer in South Africa's Transkei*. Aldershot: Ashgate.

———. 2002. "Labour and Beer in Africa: Xhosa Work Parties." In *African Identities: Contemporary Political and Social Challenges*, edited by Pel Ahluwalia and Abebe Zegeye, 160–70. Aldershot: Ashgate.

———. 2006. *Xhosa Beer Drinking Rituals: Power, Practice and Performance in the South African Rural Periphery*. Durham, NC: Carolina Academic Press.

McClendon, Thomas V. 2002. *Genders and Generations Apart: Labor Tenants and Customary Law in Segregation-Era South Africa, 1920s to 1940s*. Portsmouth, NH: Heinemann.

McKittrick, Meredith. 1996. "The 'Burden' of Young Men: Property and Generational Conflict in Namibia, 1880–1945." *African Economic History* 24:115–29.

McLaren, Anne E. 2010. "Marriage by Abduction in Twentieth Century China." *Modern Asian Studies* 35, no. 4: 953–84.

Meillassoux, Claude. 1981. *Maidens, Meal and Money Capitalism and the Domestic Community*. Cambridge: Cambridge University Press.

Menkiti, Ifeanyi. 1984. "Person and Community in African Traditional Thought." In *African Philosophy: An Introduction*, edited by Richard A. Wright, 171–82. Lanham, MD: University Press of America.

Mesatywa, Nontando Jennifer. 2014. "Validating the Evidence of Violence in Partner Relationships with Regard to Xhosa African Women." *Social Work* 50, no. 2: 235–57.

Metz, Thaddeus. 2011. "Ubuntu as a Moral Theory and Human Rights in South Africa." *African Human Rights Law Journal* 11, no. 2: 532–59.

———. 2014. "African Values and Human Rights as Two Sides of the Same Coin: A Reply to Oyowe." *African Human Rights Law Journal* 14, no. 2: 306–21.

Mfecane, Sakhumzi. 2011. "To Drink or Not to Drink? Identity Dilemmas of Men Living with HIV." *Agenda* 25, no. 4: 37–41.

———. 2016. "Ndiyindoda [I Am a Man]: Theorising Xhosa Masculinity." *Anthropology Southern Africa* 39, no. 3: 204–14.

———. 2018. "Towards African-Centred Theories of Masculinity." *Social Dynamics* 44, no. 2: 291–305.

———. 2020. "Decolonising Men and Masculinities Research in South Africa." *South African Review of Sociology* 51, no. 2: 1–15.

Mkhonto, Flora, and Ingrid Hanssen. 2018. "When People with Dementia Are Perceived as Witches. Consequences for Patients and Nurse Education in South Africa." *Journal of Clinical Nursing* 27, no. 1–2: e169–e176.

Mnisi Weeks, Sindiso. 2010. *Reconciling Living Customary Law and Democratic Decentralisation to Ensure Women's Land Rights Security*. Cape Town: Institute for Poverty, Land, and Agrarian Studies, University of the Western Cape.

———. 2011. "Beyond the Traditional Courts Bill: Regulating Customary Courts in Line with Living Customary Law and the Constitution." *SA Crime Quarterly*, no. 35: 31–40.

———. 2017. *Access to Justice and Human Security: Cultural Contradictions in Rural South Africa*. London: Routledge.

Mnisi Weeks, Sindiso, and Aninka Claassens. 2011. "Tensions between Vernacular Values That Prioritise Basic Needs and State Versions of Customary Law That Contradict Them: We Love These Fields That Feed Us, but Not at the Expense of a Person." *Stellenbosch Law Review* 3:823.

Moffett, Helen. 2006. "'These Women, They Force Us to Rape Them': Rape as Narrative of Social Control in Post-apartheid South Africa." *Journal of Southern African Studies* 32, no 1: 129–44.

Mokgoro, Justice Yvonne. 1998. "Ubuntu and the Law in South Africa." *Potchefstroom Electronic Law Journal* 1, no. 1: n.p.

Molefe, Motsamai. 2018. "Personhood and Rights in an African Tradition." *Politikon* 45, no. 2: 217–31.

Monyane, Chelete. 2013. "Is *Ukuthwala* Another Form of 'Forced Marriage'?" *South African Review of Sociology* 44, no. 2: 64–82.

Moodie, Dunbar T. 1992. "Ethnic Violence on South African Gold Mines." *Journal of Southern African Studies* 18, no. 3: 584–613.

Moodie, Dunbar T., and Vivienne Ndatshe. 1994. *Going for Gold: Men, Mines, and Migration*. Berkeley: University of California Press.

Moore, Henrietta L., and Todd Sanders, eds. 2003. *Magical Interpretations, Material Realities: Modernity, Witchcraft and the Occult in Postcolonial Africa*. London: Routledge.

Morrell, Robert. 1998. "Of Boys and Men: Masculinity and Gender in Southern African Studies." *Journal of Southern African Studies* 24, no. 4: 605–30.

———. 2002. "Men, Movements, and Gender Transformation in South Africa." *Journal of Men's Studies* 10, no. 3: 309–27.

Morrell, Robert, Rachel Jewkes, and Graham Lindegger. 2012. "Hegemonic Masculinity/Masculinities in South Africa: Culture, Power, and Gender Politics." *Men and Masculinities* 15, no. 1: 11–30.

Mphaphuli, Memory, and Letitia Smuts. 2021. "'Give It to Him': Sexual Violence in the Intimate Relationships of Black Married Women in South Africa." *Signs: Journal of Women in Culture and Society* 46, no. 2: 443–64.

Mupotsa, Danai. 2015. "The Promise of Happiness: Desire, Attachment and Freedom in Post/Apartheid South Africa." *Critical Arts* 29, no. 2: 183–98.

Mwambene, Lea, and Julia Sloth-Nielsen. 2011. "Benign Accommodation? Ukuthwala, 'Forced Marriage' and the South African Children's Act." *African Human Rights Law Journal* 11, no. 1: 1–22.

Nattrass, Nicoli. 2006. "Trading off Income and Health? AIDS and the Disability Grant in South Africa." *Journal of Social Policy* 35, no. 1: 3–19.

Nedelsky, Jennifer. 2011. *Law's Relations: A Relational Theory of Self, Autonomy, and Law*. Oxford: Oxford University Press.

Newell, Sasha. 2012. *The Modernity Bluff: Crime, Consumption and Citizenship in Cote d'Ivoire*. Chicago: University of Chicago Press.

Nguyen, Thi Huong, Pauline Oosterhoff, and Joanna White. 2011. "Aspirations and Realities of Love, Marriage and Education among Hmong Women." *Culture, Health and Sexuality* 13, suppl. 2: S201–S215.

Ngwane, Zolani. 2001. "'Real Men Reawaken Their Fathers' Homesteads, the Educated Leave Them in Ruins': The Politics of Domestic Reproduction in Post-Apartheid Rural South Africa." *Journal of Religion in Africa* 31:402–26.

Nkosi, Makho, and Johan Wassermann. 2014. "A History of the Practice of *Ukuthwala* in the Natal/KwaZulu-Natal Region up to 1994." *New Contree* 70:131–46.

Ntsebeza, Lungisile. 2002. "Structures and Struggles of Rural Local Government in South Africa: The Case of Traditional Authorities in the Eastern Cape." PhD thesis, Rhodes University, Grahamstown.

Nyamnjoh, Francis. 2004. "Reconciling the 'Rhetoric of Rights' with Competing Notions of Personhood and Agency in Botswana." In *Rights and the Politics of Recognition in Africa*, edited by Harri Englund and Francis Nyamnjoh, 33–63. London: Zed.

Nyatsanza, Tarcisio. 2000. "A Case for Human Rights Education in an African Context: The Concept and the Practice." Paper presented at the Democratic Transformation of Education in South Africa Conference, University of Stellenbosch, September 27–28, 2000.

OECD (Organisation for Economic Co-operation and Development). 2020. "Building an Inclusive Social Protection System in South Africa." https://www .oecd.org/southafrica/building-an-inclusive-social-protection-system-in-south -africa-e01d1e09-en.htm.

Okome, Mojúbàolú. 2001. "African Women and Power: Reflections on the Perils of Unwarranted Cosmopolitanism." *Jenda Journal* 1, no. 1: 1–14.

Okyere-Manu, Beatrice Dedaa, and Elias Konyana. 2018. "Who Is *Umuntu* in *Umuntu ngumuntu ngabantu*? Interrogating Moral Issues Facing Ndau Women in Polygyny." *South African Journal of Philosophy* 37, no. 2: 207–16.

Oomen, Barbara. 2004. "Vigilantism or Alternative Citizenship? The Rise of Mapogo a Mathamaga." *African Studies* 63, no. 2: 153–71.

Osman, Fatima. 2020. "The Omission of the Opt-Out Clause. The Revised (and Improved?) Traditional Courts Bill 2017." *SA Crime Quarterly* 69:69–79.

Oyěwùmí, Oyèrónkì. 2004 "Conceptualizing Gender: The Eurocentric Foundations of Feminist Concepts and the Challenge of African Epistemologies." In *African Gender Scholarship: Concepts, Methodologies and Paradigms*, edited by Arnfred, Signe, Bibi Bakare-Yusuf, and Eduard Waswwa Kisiang'ani, n.p. Dakar: Codesria.

Oyowe, Oritsegbubemi A., and Olga Yurkivska. 2014. "Can a Communitarian Concept of African Personhood Be Both Relational and Gender-Neutral?" *South African Journal of Philosophy* 33, no. 1: 85–99.

Paley, Julia. 2001. *Marketing Democracy Power and Social Movements in Post-Dictatorship Chile*. Berkeley: University of California Press.

Parliamentary Monitoring Group. 2018. "Urbanisation." https://pmg.org.za/page /Urbanisation.

Pauli, Julia, and Rijk van Dijk. 2016. "Marriage as an End or the End of Marriage? Change and Continuity in Southern African Marriages." *Anthropology Southern Africa* 39, no. 4: 257–66.

Peires, Jeff. 1987. "The Central Beliefs of the Xhosa Cattle-Killing." *Journal of African History* 28, no. 1: 43–63.

Peveri, Valentina. 2014. "Approaching Abduction through Narratives: Love and Violence in a Hadiya Village, Southwestern Ethiopia." *Paideuma* 60:205–26.

Phaswana-Mafuya, Nancy, Karl Peltzer, and George Petros. 2009. "Disability Grant for People Living with HIV/AIDS in the Eastern Cape of South Africa." *Social Work in Health Care* 48, no. 5: 533–50.

Piot, Charles. 1999. *Remotely Global: Village Modernity in West Africa*. Chicago: University of Chicago Press.

———. 2010. *Nostalgia for the Future: West Africa after the Cold War*. Chicago: University of Chicago Press.

Posel, Deborah. 1995. "State, Power and Gender: Conflict over the Registration of African Customary Marriage in South Africa c. 1910–1970." *Journal of Historical Sociology* 8, no. 3: 223–56.

———. 2004. "Afterword: Vigilantism and the Burden of Rights: Reflections on the Paradoxes of Freedom in Post-Apartheid South Africa." *African Studies* 63, no. 2: 231–36.

———. 2005. "The Scandal of Manhood: 'Baby Rape' and the Politicization of Sexual Violence in Post-Apartheid South Africa." *Culture, Health and Sexuality* 7, no. 3: 239–52.

Posel, Dorrit, Stephanie Rudwick, and Daniela Casale. 2011. "Is Marriage a Dying Institution in South Africa? Exploring Changes in Marriage in the Context of *Ilobolo* Payments." *Agenda* 25, no. 1: 37–41.

Qayiso, Percy. 1964. "Xhosa Morality." Unpublished typescript. Cory Library, Grahamstown, MS, Folder 13.

Rangan, Haripriya, and Mary Gilmartin. 2002. "Gender, Traditional Authority, and the Politics of Rural Reform in South Africa." *Development and Change* 33, no. 4: 633–58.

Ratele, Kopano. 2013. "Masculinities without Tradition." *Politikon* 40, no. 1: 133–56.

———. 2015. "Working through Resistance in Engaging Boys and Men towards Gender Equality and Progressive Masculinities." *Culture, Health and Sexuality* 17, no. 2: 144–58.

———. 2018. "Concerning Tradition in Studies on Men and Masculinities in Ex-Colonies." In *Gender Reckonings: New Social Theory and Research*, edited by Messerschmidt, James W., Martin, Patricia T., Messner, Michael A., Connell, Raewyn, 211–32. New York: New York University Press.

Rebhun, Linda-Anne. 1999. *The Heart Is Unknown Country: Love in the Changing Economy of Northeast Brazil*. Redwood City, CA: Stanford University Press.

Redding, Sean. 2006. *Sorcery and Sovereignty: Taxation, Power, and Rebellion in South Africa, 1880–1963*. Athens: Ohio University Press.

Reddy, Trusha, and Andile Sokomani. 2008. "Corruption and Social Grants in South Africa." Monograph No. 154. Pretoria: Institute for Security Studies.

Reid-Cunningham, Alison R. 2009. "Anthropological Theories of Disability." *Journal of Human Behavior in the Social Environment* 19, no. 1: 99–111.

Rice, Kathleen. 2014. "*Ukuthwala* in Rural South Africa: Abduction Marriage as a Site of Negotiation about Gender, Rights and Generational Authority among the Xhosa." *Journal of Southern African Studies* 40, no. 2: 381–400.

———. 2017. "Rights and Responsibilities in Rural South Africa: Implications for Gender, Generation, and Personhood." *Journal of the Royal Anthropological Institute* 23, no. 41: 28–41.

———. 2018. "Understanding *Ukuthwala*: Bride Abduction in the Rural Eastern Cape, South Africa." *African Studies* 77, no. 3: 394–411.

Riesman, Paul. 1986. "The Person and the Life Cycle in African Social Life and Thought." *African Studies Review* 29, no. 2: 71–138.

Rosenberg, Harriet G. 1990. "Complaint Discourse, Aging, and Caregiving among the !Kung San of Botswana." In *The Cultural Context of Aging: Worldwide Perspectives*, edited by Jay Sokolovsky, 20–41. New York: Bergin & Garvey.

Rudwick, Stephanie, and Magcino Shange. 2009. "Hlonipha and the Rural Zulu Woman." *Agenda* 23, no. 82: 37–41.

Salenda, Kasjim. 2016. "Abuse of Islamic Law and Child Marriage in South-Sulawesi Indonesia." *Al-Jami'ah: Journal of Islamic Studies* 54, no. 1: 95–121.

SA News (South African Government New Agency). 2015. "New Biometric Card to Boot Out Social Grant Fraud." http://www.sanews.gov.za/south-africa/new-biometric-card-boot-out-social-grant-fraud/.

Sanger, Andreas. 2002. "Identity Management and Old Age Construction among Xhosa-Speakers in Urban South Africa: Complaint Discourse Revisited." In *Aging in Africa: Sociolinguistic and Anthropological Approaches*, edited by Sinfree Makoni and Koenraad Stroeken, 43–66. Aldershot: Ashgate.

Schane, Sanford. 2002. "Ambiguity and Misunderstanding in the Law." *Thomas Jefferson Law Review* 25:167–94.

Schlemmer, Arina, and Bob Mash. 2006. "The Effects of a Language Barrier in a South African District Hospital." *South African Medical Journal* 96, no. 10: 1084–87.

Scorgie, Fiona. 2002. "Virginity Testing and the Politics of Sexual Responsibility: Implications for AIDS Intervention." *African Studies* 61, no. 1: 55–75.

Seekings, Jeremy, and Heidi Matisonn. 2010. "The Continuing Politics of Basic Income in South Africa." UCT CSSR Working Paper No. 286, 2010. https://open.uct.ac.za/bitstream/handle/11427/19173/Seekings_continuing_politics_2010.pdf?sequence=1&isAllowed=y.

Segar, Julia. 1994. "Negotiating Illness: Disability Grants and the Treatment of Epilepsy." *Medical Anthropology Quarterly* 8, no. 3: 282–98.

Settersten, Richard A., Jr., and Gunhild O. Hagestad. 2015. "Subjective Aging and New Complexities of the Life Course." *Annual Review of Gerontology and Geriatrics* 35, no. 1: 29–53.

Seymour, Wilfred Massingham. 1982. *Seymour's Customary Law in Southern Africa.* Cape Town: Juta.

Shefer, Tamara, Mary Crawford, Anna Strebel, Leickness C. Simbayi, Nomvo Dwadwa-Henda, Allanise Cloete, Michelle R. Kaufman, and Seth C. Kalichman. 2008. "Gender, Power and Resistance to Change among Two Communities in the Western Cape, South Africa." *Feminism and Psychology* 18, no. 2: 157–82.

Shisana, Olive, Thomas Rehle, Khangelani Zuma, Sean Jooste, Nompumelelo Zungu, Demetre Labadarios, and Dorina Onoya. 2014. *South African National HIV Prevalence, Incidence and Behavioural Survey, 2012.* Cape Town: HSRC Press.

Shope, Janet Hinson. 2006. "'Lobola Is Here to Stay': Rural Black Women and the Contradictory Meanings of Lobolo in Post-apartheid South Africa." *Agenda* 20, no. 68: 64–72.

Shutte, Augustine. 2001. "*Ubuntu*: An Ethic for a New South Africa." Pietermaritzburg: Cluster.

Sideris, Tina. 2004. "'You Have to Change and You Don't Know How!': Contesting What It Means to Be a Man in a Rural Area of South Africa." *African Studies* 63, no 1: 29–49.

Silberschmidt, Margrethe. 2011. "What Would Make Men Interested in Gender Equality?" In *Men and Development: Politicizing Masculinities*, edited by Andrea Cornwall, Jerker Edström, and Alan Greig, 98–110. London: Zed.

Simchowitz, Brett. 2004. "Social Security and HIV/AIDS: Assessing 'Disability' in the Context of ARV Treatment." CSSR Working Paper No. 99, Centre for Social Science Research, University of Cape Town.

Smit, W. Jaco, and Catriens Notermans. 2015. "Surviving Change by Changing Violently: *Ukuthwala* in South Africa's Eastern Cape Province." *Anthropology Southern Africa* 38, no. 1: 29–46.

Smith, Nicholas R. 2019. *Contradictions of Democracy: Vigilantism and Rights in Post-Apartheid South Africa.* London: Oxford University Press.

Soga, John Henderson. [1933] 2013. *The Ama-Xosa: Life and Customs.* Cambridge: Cambridge University Press.

Spronk, Rachel. 2009. "Media and the Therapeutic Ethos of Romantic Love in Middle-Class Nairobi." In *Love in Africa*, edited by Jennifer Cole and Lynn Thomas, 181–203. Chicago: University of Chicago Press.

Staples, James, and Nilika Mehrotra. 2016. "Disability Studies: Developments in Anthropology." In *Disability in the Global South*, edited by Shaun Grech and Karen Soldatic, 35–49. New York: Springer.

Statistics South Africa. 2016. "Community Survey." http://cs2016.statssa.gov.za/.

———. 2019. "Five Facts about Poverty in South Africa." https://www.statssa.gov.za/?p=12075.

Steele, Mark. 2006. *Report on Incentive Structures of Social Assistance Grants in South Africa.* Pretoria: Department of Social Development.

Steinberg, Jonny. 2013. "Working through a Paradox about Sexual Culture in South Africa: Tough Sex in the Twenty-First Century." *Journal of Southern African Studies* 39, no. 3: 497–509.

Stross, Brian. 1974. "Tzeltal Marriage by Capture." *Anthropological Quarterly* 47, no. 3: 328–46.

Suggs, David N. 1996. "Mosadi Tshwene: The Construction of Gender and the Consumption of Alcohol in Botswana." *American Ethnologist* 23, no. 3: 597–610.

———. 2001. "'These Young Chaps Think They Are Just Men, Too': Redistributing Masculinity in Kgatleng Bars." *Social Science and Medicine* 53:241–50.

Sultanalieva, Syinat. 2021. "Another Woman Killed in Scourge of Kyrgyzstan 'Bride Kidnapping.'" Human Rights Watch, April 9, 2021. https://www.hrw.org/node/378456/printable/print.

Taylor Commission. 2002. *Report of the Committee of Inquiry into a Comprehensive System of Social Security for South Africa "Transforming the Present Protecting the Future."* https://pmg.org.za/committee-meeting/2551/.

Taylor, John P. 2008. "The Social Life of Rights: 'Gender Antagonism,' Modernity and *Raet* in Vanuatu." *Australian Journal of Anthropology* 9:165–78.

Thomas, Philip. 2002. "The River, the Road, and the Rural-Urban Divide: A Postcolonial Moral Geography from Southeast Madagascar." *American Ethnologist* 29, no. 2: 366–91.

Thornberry, Elizabeth. 2019. *Colonizing Consent: Rape and Governance in South Africa's Eastern Cape.* Cambridge: Cambridge University Press.

Thornberry, Elizabeth, Annie Bunting, Benjamin Lawrance, and Richard Roberts. 2016. "Ukuthwala, Forced Marriage, and the Idea of Custom in South Africa's Eastern Cape." In *Marriage by Force? Contestation over Consent and Coercion in Africa,* 137–59. Athens: Ohio University Press.

UNHROHC (United Nations Human Rights Office of the High Commissioner). 2018. "Culture of Abduction, Rape and Forced Marriage Violates Women's Rights in Kyrgyzstan, UN Experts Find." https://www.ohchr.org/EN/NewsEvents/Pages/DisplayNews.aspx?NewsID=23583&LangID=E.

United Nations. 2015. "Despite Progressive Laws, Gender-Based Violence 'Pervasive' in South Africa, UN expert warns." http://www.un.org/sustainabledevelopment/blog/2015/12/despite-progressive-laws-gender-based-violence-pervasive-in-south-africa-un-expert-warns/.

Van der Drift, Roy. 2002. "Democracy's Heady Brew: Cashew Wine and the Authority of Elders among the Balanta of Guinea-Bissau." In *Alcohol in Africa,* edited by Deborah Bryceson, 179–96. Portsmouth: Heinemann.

Van der Geest, Sjaak. 2007. "Complaining and Not Complaining: Social Strategies of Older People in Kwahu, Ghana." *Global Ageing* 4, no. 3: 55–66.

Van der Vliet, Virginia. 1991. "Traditional Husbands, Modern Wives? Constructing Marriages in a South African Township." *African Studies* 50, no. 1: 219–41.

Vasconcelos, Joana. 2010. "The Double Marginalisation: Reflections on Young Women and the Youth Crisis in Sub-Saharan Africa." In 7° *Congresso Ibérico de Estudos Africanos, 9, Lisboa, 2010—50 Anos Das Independências Africanas: Desafios Para a Modernidade : Actas.* Lisbon: Centro de Estudos Internacionais.

Venter, Christine M. 1995. "The New South African Constitution: Facing the Challenges of Women's Rights and Cultural Rights in Post-Apartheid South Africa." *Journal of Legislation* 21:1–22.

Vincent, Louise. 2006. "Virginity Testing in South Africa: Re-traditioning the Postcolony." *Culture, Health and Sexuality* 8, no. 1: 17–30.

———. 2008. "'Boys Will Be Boys': Traditional Xhosa Male Circumcision, HIV and Sexual Socialisation in Contemporary South Africa." *Culture, Health and Sexuality* 10, no. 5: 431–46.

von Schnitzler, Antina. 2014. "Performing Dignity: Human Rights, Citizenship, and the Techno-politics of Law in South Africa." *American Ethnologist* 41, no. 2: 336–50.

———. 2016. *Democracy's Infrastructure: Techno-politics and Protest after Apartheid.* Princeton, NJ: Princeton University Press.

Walker, Cherryl. 1990. Women and Gender in South Africa to 1945: An Overview. In *Women and Gender in South Africa to 1945,* edited by Cherryl Walker, 1–32. London: James Currey.

Wardlow, Holly. 2006. *Wayward Women: Sexuality and Agency in a New Guinea Society.* Berkeley: University of California Press.

Wardlow, Holly, and Jennifer Sue Hirsch, eds. 2006. *Modern Loves: The Anthropology of Romantic Courtship and Companionate Marriage.* London: Macmillan.

Watt, Melissa H., Frances M. Aunon, Donald Skinner, Kathleen J. Sikkema, Jessica C. MacFarlane, Desiree Pieterse, and Seth C. Kalichman. 2012. "Alcohol-Serving Venues in South Africa as Sites of Risk and Potential Protection for Violence against Women." *Substance Use and Misuse* 47, no. 12: 1271–80.

Weiss, Brad, ed. 2004. *Producing African Futures: Ritual and Reproduction in a Neoliberal Age.* Leiden: Brill.

Werner, Cynthia. 2009. "Bride Abduction in Post-Soviet Central Asia: Marking a Shift towards Patriarchy through Local Discourses of Shame and Tradition." *Journal of the Royal Anthropological Institute* 15, no. 2: 314–31.

Werner, Cynthia, Christopher Edling, Charles Becker, Elena Kim, Russell Kleinbach, Fatima Esengeldievna Sartbay, and Woden Teachout. 2018. "Bride Kidnapping in Post-Soviet Eurasia: A Roundtable Discussion." *Central Asian Survey* 37, no. 4: 582–601.

West, Candace, and Don Zimmerman. 1987. "Doing Gender." *Gender and Society* 1, no. 2: 125–51.

White, Hylton. 2001. "Tempora et Mores: Family Values and the Possessions of a Post-apartheid Countryside." *Journal of Religion in Africa* 31, no. 4: 457–79.

————. 2010. "Outside the Dwelling of Culture: Estrangement and Difference in Postcolonial Zululand." *Anthropological Quarterly* 83, no. 3: 497–518.

————. 2015. "Custom, Normativity and Authority in South Africa." *Journal of Southern African Studies* 41, no. 5: 1005–17.

Whooley, Patrick. 1975. "Marriage in Africa: A Study of the Ciskei." In *Church and Marriage in Modern Africa*, edited by Trevor David Verryn, 245–67. Pretoria: Ecumenical Research Unit.

Wickström, Annette. 2014. "'Lungisa'—Weaving Relationships and Social Space to Restore Health in Rural KwaZulu Natal." *Medical Anthropology Quarterly* 28, no. 2: 203–20.

Willen, Sarah. 2015. "Lightning Rods in the Local Moral Economy: Debating Unauthorized Migrants' Deservingness in Israel." *International Migration* 53, no. 3: 70–86.

Williams, Raymond. 1973. *The Country and the City*. London: Oxford University Press.

Wilson, Monica. 1977. *For Men and Elders: Changes in the Relations of Generations and of Men and Women among the Nyakyusa and Ngonde*. London: International African Institute.

————. 1981. "Xhosa Marriage in Historical Perspective." In *Essays on African Marriage in Southern Africa*, edited by Eileen Jensen Krige and John L. Comaroff, 133–147. Cape Town: Juta.

Wilson, Monica, S. Kaplan, T. Maki, and E. M. Walton. 1952. *Social Structure. Keiskammahoek Rural Survey*. Pietermaritzburg: Shooter & Shuter.

Wiredu, Kwasi. 1992. "The Moral Foundations of an African Culture." In *Person and Community: Ghanaian Philosophical Studies*, Vol. I, edited by Kwame Gyekye and Kwasi Wiredu, 193–206. Washington, DC: Council for Research in Values and Philosophy.

Wojcicki, Janet Maia. 2002. "'She Drank His Money': Survival Sex and the Problem of Violence in Taverns in Gauteng Province, South Africa." *Medical Anthropology Quarterly* 16, no. 3: 267–93.

Wolff, Brent, Joanna Busza, Leonard Bufumbo, and Jimmy Whitworth. 2006. "Women Who Fall by the Roadside: Gender, Sexual Risk and Alcohol in Rural Uganda." *Addiction* 101, no. 9: 1277–84.

Wolpe, Harold. 1972. "Capitalism and Cheap Labour-Power in South Africa: From Segregation to Apartheid." *Economy and Society* 1, no. 4: 425–56.

Wood, Kate. 2005. "Contextualizing Group Rape in Post-apartheid South Africa." *Culture, Health and Sexuality* 7, no. 4: 303–17.

Wood, Kate, and Rachel Jewkes. 2001. "'Dangerous' Love: Reflections on Violence among Xhosa Township Youth." In *Changing men in Southern Africa*, edited by Robert Morrell, 95–102. Pietermaritzburg: University of Natal Press.

Worden, Nigel. 2011. *The Making of Modern South Africa: Conquest, Apartheid, Democracy*. London: John Wiley & Sons.

Wyrod, Robert. 2008. "Between Women's Rights and Men's Authority: Masculinity and Shifting Discourses of Gender Difference in Urban Uganda." *Gender and Society* 22, no. 6: 799–823.

Yan, Yunxiang. 2003. *Private Life under Socialism: Love, Intimacy, and Family Change in a Chinese Village, 1949–1999*. Redwood City, CA: Stanford University Press.

Zelizer, Viviana A. 2000. "The Purchase of Intimacy." *Law and Social Inquiry* 25, no. 3: 817–48.

INDEX

Note: Italicized page numbers indicate illustrations.

Adam, Heribert, 144n13

Africanist anthropology, 9, 12, 98. *See also* ethnographic research; scholarship on South Africa

African National Congress (ANC), 46, 145n3

aging: cultural markers of, 60–61, 63–64, 65; and industrial notions of productivity, 64; moral ambiguities in, 60; and requirements for old-age pensions, 61–62

amalungelo (relational moral rightness): concept of, 49–50; moral order based on, 125; reconciliation with *irhayti*, 122, 127, 129, 131; tensions with *irhayti*, 44, 57, 58; *ubuntu* and, 128

Apartheid: about, 137n3; ANC and, 145n3; and control over women, 114–15; human rights and, 45, 66; internalized racism from, 144n13; rural/urban divide from, 12, 85; and segregated reserves, 11. *See also* Customary Law; urban/rural divide

autonomy: and *amalungelo*, 130; in behavior of people in Mhlambini, 3–4; democracy's privileging of, 124; and dependence on domestic labor, 94–95; and dignity, 130; and equitable access to grants, 72; and human rights, 96–97, 129; *irhayti* and, 128; marriage and, 17–18; social relations and

value of, 48–49; *ukuthwala* and, 118; young women's desire for, 75, 76–77, 123

Bantustan system, 11, 12, 18, 73, 145n5

beer, consumption of, 79–81

Boyd, Lydia, 51

bride abduction. See *ukuthwala* (bride abduction)

bridewealth (*lobola*): and acquisition of domestic labor, 7, 97; and alleviation of poverty, 87; flexibility in, 15; gender equality and, 90–91, 92; and love marriages, 92; low payments of, 139n19; and premarital childbearing, 89; and sexuality rights, 116; *ukuthwala* and, 22, 99, 100, 102, 110, 112; unemployment and, 18, 58, 101, 105, 141n34; values and meanings of, 7, 89–90

Chowdhury, Romit, 55

cohabitation, 100, 106–7, 139n19, 146n9

Cole, Jennifer, 98

community meetings: compensation orders, 79; and employment, 29; village politics and, 16

Cook, Peter Alan Wilson, 13

culture, rights to, 46–47, 140n29

KATHLEEN RICE is Assistant Professor in the Department of Family Medicine at McGill University, where she holds the Tier II Canada Research Chair in the Medical Anthropology of Primary Care. *Rights and Responsibilities in Rural South Africa: Gender, Personhood, and the Crisis of Meaning* is her first book.

For Indiana University Press

Tony Brewer, Artist and Book Designer
Brian Carroll, Rights Manager
Gary Dunham, Acquisitions Editor and Director
Anna Francis, Assistant Acquisitions Editor
Brenna Hosman, Production Coordinator
Katie Huggins, Production Manager
Nancy Lightfoot, Project Editor and Manager
Dan Pyle, Online Publishing Manager
Jennifer Witzke, Senior Artist and Book Designer
Stephen Williams, Marketing and Publicity Manager